新视界商务英语系列教材

总顾问 / 叶兴国　王立非

总主编 / 郭桂杭　刘白玉

The Contrast of Chinese and Western Cultures

中西文化对比教程

（第二版）

主　编　刘春芳

副主编　马　骞　张　洁　马海歆　张　续

中国人民大学出版社

·北京·

导读

文化是一个极为宽泛的概念，文化学习是一种对代代相传的总体行为模式进行了解的过程。由于这种总体行为模式涵盖了深厚的历史，涉及社会中的不同层级和不同方面，因此学生在学习过程中会感到知识庞杂而无从下手。其实，正因为文化本身包含了社会生活的许多方面，所以应该是丰富生动、五彩缤纷的，研习文化也应是一个充满惊喜与快乐的过程。英国人类学家爱德华·泰勒认为："文化是一个错综复杂的整体，它包括知识、信仰、艺术、法律、道德、习俗以及作为社会成员的人所获得的其他一切能力和习惯。"换言之，对文化的了解和掌握是通过一个社会不同层面的表现方式来进行的，这些层面可分为有形和无形两个部分。有形文化指的是人们的行为方式，包括语言、习俗等，也包括特定的文化产品，如文学、艺术、音乐等。无形的层面则包括人的价值取向、信仰和道德观等。从地理环境到历史发展脉络，西方社会与我们的民族存在着巨大差异，在此基础上衍生出的文化也与我们迥然不同。作为生活在国际化、信息化和数字化时代的青年学生，极有必要对西方文化进行深入了解，对中西文化进行多维比较，从而既了解西方文化的起源、特点，又了解中华文化的深刻内涵与独特风貌。唯有如此，才能在当今文化交融、文化碰撞的时代保持清醒的头脑。

对于中西文化对比的学习，需要注意以下几个问题：

一是要抓住中西方文化的发展脉络与主要精神。同学们在学习时，面对体系庞大与繁杂的西方文化有时会感到迷茫和困惑，面对崭新的文化思想和浩瀚的知识会产生力不从心之感。在这里，我希望用一个小小的比喻来解决大家的困惑。我们可以尝试把西方文化的发展比作一个人的成长过程，以剥离西方文化史的神秘抽象之感，对其形成生动而具体的认识。马克思曾说，"希腊人是正常的儿童"，也就是说，希腊文化中所表现出来的随心所欲、张扬纵性的特点恰如小小的孩童，凡事以自己的所欲所求为中心，很少考虑外在规范与社会价值体系。沿着这种思路思考下去，想哭就哭、想闹就闹的孩童很快便会进入深受家长与老师管束的时期。我们可以把这个时期视作神学思想统治一切、人性备受压制的中世纪。长期的压制激发了人们对人性的渴望与追求，因此当儿童长大成人并逐渐成熟，开始对自我逐渐进行肯定并歌颂时，西方文化历史也就进入了以人文主义思想为主要特点的文艺复兴时期。这个时期对人性的颂扬是极其热烈的，人是"宇宙的精华、万物的灵长"是这一时期的人性宣言。文艺复兴虽高扬人性的大旗，开创了人类历史崭新的一页，但是这一时期也存在着青春期般的特点，热烈有余而理性思考不足。在此基础上，人的发展与成长越发成熟与理性，西方文化也进入了以理性为主要特点的时代。理性的发展促使人能够不断地成功、不断地征服，进一步印证人的理性之伟大，这便是以理性为核心，以科技发展为主要成就的启蒙主义时期，也可以说与青春期过后的理性人生相对。理性的思索与理性的行为模式虽然使人不断地取得了外在的成功，但却使人内心的情感世界逐渐失落与衰微，于是，渴盼激情的人们便发起了一场以情感为内核的思想革命，即浪漫主义大张旗鼓地在欧洲各国盛行。之后，人的发展在经历过这种激情变奏后，进入了更为冷静、更为现实的中年时期，这便是西方文化史上的现实主义时期。这是一个浪漫的理想逐渐褪色、对现实的认识和思考更为客观的时期。如果没有意外的事件，西方本来可以沿着这条冷静而客观的道路缓缓前行。然而，令人震惊的是，历史上却发生了令人精神崩溃的两次世界大战。残酷的战争摧毁了人们对未来的期待、对信仰的依赖以及追求善与美的信心。由此，西方的思想界承受了前所未有的打击。"上帝死了"等话语将西方世界宁静的状态打破，当代西方文化由此充满了对人性的怀疑、对人类未来的怀疑、对世界发展的不信任等黑色与荒诞的因素。因此，当代西方文化没有在物质丰富的背景下走向丰盈与完满，反而越发变得支离破碎。这种境遇像不像一个虽然拥有无尽财富，却因心灵无处归依而感到落寞与孤独的中年人呢？以人的发展来比喻西方文化的发展虽有片面之嫌，但是希望这个比喻能帮助大家理清西方文化发展史的主要脉络，聚焦这个脉络中出现的事件和人物大都具有的某些共同特点。相比之下，中华文化从一开始就有比较深刻的自制力与约束性，好比人很早就摆脱了童年的随性与张扬，迅速进入谨慎的成熟期。我们都非常熟悉的"孔融让梨"的故事，不正是体现了这一特性吗？小小的孩童已经明白要克制自己的欲望，服从社会的规范。

二是要树立文化比较的视野。多年的教学经验使我感到，我们的青年学生面对与中华文化迥异的西方文化时常常有两种反应。一种反应是对西方文化甚为崇拜，从而对中国文化产生轻视之感。面对与我们有着很多差异的西方文化，他们常常会对自身的文化产生怀疑。这种怀疑形成的根源是对中华文化的理解不深、对西方文化的了解也不够。文化的形成有其独特的背景，中华文化的悠久历史与传统包含着西方文化所没有的智慧。中华文化素来未以科技发展为其重要目标，但是以滋养内心、培养人格为其重要指向。在这种文化氛围的影响下，中华文化中的优秀人物大都是有着良好的教养与高贵的人格，而非德行欠佳、空有一技之长之人。西方文化注重个性的文化氛围固然造就了西方近代科技的发展，但西方文化中单向竞争与个性张扬的思想，加上积淀了不断征服、不断掠夺的性格底蕴，导致当今世界被战争阴云威胁，西方人自己的内心也因此失去了精神依托而被无助感和荒诞感所笼罩。西方当代文化面临困境，正是由于其过于强调科学精神而忽略了人文气质。我们学习西方文化，就是要了解其发展脉络、发生背景，学习其擅长理性思维、投身科技发展的科学精神，也要批判其忽略人文意蕴和高尚情操的价值取向。另一种反应则是由于对中华文化极其热爱，拒绝学习和了解西方文化，认为西方文化不足以和中华文化相提并论。这种思想的根源也在于没有深入了解这两种文化。中华文化固然博大精深，充满智慧，但不能因此否认西方文化的自身价值，或者因此就对西方文化嗤之以鼻。西方文化与中华文化孕育发展的背景截然不同，其形成的文化思想也有着巨大差异。学习西方文化中的优点，避免其不完善的地方，包容文化的差异性，并在相互尊重的基础上相互学习，取长补短才是最佳策略。

三是文化比较要注意避免草率下结论，避免片面得出孰优孰劣的推断。文化的学习就像打开了一扇大门，推开门后看到的是从未见过的五彩缤纷的花朵，正如郁金香与牡丹花难分伯仲一样，文化现象也难以从主观上判断好坏。正确的学习态度是了解差异、比较差异，不断进行学习与研究。文化是复杂因素的产物，绝不是一句好坏便可评判的。如果碰到什么问题和困难，最好的办法是与老师和同学沟通，同时阅读大量的资料文献，辩证地看待观点论断，从而形成更加全面、深刻的认识，而非简单地对文化现象下结论。

以上是编者综合多年来的教学经验与体会，针对中西文化对比的学习中出现的一些问题所给予的一些解释。具体到《中西文化对比教程》本身，其编写特点有以下四点：

第一，本书致力于贯彻翻转课堂的授课模式。笔者从事高校英语教育二十余年，一直致力于钻研英语教学法的提高与改进。作为一种适应现代社会技术与发展，注重新型师生关系与各自的主体地位的教学方式，翻转课堂在越来越多的课程中得到了不同程度的运用。而在英语教学过程中，笔者认为文化类课程，尤其是中西文化对比课程，比其他英语课程更加适用翻转课堂的教学模式。一是因为中西文化对比探讨的是较为宽泛和宏观的文化现象，因此不需要像其他英语课程一样以教师讲授为主、学生听课为辅。相反，在了解了基本文化现象后，这门课程更需要将重点放在探讨方面。二是许多文化问题本身是开放的，并没有明确的固定答案，而是需要学生从不同角度和层面进行理解，这就更加突出了课前阅读与课后研读的重要意义。根据这些特点，基于多年的教学经验，我们将翻转课堂的教学理念运用在该教材的编写中，致力于使这本教材成为翻转课堂教学的典型教材。因此，本书每一节大致分为课前阅读、课堂讨论与课后研读三大部分，条理清晰地将翻转课堂的运作方式展现出来。同时，配备了精美的PPT课件，为教师备课提供了充分的资料，也为学生们的课前学习提供了齐全的材料。

第二，本书对各种文化现象进行了精心选择，认真研究，使本教材没有按部就班地对文化现象进行简单罗列，而是将有对比意义和对比空间的一些现象进行重点比较，并在比较过程中给出要思考的具体问题，促进学生在学习过程中主动有效地进行思考。限于篇幅与课堂授课的时间，我们重点选择了有对比意义的中西材料，如在“中西方神话中的英雄对比”一节中，我们选择了西方神话中的阿喀琉斯和中国神话中的后羿进行中西英雄性格特点对比，而在实际上课的过程中，教师可以鼓励学生找出更多的英雄人物进行对比，如西方神话中的普罗米修斯、中国神话中的夸父等。教师可以让学生在课前搜集这些材料，也可以在授课时提出这些问题。总之，要使文化对比的范围与深度进一步加强，使课堂授课的效果更加生动，便不能局限在课本所提供的材料上，而是要从无尽的中西文化海洋中寻找更多有意义的材料，完成真正意义上的文化对比。寻找有对比意义与价值的中西方材料本身，便是很好的学习与思考过程。

第三，本教材的一大亮点是“文化反思”模块。鉴于文化问题并无明确、固定的答案，因此本教材在每一节的最后，都对文化问题和文化现象进行了综述和反思。文化反思的书写以趣味性和理论性相结合为主，注重文化对比问题的开放性与发展性。这种方式，使中西文化对比不局限在几个故事或者事件中，而是将文化对比深入化，使学生们不仅了解了文化现象，思考了文化问题，更培养了深刻严谨的思维方式，帮助其形成客观成熟的文化认知。文化反思部分是学生在阅读了相关文化对比的文本，观看了相关视频资料，进行了充分的课前准备以及热烈的课上讨论、课下总结之后，再去阅读的内容，使学生对文化对比的思想与内涵有了更加深入的把握和提升。

第四，教学手段应在以课本为依据的基础上尽量多样化，充分运用现代化教学手段，使本课程的教学不仅信息丰富，而且生动有趣。由于本课程具有提纲挈领的特点，对每个历史阶段的介绍均突出重点，语言尽量生动简洁，非常适合学生对通识课程的基本需求。同时，在教学中可根据课本的内容，进行一些教学方法的改进与探索。由于篇幅所限，本课本的图片并不多，教师在授课时可通过更多的图片展示来生动地阐释西方文化。例如，对西方典型建筑、著名绘画作品的介绍可运用该方法。此外，对于西方文化史上的重大事件、重要人物，几乎均可找到相应的影视作品，一些作品早已成为永恒的经典。在课堂教学中，可为学生播放一些视频片段，激发学生的学习兴趣，并推荐一些能拓展知识面的影片与资料让学生课后观看，然后在课堂上进行讲述与评论。再者，西方文化史的学习离不开对文化现象、文化问题、中西方文化比较与融合等问题的探讨。因此，对文化热点问题的讨论也是本课程教学的一项基本内容。问题的讨论可通过多种形式进行，使课堂教学更加丰富多彩。

总之，《中西文化对比教程》是一本生动而深刻的、对中西文化进行客观比较的教材。西方社会是一个不同寻常的社会，是经过数千年的发展整合而形成的。它的文化既表现出一致性，又呈现出复杂性和多彩性。中华文化作为世界文明古国中唯一从未中断过的文化，底蕴深厚，内涵独特，呈现出极为睿智与通达的特性。对中西文化的了解应是每个当代学生必备的，也是进一步学习和进入职场的必备前提。为了使更多的人从本书中受益，本书采用了中英文相结合的方式，同时配备英语生词表，既方便学生阅读，又为学生提高英语水平提供了良好平台。新的教学理念、生动的比较、特别的视野、高度的概括、独特的评说和深刻的反思构成了《中西文化对比教程》的基本特色。因此，笔者希望本书的出版能为通识课程的教育增添一抹亮色，为推进青年学生对中西方文化的全面了解做出一点贡献。

本书配有练习题参考答案，任课老师可登录中国人民大学出版社主页 http://www.crup.com.cn，搜索本书后下载相关资源，或联系 010-62512737，010-62515580，huangt@crup.com.cn，wangxw@crup.com.cn 索取。

刘春芳

2025 年 1 月

目 录
Contents

Chapter Four

Chapter Five

Chapter Six

Chapter Seven

Chapter One

The Contrast of Chinese and Western Myths

课前成果检测

中西方神话阅读测试题

一、填空题

1.《淮南子·览冥训》女娲炼________以补苍天，断________以立四极，杀________以济冀州，积________以止淫水。

2. ________有与日竞走的宏志，手拿两条黄蛇追赶太阳。后来，为了避免人们每天在十个烈日的炙烤下生存，________射日。

3. 白蛇传、梁祝、________和牛郎织女，并称为“中国古代四大爱情传说”。

4. 他舞动混天绫，砸下乾坤圈，打得东海龙王儿子现了原形，他就是________。

5. 古代一位道士，学仙修道时因偷吃仙炉丹药而触犯天条，天帝罚他到月宫去砍桂树。他就是________。

6. 梁山伯与祝英台的精魂化作________，形影相随，比翼双飞。

二、单选题

1. 汉字是一种象形文字，相传汉字是（　　）所造。

A. 皇帝　　B. 盘古　　C. 仓颉　　D. 女娲

2. 白蛇传发生在（　　）。

A. 洪泽湖　　B. 莫愁湖　　C. 洞庭湖　　D. 西湖

3. 盘古开天辟地完成后，力竭而亡，周身发生了很大的变化，他的血液变成了（　　）。

A. 高山　　B. 雷声　　C. 江河　　D. 天地

4. 为人类盗取火种，宙斯下令将其锁在高加索山崖上的是（　　）。

A. 潘多拉　　B. 丘比特　　C. 阿波罗　　D. 普罗米修斯

5. 夜间化身为猫头鹰的女神是（　　）。

A. 雅典娜　　B. 维纳斯　　C. 赫拉　　D. 厄里斯

6. “大力神的十二项英雄事迹”这一希腊神话中的主角是（　　）。

A. 赫拉克勒斯　　B. 宙斯　　C. 赫拉　　D. 俄狄浦斯王

三、多选题

1. 希腊神话中的英雄传说故事主要有（　　）。

A. 赫拉克勒斯的十二项英雄事迹

B. 伊阿宋取金羊毛

C. 珀尔修斯取美杜萨的头

D. 忒修斯杀死米诺斯牛

E. “提坦之战”

2. 下列选项中对希腊神话的特点的描述不正确的是（　　）。

A. 希腊神话中的神是高度人格化的，拥有人的形象和性格

B. 希腊神话体现出浓郁的神话主义色彩

C. 希腊神话的文化背景是乐观主义，充满了光明

D. 希腊神话既有浪漫夸张，又有现实描写，表现了古希腊人丰富的想象力和极大的创造力

四、阅读题

他派人问弥达斯有什么要求，他应该怎样报答他。弥达斯毫不迟疑地回答说：“请恩准使我摸到的一切都变成金子。”然而，变成金子的不仅仅是石块、花朵和屋内的陈设。他坐下吃饭时，他吃的食物和喝的水也都变成了金子。过了不久，弥达斯恳求狄俄尼索斯使他从他的那个愿望

中解脱出来，因为他饥渴交加，快要死了。狄俄尼索斯逗弄弥达斯，特别开心。他叫弥达斯前往帕克托罗斯河的源头，在河里洗个澡。弥达斯依照行事，解除了点金术，但帕克托罗斯河的沙子至今因含金而闪闪发光。

1. 这段话出自（　　）故事。

2. 如果你现在也能拥有神奇的点金术，你触碰的东西都会变成金子，你愿意拥有这样的能力吗？请说出你的理由。

五、思考题

希腊、罗马神话中都有“盗火”的故事。普罗米修斯为了使地上的人们免受虎豹豺狼的侵扰，打破对黑暗的恐惧，冒死从主神宙斯那里盗取了火种，救万民于水火。但主神宙斯大为震怒，为了惩罚普罗米修斯将火种偷到人间，将他锁在悬崖上，遭受日复一日的酷刑。我国远古神话中的两位主神盘古、女娲纷纷为人民的福祉牺牲自我：盘古开天辟地之后，力竭之时把身体变成了世间万物；女娲炼石补天之后，连同自己也化作了补天巨石。试分析中西神话中诸神形象的差异。

Section One

The Contrast of Chinese and Western Creation Myths

I. Learning Objectives

1. To know the main characters and plots of Chinese and Western creation myths

2. To make a comparison and contrast between Chinese and Western creation myths and to summarize their influences upon Chinese and Western cultures

II. Key Points and Difficult Points

1. To summarize the similarities of Western creation myths and the relations with other aspects of Western culture

2. To summarize the similarities of Chinese creation myths and the relations with other aspects of Chinese culture

3. To compare and contrast Chinese and Western creation myths

III. Lead-in Questions

1. What are the differences of the characters between the Chinese and Western creation myths?

2. Are there any differences between Chinese and Western cultural origins? If so, what are they?

3. What is the connection between the shaping of cultural characters and creation myths?

IV. Learning Contents

1. Creation Myths in Ancient Greece

In ancient Greece, some people began telling stories to explain the mysteries of life. Over much time, the stories grew rich and imaginative. The storytellers actually wove in their customs, beliefs and theories about life, death, and the wonders of nature. The myths were about gods and goddesses, fearful monsters, brave heroes, and mysterious beauties.

According to mythology, the gods and goddesses looked and acted like human. They married each other. They laughed, loved, quarreled and fought with each other. But they were immortal. They lived forever because a fluid called ichor—not blood—flowed through their veins.

The mightiest of the gods and goddesses lived in a golden palace on Olympus—a mountain so high, the top was hidden by clouds. They feasted an ambrosia and nectar—the food and drink of the gods. And whenever they wished, they could change shape and speed down to earth, to mingle with the mortals. The awesome Olympians earned their thrones on Olympus. They fought a fierce battle and won.

This is the story of how it happened. In the very beginning, there was a dark space named Chaos and Gaea. The Earth grew out of this dark space and later Gaea gave birth to Uranus, the Sky. Uranus rained down on young Gaea, and plants, animals, and rivers appeared.

Gaea became Mother Earth, mother of all living things—and mother of the first gods.

Gaea and Uranus had many children. Their first-born children were the twelve giant Titans, six girls and six boys. Later, more children were born. Three were the mighty Cyclopes—strong, one-eyed giants. Three were the Hecatoncheires, with a hundred arms and fifty heads. Uranus hated the Cyclopes and the Hecatoncheires, because they were ugly. He threw them into Tartarus—the deepest pit in the Underworld.

Gaea was furious. She urged the Titans to overthrow their father and rescue their brothers. Only the youngest, Cronus, was brave enough. He attacked Uranus with a sickle and banished him from the Earth. Cronus replaced his father as Lord of the Universe. But he was cruel and did not free his brothers from Tartarus. Cronus married his sister Rhea, and they had many children. But Cronus was afraid that one of them might overthrow him just as he had done to his father. So as each child was born, he swallowed it. Rhea was horrified. When the youngest was born, she tricked Cronus. She hid the baby Zeus in a distant cave, so Cronus would not find him. Rhea then gave Cronus a stone wrapped in a blanket. He swallowed that instead—the blanket and all.

Hidden away, Zeus was raised by gentle woodland nymphs and a nymph-goat named Amaltheia, who fed him milk. When the baby cried, the Curetes—Zeus's guards—clashed their weapons to hide the sound. Zeus grew into the strongest of all the gods and married Metis, a Titan's daughter. Rhea was still angry with her husband and wanted Zeus to depose him. But Metis, the Goddess of Prudence, was wise. She said Zeus needed help, for Cronus had the Titans on his side. Rhea found a way. With her help, Metis gave Cronus a drink she promised would make him undefeatable.

Instead, it made Cronus throw up the stone and his unharmed children—Hestia, Demeter, Hera, Zeus, Hades, and Poseidon. They were reunited, and gratefully joined their brother. Zeus freed their uncles from Tartarus, and they prepared to fight the Titans together. The Cyclopes, who were great builders and smiths, made the weapons. They armed Zeus with a thunderbolt that shook the Universe. They made Poseidon a trident that could split the seas. They gave Hades a helmet of darkness that made him invisible to his enemies. For ten years war raged between the old gods and the new gods. At last Cronus and the Titans were defeated and thrown into Tartarus, to be guarded forever by their hundred-armed brothers.

朱庇特与忒提斯

Mother Earth was finally at peace. Rule of the Universe was divided among the three brothers. Zeus was declared King of the Gods, and God of Heaven and Earth. Poseidon became God of the Sea, and Hades God of the Underworld.

单词表

mythology	*n.*	（统称）神话；某文化（或社会等）的神话
immortal	*adj.*	长生的；永世的；不朽的
ichor	*n.*	（诸神血管中的）灵液
ambrosia	*n.*	（古希腊和罗马神话中）神的食物；神肴；仙馐

nectar	*n.*	花蜜；神酒
throne	*n.*	（国王、女王的）御座，宝座
Gaea	*n.*	盖娅（大地女神）
Uranus	*n.*	乌拉诺斯（天神）
Titans	*n.*	提坦诸神
Cyclopes	*n.*	库克罗普斯（希腊神话中的独眼巨人）
Hecatoncheires	*n.*	百臂巨人
Tartarus	*n.*	塔尔塔罗斯（地狱底下暗无天日的深渊）；地狱
furious	*adj.*	狂怒的；暴怒的
Cronus	*n.*	克洛诺斯（天神乌拉诺斯和大地女神盖娅的儿子，他夺取了父亲的王位，后又被他的儿子宙斯夺走王位）
sickle	*n.*	镰刀
banish	*v.*	放逐；流放；把（某人）驱逐出境
Rhea	*n.*	瑞亚（众神之母）
Zeus	*n.*	宙斯（主神）
woodland	*n.*	树林；林地；林区
nymph	*n.*	（古希腊、罗马神话中居于山林水泽的）仙女
Metis	*n.*	墨提斯（俄刻阿诺斯和忒提斯的女儿，宙斯的第一个妻子）
depose	*v.*	罢免；废黜
prudence	*n.*	谨慎；慎重；精明
Hestia	*n.*	赫斯提（女灶神，罗马神话中称为 Vesta）
Demeter	*n.*	得墨忒耳（掌管农业、谷物、丰收之女神）
Hera	*n.*	赫拉（主神宙斯之妻）
Hades	*n.*	哈得斯（冥王）
Poseidon	*n.*	波塞冬（海神）
thunderbolt	*n.*	雷电；霹雳
trident	*n.*	三叉戟（旧时武器）

盘古开天辟地

2. 盘古开天辟地

天地混沌如鸡子，盘古生在其中，万八千岁。天地开辟，阳清为天，阴浊为地。盘古在其中，一日九变，神于天，圣于地。天日高一丈，地日厚一丈，盘古日长一丈。万八千岁，天数极高，地数极深，盘古极长。后乃有三皇。数起于一，立于三，成于五，盛于七，处于九，故天去地九万里……首生盘古，垂死化身，气成风云，声为雷霆，左眼为日，右眼为月，四肢五体为四极五岳，血液为江河，筋脉为地里，肌肉为田土，发髭为星辰，皮毛为草木，齿骨为金石，精髓为珠玉，汗流为雨泽，身之诸虫，因风所感，化为黎氓。（徐整，《三五历纪》）

V. Story Links

1. Odin: The Creation God of North Europe

Odin was a widely revered god in Norse mythology. He was closely associated with wisdom, healing, death, royalty, the gallows, knowledge, war, battle, victory, sorcery, poetry, frenzy, and the runic alphabet, and he was depicted as the husband of the goddess Frigg. Odin was also known in Old English as Wōden, meaning "lord of frenzy", or "leader of the possessed". The modern English weekday name Wednesday derives from Old English Wōdnesdæg, meaning "day of Wōden".

Old Norse texts portray Odin as the son of Bestla and Borr along with two brothers, Vili and Vé, and he fathered many sons, most famously the gods Thor (with Jörð) and Baldr (with Frigg). He is known by hundreds of names. Odin is frequently portrayed as one-eyed and long-bearded, wielding a spear named Gungnir or appearing in disguise wearing a cloak and a broad hat. He is often accompanied by his animal familiars—the wolves Geri and Freki and the ravens Huginn and Muninn, who bring him information from all over Midgard—and he rides the flying, eight-legged steed Sleipnir across the sky and into the Underworld.

2. 女娲造人

天地开辟以后，天上有了太阳、月亮和星星，地上有了山川草木、鸟兽虫鱼。不知道什么时候出现了一个神通广大的女神，叫作女娲。有一天，女娲在一个池子旁边蹲下来，顺手从池边掘起一团黄泥，揉成了第一个娃娃。她把这个小东西放到地面上，他刚一接触地面就活了起来，女娲给这个心爱的孩子取了一个名字，叫作"人"。她又继续用黄泥做了许多能说话、会走路的小人儿。她一心要让这些灵敏的小生物布满大地，但是，大地毕竟太大了。最后，她想出了一个绝妙的创造人类的方法。她从崖壁上拉下一条枯藤，将其伸进一个泥潭里，搅出了浑黄的泥浆，然后向地面一挥洒，泥点溅落的地方就出现了许多小人儿。不久，大地上就布满了人类的踪迹。

女娲造人

（资料来源：http://www.thn21.com/teach/15038.html）

VI. Did You Know?

1. 提坦（Titan）

提坦，现引申为"巨人，高人，伟人"，其形容词为 titanic，意思是"巨大的，极重要的，强大的，极艰巨的"。著名巨轮 *Titanic* 得名于此，寓意此轮船巨大且坚不可摧。

2. Achilles' Heel（致命的弱点）

直译为"阿喀琉斯之踵"，原指阿喀琉斯的脚跟。阿喀琉斯出生时被母亲握住脚踵倒浸在冥河水中，因此除未浸水的踵部外，任何武器都伤害不了他。后来他在特洛伊战争中被人射中脚踵而死。"阿喀琉斯的脚踵"现在一般是指"致命的弱点；要害"。

3. Swan Song（最后的杰作）

直译为"天鹅之歌"，后意译为"最后的杰作"或者"绝笔"。在古希腊神话中，阿波罗（Apollo）是太阳神、光明之神，由于他多才多艺，又是诗歌与音乐之神，后世奉他为文艺的保护神。天鹅是阿波罗的神鸟，故常用来比喻文艺。传说天鹅平素不唱歌，而在它死前，必引颈长鸣，高歌一曲，其歌声哀婉动听，感人肺腑。这是它一生中唯一的，也是最后的一次歌唱。

因此，西方各国就用这个典故来比喻某诗人、作家、作曲家临终前的一部杰作，或者是某个演员、歌唱家的最后一次表演。

VII. Cultural Reflection

神话是一种文化积淀，也是一种民族意识的积淀，几千年来它以潜意识的方式影响着人们的文化思维与行为习惯。中西方创世神话的差异也必然造成中西方民族意识的差异。神话的源起是因为古人面对苍茫大地而感到困惑。天与地到底是如何形成的？人到底是怎样出现的？各个不同的神话系统都试图给出自己的解释。因此，许多民族都有自己独具特色的创世神话，这也是许多民族在一定程度上对自己的困惑进行了解答。由于创世神话的源起大致相同，而早期先民们对天地万物的认识有限，所以中西方的创世神话在很大程度上是相似的。

一、中西方创世神话中的主体都是人格化的神灵

无论是西方神话中的盖娅和乌拉诺斯，还是中国神话中的盘古，都有这样的特性。盘古开天辟地，之后其巨大的身躯化为江河水脉、日月星辰，而希腊神话中的盖娅同样是自我衍生出天与地，并且将自身化为大地的万物。在对西方影响更深刻的基督教文化中，创世者神灵化的色彩则更加突出。据《圣经》记载，神用七天的时间创造了天地，也创造了星辰万物。这些创世者神灵化的普遍现象表达了先民对于天地为万物之源的敬仰，尤其是这些创世之神大多身居高位，更加充分证明了先民认为天地是自然万物、一切生命的依托的想法。

二、中西方创世神话中都有创造人类的故事

古希腊神话中提坦神普罗米修斯创造了人类，中国神话中女娲创造了人类，两者都是用泥土捏造了人类的模样，并赋予其生命。这些神话给出了人类的“我从哪里来”这个永恒之问最质朴的回答。人是神创造的，而且在中西方神话中，人都是在神创造了自然万物之后，最后才被创造出来的。这体现了人对自己在自然界中的位置的一种客观认识。同时，神大多又是按照自己的形象来创造人，或者通过神赋予人生命和灵气，体现了人为万物之灵的自豪之感。

此外，由于中西方创世神话所生发的自然环境与人文环境各不相同，因此中西方创世神话也呈现出一定的差异。

一、西方神话呈现理性内核的体系性，而中国神话则是感性内核的体悟性

西方创世神话中的每个神都有非常清晰的来龙去脉，在神的谱系中有非常明确的定位。神和神的关系也都非常明晰，即使是两个神之间既有夫妻关系，又有母子关系——如盖娅和乌拉诺斯，其关系的源起与发展也都很有逻辑性。相对来说，中国创世神话中的神比较孤立，很难找到神与神之间的明确关系。盘古和女娲都是创世神话的重要人物，但是他们之间的关系却有

各种解读，并不明确。西方神话从本质上体现了一种严谨、富于逻辑性的思维模式。这一思维模式在西方启蒙时期得到了前所未有的发扬，也奠定了西方人崇尚科学的基础。中国神话则更多的是单个神灵的故事，体现了中华文化中感性思维更占优势的特点。同时，由于中国古代文明发展较快，文字成熟较早，中国社会在神话的保存和流传过程中，一般采用文字的形式。可是文字在春秋战国时期主要承担着诸子百家表达他们的哲学思想和政治理念的任务，承载“齐家、治国、平天下”的现实诉求，因此神话并没有被过多地发扬光大，而是短小、零散，不成体系地散见于一般的文章中。西方神话是由民间唱诗的歌手所传承，他们往往加入一些个人的想象和润色，而且他们的职责要求他们必须以故事情节和内容的丰富取胜。因而西方神话动辄便是长篇大作，如荷马史诗，包括《伊利亚特》和《奥德赛》，共 279 298 行。

二、西方神话体现了二元对立的思想，中国神话体现的是天人合一的思想

在西方的创世神话中，神从混沌中孕育而出，便与自然世界有了区分。神将神之外的自然界作为对象加以考察认识，划清主体与客体的界限，形成了天人相分的理性自然观。自然成为人认识、利用和征服的对象，这意味着西方创世神话中具有外向性的思维特点。上帝照着自己的形象造人，又以上帝的名义赋予人类合法地对自然进行奴役和征服的权利。西方创世神话中，大多数的神都是冒险家、掠夺者和征服者。思维的外向性体现在西方人的冒险、开放、自由、积极进取、攻击性强、弃旧迎新等方面。西方文化逐渐形成了以逻辑分析为主要方法、以对象化的眼光打量和研究外物的思维模式，造就了西方文化强调个体意识与个性独立的文化个性；同时，这种观念也进一步激发了人们探索自然、征服自然的强烈欲望，导致人与自然形成了长期的竞争关系。

在中国创世神话中，化生型是一种典型的造物方式。盘古死后身体化为世间万物，人与自然融为一体，人与万物都被赋予了灵气。中国人不把自然看成是无生命的物质，而是看成人的有机体的一部分，是连续性的有机生命世界；天、地、人、自然属于同源、同构、同体，世界是由原始亲体产生。中国传统思维中不是以自然为认识对象，而是将自然人化，从主体自身出发，经过直观经验后直接回到主体自身，追求主客体统一，实现尽善尽美的人与自然、人与人的整体和谐。也就是说，神与人、神与自然和谐统一，没有间隔，自然是神的化身。此外，在中国的造人神话中，人的生命和灵魂都来自土地，因此，人不是内在分裂的，并没有灵与肉的冲突。因此“与天地合其德，与日月合其明，与四时合其序，与鬼神合其吉凶，先天而天弗违，后天而奉天时”（《周易·乾卦》）就成为中国哲学所倡导的人生最高的理想境界。基于“天人合一”的哲学思想，在人与自然的关系上，中华文化走向了提倡与天地参合、尊崇自然、人与自然相互融合并和谐共处的方向；而在价值取向上，中华文化提倡把个人目标与集体目标融为一体，强调个人对集体的依赖、责任和义务，形成了崇尚集体主义的文化个性。同时，在这一思想的

影响下，注重事物的整体概念和普遍联系也成为中华文化的主要特点之一。

三、西方创世神话的排异性与中国创世神话的包容性

西方创世神非常热衷于扩张，借以增强自身的力量，提高自身地位，因为谁的力量最强大，谁就是众神之王，而众神之王也时刻提防和打击其他企图超过自己的神。在希腊创世神话中，克洛诺斯杀死自己的父亲乌拉诺斯并夺得王位。这导致他最大的恐惧来源于自己的孩子——他害怕自己的孩子也会像他一样弑父夺权。因此他每生出一个孩子，便亲口把他吞掉以绝后患。这种文化绝对不会被以血缘为基础的中华文化所理解。后来，在母亲的保护下存活下来的孩子宙斯，杀死父亲克洛诺斯之后成为诸神之王，也同样把对手扔到冥界最深的地洞之中，使其永世不得出来。这何止是排异这么简单，这是连父子亲情都不能相容的权力意志。

而在中国，创世神话则更多地体现了包容性。我们知道，中国是一个多民族的国家，民族关系复杂，宗教信仰亦很复杂。几千年来，活跃在中国大地上的有道教、佛教、伊斯兰教、基督教等许多宗教派别，但信仰不同的教派却终能相安无事，不敌对，不冲突，这不能不让人惊奇。这与中国创世神话中深刻的包容意识分不开。

一是中国创世神话没有发展成宗教。若各民族的创世神话得到完善发育，并为后世统治集团所利用而变为宗教，那么现今诸民族因宗教信仰的差异而产生的分歧与冲突一定会更加复杂。

二是尽管中国各民族都有自己的创世神话观念，许多民族共尊一个创世神的情况并不少见，汉族也接受少数民族的创世神观念。

三是神话的历史化。创世神历史化为民族始祖，他们被搬进人类所建立的宗庙后，虽然失去了成为宗教神的可能，但由于中国伦理观念重“孝悌”，神可以不敬，但祖宗却绝对不可不敬。变成始祖神后的创世神在人们心目中的地位是其他外来神不能撼动的。

一直有观点认为，中国人的宗教观念非常淡薄，究其根本，就是因为我们的创世神话具有这种宽厚的包容性，使得没有一种宗教能够排他而独存。

VIII. Homework

东西方创世神话中的神人关系探究（小组协作讨论）

先解释词语，然后分析中西方创世神话中的神人关系差异。

词语解释：潘多拉魔盒、普罗米修斯盗火种、洪水灭世、共工怒触不周山、女娲补天

希伯来神话 ____

希腊神话 ____

中国神话 ____

Section Two

The Contrast of Chinese and Western Heroes of Myths

I. Learning Objectives

1. To learn about the names of the main characters and their stories in Chinese and Western myths
2. To learn about the personality and behavior of the main characters in Chinese and Western myths
3. To select one or two pairs of characters respectively in Chinese and Western myths to make a comparison
4. To compare and contrast the main characters in Chinese and Western myths and then to summarize the similarities and differences between the main characters in Chinese and Western myths

II. Key Points and Difficult Points

1. To spell and pronounce the main characters in Western myth
2. To make a summary of the characteristics of the main characters in Western myth
3. To select a proper pair of figures when a comparison is made
4. To summarize the characteristics of the main characters in Chinese myths
5. To conclude the similarities and differences between the main characters in Western and Chinese myths

III. Lead-in Questions

1. Do you know the characteristics of such important heroes as Prometheus and Achilles and their stories?

2. Do you know stories of such main heroes as Pangu and Houyi in Chinese myth?

3. What are the similarities and differences between the main characters in Chinese and Western myths in behavior and their pursuit of ideal?

4. Achilles had learned well about his destiny before he went to the war against Troy: If he stayed home, he would live a long and tranquil life with a beautiful wife and a group of children and grand-children, but he would soon be forgotten; If he left home for the war against Troy, he would die on field and become immortal. Finally he chose to join the war against Troy. What can you learn about the definition of hero from Achilles' choice to go to field? Were there any such figures in Chinese myth? What are the similarities and differences between them?

5. What are the heroic figures and the shaping of cultural character?

IV. Learning Contents

1. Achilles

The warrior Achilles is one of the great heroes of Greek mythology. According to legend, Achilles was extraordinarily strong, courageous and loyal, but he had one vulnerability—his "Achilles' heel". Homer's epic poem *The Iliad* tells the story of his adventures during the last year of the Trojan War.

Like most mythological heroes, Achilles had a complicated family tree. His father was Peleus, the mortal king of the Myrmidons—a people who, according to legend, were extraordinarily fearless and skilled soldiers. His mother was Thetis, a Nereid.

Thetis dunked him into the River Styx, whose waters were said to confer the invulnerability of the gods. However, she gripped him tightly by the foot as she dipped him into the river—so tightly that the water never touched his heel. As a result, Achilles was invulnerable everywhere but heels.

When he was nine years old, a seer predicted that Achilles would die heroically in battle against the Trojans. When she heard about this, Thetis disguised him as a girl. To be a great warrior was Achilles' fate, however, and he soon left Skyros and joined the Greek army.

According to legend, Achilles has led one battle after another. He has met with great success—in fact, he is undefeated in battle—but the war itself has reached a stalemate.

There was the internecine quarrel between Achilles and Agamemnon, the leader of the Achaean armies and Menelaus' brother. In a battle, Agamemnon had taken as a concubine a young Trojan woman named Chryseis. Chryseis' father was a priest of the god Apollo, so Apollo punished the Greek armies by sending a plague to kill the soldiers one by one. As his ranks thinned, Agamemnon finally agreed to allow Chryseis to return to her father. However, he demanded a replacement concubine in exchange: Achilles' wife, the Trojan princess Briseis.

Achilles did as his commander asked and relinquished his bride. Then, he announced that he would no longer fight on Agamemnon's behalf. He gathered his belongings, including the armor Hephaestus had made, and refused to come out of his tent.

With the Greeks' greatest warrior off the battlefield, the tide began to turn in favor of the Trojans. The Greeks lost one battle after another. Eventually, Achilles' best friend, the soldier Patroclus, was killed by Trojan prince Hector.

Furious, Achilles vowed to take revenge. He chased Hector back to Troy, slaughtering Trojans all the way. When they got to the city walls, Hector tried to reason with his pursuer, but Achilles was not interested. He stabbed Hector in the throat, killing him.

According to later legends, the warrior returned to Troy after Hector's funeral to exact further revenge for Patroclus' death. However, the still-vengeful Apollo told Hector's brother Paris that Achilles was coming. Paris, who was not a brave warrior, ambushed Achilles as he entered Troy. He shot his unsuspecting enemy with an arrow, which Apollo guided to the one place he knew Achilles was vulnerable: his heel, where his mother's hand had kept the waters of the Styx from touching his skin. Achilles died on the spot, still undefeated in battle.

（资料来源：http://www.history.com/topics/ancient-history/achilles）

单词表

The Iliad		《伊利亚特》
Peleus	*n.*	珀琉斯
Myrmidons	*n.*	密耳弥多涅人
Thetis	*n.*	忒提斯（海中仙女之一）
Nereid	*n.*	涅瑞伊得斯（希腊神话中海的女神）
dunk	*v.*	扣篮；泡；浸
River Styx		冥河斯提克斯

confer	*v.*	授予；给予
seer	*n.*	预言家；先知
Skyros	*n.*	斯基罗斯岛（位于爱琴海西部的一个岛）
stalemate	*n.*	僵局；困境
internecine	*adj.*	两败俱伤的；互相残杀的；致命的
Agamemnon	*n.*	阿伽门农（特洛伊战争中希腊军队的统帅）
Achaean	*adj.*	亚加亚的；与亚加亚人有关的
Menelaus	*n.*	墨涅拉俄斯（斯巴达国王）
concubine	*n.*	妾；情妇；妃子
relinquish	*v.*	放弃；放手
Hephaestus	*n.*	火神赫菲斯托斯
Hector	*n.*	赫克托尔
ambush	*v.*	埋伏

2. 后羿

故事一：传说中后羿是尧时候的人。神话说，帝尧之时，天上有十个太阳同时出现，把土地都烤焦了，庄稼也干枯了，人们热得喘不过气来，倒在地上昏迷不醒。因为天气酷热的缘故，一些怪禽猛兽，也都从干涸的江湖和烧焦的森林里跑出来，在各地残害人民。后羿立即开始了射日的战斗。他从肩上取下那红色的弓，取出白色的箭，一支一支地向骄横的太阳射去，顷刻间十个太阳被射去了九个。

后羿雕像

后羿战巴蛇

故事二：后羿诛杀的第一个恶兽是在中原猖狂作恶的猰貐（yà yǔ）。猰貐原是个人面蛇身的天神。黄帝时代，猰貐被同为人面蛇身的天神贰负和危谋害。黄帝命人把被害死的猰貐抬到昆仑山上用不死药救他。猰貐复活后迷失了本性，变成了一只形状像牛，人脸、马蹄、浑身披着红色长毛的可怕怪物，被它吞食的人畜不计其数。后来后羿来到中原，猎杀了猰貐，为民除害。

（资料来源：http://baike.baidu.com/item/%E5%90%8E%E7%BE%BF/1504）

V. Story Links

1. Hercules（赫拉克勒斯）

Hercules was the son of Zeus and the mortal Alcmene. Hercules is famous for his strength and numerous far-ranging adventures. He was the greatest of the Greek heroes, a paragon of masculinity. Hercules used his wits on several occasions when his strength did not suffice, such as when laboring for the king Augeas of Elis, wrestling the giant Antaeus, or tricking Atlas into taking the sky back onto his shoulders. Together with Hermes he was the patron and protector of gymnasia and palaestrae. By conquering dangerous archaic forces he is said to have "made the world safe for mankind" and to be its benefactor.

2. 大禹

大禹是黄帝的后代，三皇五帝时期，黄河泛滥，鲧、禹父子二人受命于尧、舜二帝，任崇伯和夏伯负责治水。大禹率领民众，与自然灾害中的洪水斗争，最终获得了胜利。面对滔滔洪水，大禹从鲧治水的失败中吸取教训，改变了"堵"的办法，对洪水进行疏导，体现出他具有带领人民战胜困难的聪明才智。大禹为了治理洪水，常年在外与民众一起奋战，置个人利益于不顾，"三过家门而不入"。大禹治水 13 年，耗尽心血与体力，终于完成了治水的大业。

VI. Did You Know?

1. The Trojan Horse

指"木马计、暗藏的危险或者奸细"，出自荷马史诗《奥德赛》。

2. Procrustean Bed

亦作 the Procrustes' bed 或 the bed of Procrustes，直译是"普洛克路斯忒斯的床"，源自古希腊神话中的典故，常用以表示 an arrangement or plan that produces uniformity by violent and arbitrary measures 之意。该词语与中国成语"削足适履""截趾穿鞋"颇为相似，也类似于"强求一律"的说法。

VII. Cultural Reflection

中西神话中都有令人景仰的英雄形象，这些英雄形象沉淀为民族精神的外在表现，内化为民族性格的重要组成部分。可以说，神话中的英雄充分展示了人类的人格理想。他们大多具有敢于为他人牺牲的崇高理想，有英勇顽强的战斗精神，凭借自己的力量和智慧战胜人类的敌人，为本民族的发展和壮大起到巨大的作用。西方神话中的英雄没有我们今天的正义和非正义战争的观念。他们不仅保卫家园，而且征服其他部落，抢掠财物，杀死男子，俘获女子作为奴隶。中国神话中的黄帝同炎帝为了部落栖息之地而爆发战争，上古的神话史便是炎、黄两大部族的残酷斗争史，然而后代子孙对炎帝、黄帝同样崇敬，把他们奉为中华民族的祖先。中西神话中的英雄虽然有共同的特点，但更多地表现出来的却是代表不同文化内涵的巨大差异。

一、西方神话更强调个体意志，中国神话更注重集体利益

西方神话中的著名英雄当属阿喀琉斯。他勇武过人，力大无比。在特洛伊的战场上，因为有他的加盟，希腊军队一路高歌，逢战必胜。然而阿喀琉斯却因为主帅阿伽门农占有了他的一个女俘而拒绝再度参战，并眼看着希腊军队节节败退而无动于衷。后来阿伽门农亲自前来赔罪并乞求，阿喀琉斯依然坚持不出战。直至后来他的挚友因为渴望胜利而独赴沙场，被特洛伊大王子赫克托尔杀死，才使阿喀琉斯因复仇心切而再次参战。阿喀琉斯的选择完全听从于他个人的主观意志，把自我的情绪作为行动的指南，将个性化的个体展现到极致。

在中国神话中，大多数的中国英雄很少体现个人的意志。对于后羿，神话中没有描述过他的内心矛盾和斗争。《山海经・海内经》云：“帝俊赐羿彤弓素矰，以扶下国，羿是始去恤下地之百艰。”只知道他是受命于帝俊降临人间铲除祸害。在完成七件大功之后，后羿觉得自己没有辜负帝俊的委命，把在桑林擒获的大野猪杀了，剁得细细的并蒸成肉膏，奉献给天帝，满以为天帝会嘉许他，结果却出乎意料。后羿在功成之后首先想到的是得到帝俊的认可，但是他失望了。大概因为他射死人家九个儿子，所以被天帝革除了神籍，从此不能上天做神了。从神仙降落为凡人，后羿经常听到嫦娥的抱怨和责怪，最后后羿下决心排除万难去昆仑山向西王母寻得了两份不死之药，没想到嫦娥贪心，独自把不死药都吞了，结果飞上了月宫。而后羿从此性情大变，每日到处浪游，消磨时光。这是个例还是共性？究其根源何在？中国自古以来一直是“以群体为本位”的社会，人们世世代代以家族为单位的农耕生活，铸就了相互关心、相互依存的心理，人们从整体的存在中实现自我价值取向，具有“重整体，尚人伦，贵和持中的特点”。中国人把人和自然、人和人的关系，特别是男人和女人的关系，视为相依为命、休戚相关、患难相扶的关系，体现出和谐共荣的文化理念。

二、西方神话中的英雄张扬欲望，而中国神话中的英雄则更注重世俗道德

除了对个体意志的尊崇与张扬，希腊神话中的英雄人物也体现出对自我欲望的直面与认可。阿喀琉斯为一女俘愤而罢战，美神阿芙洛狄忒与战神阿瑞斯婚外偷情；厄洛斯和普赛克为了爱情历尽艰辛。诸神及英雄们的欲望常常不受道德控制，最典型的应当属地位最高的天神宙斯。希腊故事中有很多讲述他追求不同女子的情爱故事。尽管有漂亮的赫拉天后，但他仍不满足，在天上地下四处猎取美色，留情遗种，而且为达目的不择手段。他们直面个体欲望，张扬个体欲望。马克思认为，“希腊人是正常的儿童”。古希腊文化真的在这一点上做到了儿童般地想什么就表达什么，想什么就直接追求什么。由此，我们不难理解，西方中世纪骑士文学赞美骑士与贵妇人私通，《十日谈》大谈男女性事，或许都生动地体现了希腊神话中对张扬欲望精神的不断传承。

相反，中国的创世神对“性”则采取讳莫如深的态度。创世神从流传于汉族的盘古、女娲，到蒙古族的麦德尔神女，没有一个有生活作风问题。甚至在这些创世神话里很难找到谈及“性”的字句。就算偶有提到男女创世神结合生育造人亦提得很隐晦。如阿昌族神话《遮帕麻与遮米麻》中遮帕麻对遮米麻说：“你能织地，我会造天，让我们结合在一起来创造人类吧。”他们又怕无人为其说媒定亲，不能名正言顺而“违背天意”，非得隔山生烟交合才肯结合。生育也不是直接说生下了孩子，而是说生下一颗葫芦籽，种下后得了一个大葫芦，破开得九子，慎之又慎。神话中这种对“性”的过分严谨态度使得后人谈“性”变色。古代文学里，凡英雄豪杰定是不近女色，如《三国演义》和《水浒传》中的众多好汉便是如此。

三、西方神话中的英雄多暴力行为，而中国神话中的英雄则多牺牲精神

西方神话中充满了暴力行为及对暴力的热衷。诸位神灵英雄探索如何使自己变得更强大有力，是为争夺或保护至高无上之权力地位。盖娅因为乌拉诺斯扔掉了面目丑陋的孩子，就怂恿自己的儿子们杀掉父亲，以泄私恨。她的小儿子克洛诺斯在杀死自己的父亲称王之后，害怕自己的孩子将来也推翻自己，因此吃掉了自己所有的亲生孩子（除了被藏起来的宙斯）。宙斯以酷刑折磨普罗米修斯，不仅是因为后者为人间盗火，还因为他知道宙斯将被另外的神推翻的秘密。对暴力的推崇是个性发展的结果，即为了达到目的而不惜一切手段的意志。暴力行为也是冒险精神所必备的要素之一，没有面对暴力毫不胆怯的心态，便无法实现在陌生领域的冒险和对外面世界的征服。可以说，对个性的追求助长了暴力行为的发生，而对暴力行为的推崇又助长了冒险精神的发生。冒险与求知带来大量的探险活动，哥伦布在探险中发现了美洲新大陆，以《鲁滨孙漂流记》为代表的探险文学也应运而生。这种文化传承使得每个人的个性与创造力都得到最大限度的张扬与扩充，社会充满活力，却也因此常使民族精神的内聚力不强，大家各行其是，社会问题层出不穷。这也解释了在西方社会中，共同规范与规则的重要意义。

中国神话中的英雄则更多地体现了牺牲精神。盘古开天之后倒下，身体变为大地万物；夸父为了追赶太阳而累到付出生命；精卫为了填海经年不息地为不可能达到的目标而努力。大家耳熟能详的恐怕当属大禹治水的故事了。他为了治理水患三过家门而不入，以牺牲自己的享受和家庭来实现对事业的忠诚。

这种牺牲精神背后是强烈的责任意识和务实精神，这种精神对民族的发展起着积极作用，它成为原始社会民族内聚力和社会一体化的促进力，有利于集大众之力于一个目标，更好地与大自然做斗争。务实精神使中华民族形成了丰富多彩的本土文化和传统。

总之，西方神话中的英雄随心所欲，关乎自然欲望而不关乎道德。他们是伟大的创世者和救世者，但也是灭世者。而中国神话中的英雄虽多半人半兽，但大多是真、善、美的化身，承担维护宇宙和世界秩序的重大责任，是人类的创造者、保护者。中国神话中的英雄具有崇拜、服从、塑造和神化权威的倾向，反映在思维方式上是唯上和唯贤，道德至上。西方神话中的英雄则体现出对个性的推崇，对权威的怀疑，对未知世界充满了探索欲望，是一种外向征服的文化，而中国的文化则是内省的，重视身心和谐以及道德完善，更具宽容性与和谐基因。

VIII. Homework

1. 中西方神话中的英雄形象探索

请将中国神话人物与西方神话人物对应起来，并说出选择的理由。

中国神话人物	西方神话人物
刑天	普罗米修斯
黄帝	阿喀琉斯
夸父	赫拉克勒斯
后羿	宙斯
女娲	阿瑞斯
大禹	

选择的理由是：________________________________

2. 头脑风暴

通过阅读、学习神话人物事迹和中西方神话人物的对比，你对中西方神话中的英雄人物性格有多少了解呢？我们一起来进行头脑风暴吧！

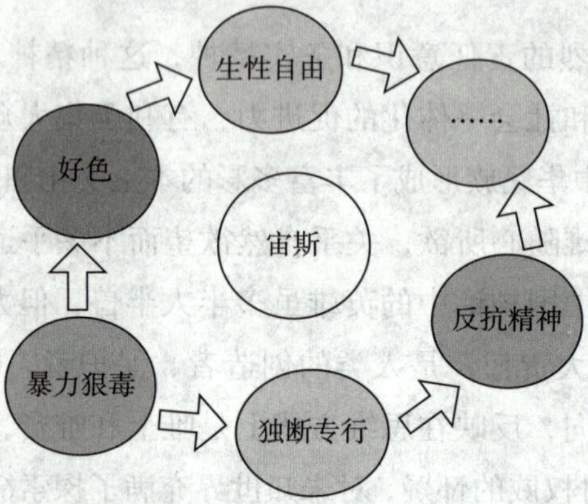

关于宙斯的性格，你还有什么想法吗？

说一说下列神话人物的性格特征吧！

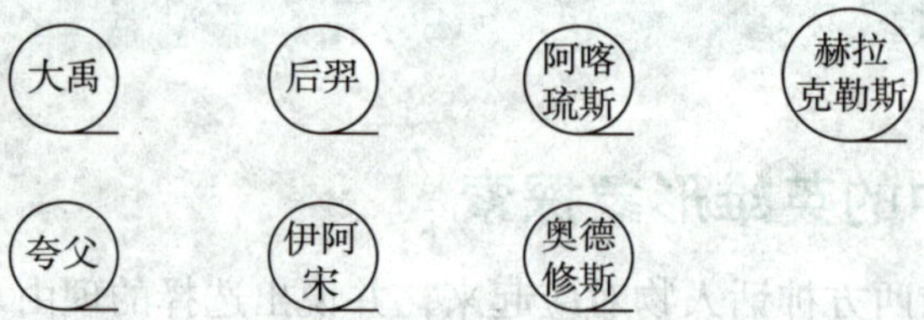

3. 小组协作

角色扮演人数：2～4 人

如果你将经历一次时空穿越，你可以跟中西方的神话英雄在 QQ、微信上即时交流，你最想跟哪位英雄聊天呢？你想问他 / 她哪些问题呢？你又能回答他 / 她的哪些问题呢？聊天内容不仅要生动有趣，而且要兼顾深度和广度。

小组成员 A：扮演神话英雄　　小组成员 B：你自己

对话范例如下：请你和同伴一起，进行一次有趣的对话吧！

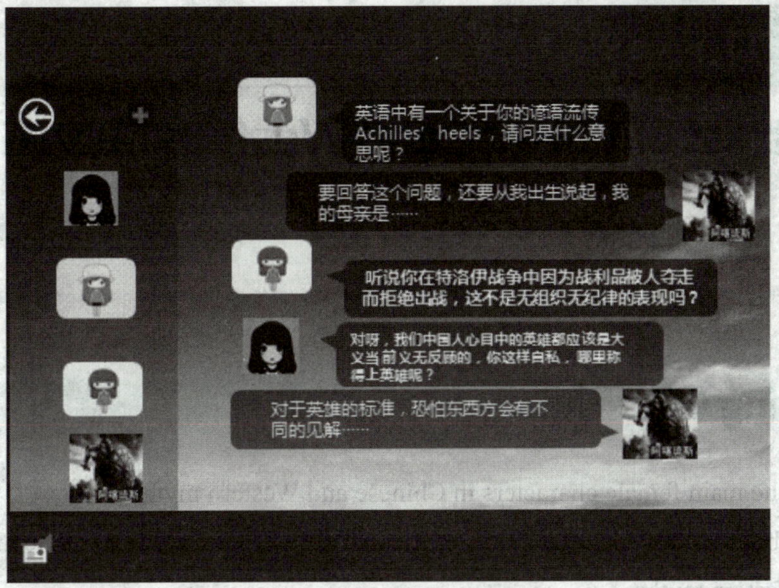
英语中有一个关于你的谚语流传Achilles' heels，请问是什么意思呢？
要回答这个问题，还要从我出生说起，我的母亲是……
听说你在特洛伊战争中因为战利品被人夺走而拒绝出战，这不是无组织无纪律的表现吗？
对呀，我们中国人心目中的英雄都应该是大义当前义无反顾的，你这样自私，哪里称得上英雄呢？
对于英雄的标准，恐怕东西方会有不同的见解……

Section Three

The Contrast of Chinese and Western Myth Goddesses

I. Learning Objectives

1. To know the main female characters in Chinese and Western myths

2. To learn about the personalities, ways of life and attitudes toward love of the main female figures in Chinese and Western myths

3. To make a comparison of the world views and values of the female figures between Chinese and Western myths

4. To summarize the similarities and differences of the characters of female figures in Chinese and Western myths and trace the cultural roots of these differences

II. Key Points and Difficult Points

1. To master the life courses of female figures in Western myths

2. To master the values and world views of female figures in Western myths

3. To select the point from which a comparison and contrast of Chinese and Western female figures can be made

4. To compare and contrast the personalities between Chinese and Western female figures

5. To understand the cultural sources for these similarities and differences mentioned above

III. Lead-in Questions

1. What are the differences of the goddesses between Chinese and Western myths?

2. How different are the attitudes of goddesses between Chinese and Western myths toward love

and family?

3. What are the different destinies of goddesses between Chinese and Western myths?

4. What is the connection between cultural origins and creation myths?

5. What is the connection between the shaping of cultural characters and creation myths?

IV. Learning Contents

1. Helen and Paris

Helen was the most beautiful woman of the world in Western myth. She was an infamous lady. She lighted the flames of the Trojan war and brought extreme destruction on the city of Troy. Helen was the daughter of Zeus. Helen's matchless beauty and charms drew towards her many heroes from all parts of Greece.

When still small she was carried off by Theseus, who wished to have a divine wife. But she was rescued later by her brother Castor, and brought back to her native land. Her stepfather married her to Menelaus, king of Sparta.

Nothing of importance had happened to her married life until Paris came to visit Sparta. Helen was attracted by Paris' lovely face. They stole one another's love in the absence of Menelaus and then eloped on board a ship to Troy. Helen left her young daughter behind. To get Helen back, the Greek army sailed across and laid a long siege to the city of Troy.

帕里斯和海伦

Helen was quietly weaving her story into a web of golden carpet one day when she was called up the city walls of Troy to look at the fighting between Menelaus and Paris. Menelaus was determined to kill Paris in the battle. Sitting by the side of King Priam, she told the chiefs of the Greek side to him. Tears of love filled up her eyes when she saw her first husband down below. After Paris fled the field she had the feelings of love and scorn. She encouraged Hector and Paris to take the field again and sincerely mourned the death of the true hero Hector. But when Odysseus and Diomedes came in disguise to steal the Palladium, she helped them to do so as much as she could. After Paris died in battle she became the wife of another son of Priam.

In the meantime Menelaus was anxiously searching for Helen in the ruined palaces of Troy. Aphrodite had made Helen more beautiful, so when he finally found her trembling in a corner, Menelaus was most unwilling to bring his sword down on her charming face. Menelaus felt secretly overjoyed to have his wife back again. Following Menelaus through the ruins of the city, Helen felt ashamed of her impure behavior. And she was truly scared at the terrible fate she was to have in the Greek Camp.

Once more her beauty saved her. No one could bring himself to thrust his sword into such a charming and graceful lady. In the tent of Menelaus she threw herself at the feet of the Spartan king, asking for forgiveness. Moved by the scene, Menelaus helped her up and let her forget the past. He held her in his arms while she had tears of grief and happiness. The pair loved each other like before and vanished in the far west.

单词表

infamous	*adj.*	声名狼藉的，无耻的，伤风败俗的
Trojan	*adj.*	特洛伊的
Zeus	*n.*	宙斯
carry off		抢走，赢得
Theseus	*n.*	忒修斯
divine	*adj.*	神圣的，极好的
Menelaus	*n.*	斯巴达王
Sparta	*n.*	斯巴达
elope	*v.*	私奔
siege	*n.*	围攻，围困，包围，封锁

weave	*v.*	编，织
chief	*n.*	首领，酋长
flee	*v.*	逃走，逃掉
scorn	*n.*	轻蔑，鄙视，看不起
mourn	*v.*	哀痛，哀悼
Odysseus	*n.*	奥德修斯（古希腊荷马所作史诗《奥德赛》中的主人公，伊塞卡国王，在特洛伊战中献木马计）
Diomedes	*n.*	狄俄墨得斯（古希腊男性英雄之一，为特洛伊战争之希腊联军英雄）
disguise	*n.*	伪装，化装，掩饰
Priam	*n.*	普里阿摩斯（特洛伊末代国君）
Aphrodite	*n.*	阿芙洛狄忒（古希腊神话中的爱与美之女神，是奥林匹斯十二主神之一，在罗马神话中被称为维纳斯）
thrust	*v.*	猛推，刺入
sword	*n.*	剑
grief	*n.*	悲伤，悲痛
vanish	*v.*	消失，突然不见

2. 娥皇和女英的故事

传说中聪明美丽的娥皇和女英，是上古时部落酋长尧帝的两个女儿。尧帝晚年，想物色一个满意的继承人。他看到舜是个德才超群的人，于是就把帝位传给了舜，并让娥皇和女英做了舜的妻子。娥皇被封为后，女英被封为妃。舜不负尧的信任，让禹治理洪水，使人民过上了安定的生活，娥皇、女英也鼎力协助舜为百姓做好事。舜帝晚年时，九嶷山一带发生战乱，舜想到那里视察一下实情。舜把这个想法告诉娥皇、女英，两位夫人想到舜年老体衰，争着要和舜一块去。舜考虑到山高林密，道路曲折，只带了几个随从，悄悄地离去。娥皇、女英知道舜已走的消息，也立即起程。追到扬子江边遇到了大风，一位渔夫把她们送上洞庭山。后来，她们俩得知舜帝已死，被埋在了九嶷山下，便日日扶竹向九嶷山方向泣望，把那里的竹子染得泪迹斑斑。最后，她们俩投湘水而亡，成了湘水之神。

娥皇和女英

V. Story Links

1. Niobe（尼俄柏）

Niobe is one of the most tragic figures in Greek mythology. She and her husband, Amphion, had fourteen children, known as the Niobids. In a moment of hubris, Niobe boasted about her seven sons and seven daughters during a ceremony honoring Leto, the daughter of the Titans Coeus and Phoebe. She mocked Leto for having only two children: Apollo, the god of prophecy and music, and Artemis, the virgin goddess of the wilderness. Leto, deeply insulted, retaliated by sending Apollo and Artemis to earth to slaughter all of Niobe's children. Overwhelmed by grief at the sight of his dead sons, Amphion is said to have either committed suicide or died of despair. In any case, Niobe's entire family was annihilated in mere moments. Devastated, Niobe cradled her youngest daughter in her arms before fleeing to Mount Sipylus in Asia Minor. There, consumed by sorrow, she was transformed into stone, and from the rock, a stream—identified as the Achelous—flowed, formed by her endless tears. Niobe thus became a poignant symbol of eternal mourning.

2. 嫘祖养蚕缫丝

相传嫘祖是中国远古时代的帝王黄帝的妻子。她勤劳、贤惠，不仅操持家，而且帮黄帝处理国家大事，而其最大的功劳就是教会了老百姓养蚕、缫丝。那时候，大地上有一个蚕神，每天趴在大桑树上，不停地吐着银白闪亮的细丝，但是人们却不知道利用它来织绸做衣服。有一次，黄帝打了大胜仗，善良的蚕神也把吐的丝作为礼物送给了黄帝。黄帝把蚕丝拿给妻子嫘祖，嫘祖看到蚕丝轻若浮云，柔似流水，便用这些丝织成绢做衣服。老百姓们看到嫘祖养蚕、织绢，也都纷纷来仿效，嫘祖就把这方面的技术耐心地教给他们，这样，养蚕便在中国盛行起来，丝绸也就成了中国的特产。

VI. Did You Know?

1. Helen of Troy

这个短语的中文意思是“红颜祸水”。由于 Helen 导致了特洛伊城的沦陷，因此 Helen of Troy 就成了“红颜祸水”的代名词。

2. An Apple of Discord

意为“争斗之源，不和之因”，直译为“纠纷的苹果”，出自荷马史诗《伊利亚特》。

3. Pandora's Box

潘多拉的盒子。英语中常用 Pandora's box 喻指“灾祸之源”，用 open Pandora's box 表示“引起种种祸患”。例：When I asked Ella about her grades, I didn't know I had opened Pandora's box.

4. Win/Gain Laurels

获得荣誉；赢得声望。look to one's laurels 爱惜名声；保持纪录。rest on one's laurels 坐享清福；吃老本。这一说法源自希腊神话中太阳神阿波罗（Apollo）与河神珀涅俄斯（Peneus）的女儿达弗涅（Daphne）的爱情故事。

5. A Penelope's Web

亦作 The Web of Penelope，直译为“珀涅罗珀的织物”，指“故意拖延的策略；永远做不完的工作”，典故出自荷马史诗《奥德赛》。

VII. Cultural Reflection

女性是神话中一个特殊的群体，她们或美或丑，或善或恶，都引发人们的无限关注。而且，中西神话中的女性也是后世女性形象、女性思想以及女性文学的根基。中西方文化中的女性都服从男子的管制，处于较低的地位，社会事务一般不为女性所关注。除了这些屈指可数的相同之处，中西方神话中的女性体现出来的差异值得注意。

一、西方神话中的女性敢爱敢恨，中国神话中的女性贤良谦让

西方神话中的女性群星闪耀，性格各异。这些女神的性格特点非常突出，尤其是在爱恨情仇的选择上，表现出相当强烈的主动性。赫拉会对宙斯的情人不遗余力地进行报复，毫不掩饰自己的嫉妒之心；月亮女神狄安娜爱上了恩底弥翁，便大胆主动地追求；一位海洋女神克吕提厄痴迷于太阳神阿波罗，即使最终化为一株向阳花也不改初心……最令人印象深刻的恐怕还是为爱情不惜抛弃家人的美狄亚了。美狄亚为了追求自己的爱情，背叛了父亲，残酷地杀死了弟弟，并为自己的爱人伊阿宋奉献了智慧与勇气。当她看到伊阿宋移情别恋后，又不惜杀死其新欢，甚至杀死了自己的两个儿子。她的行为凌厉而果敢，甚至可以说残忍而血腥。对于这个不惜动用一切手段的女人，希腊神话对她是宽容的，美狄亚离开伊阿宋之后，最后成为雅典王埃勾斯的妻子。

中国神话体系中，女神们的个性特征没有这么鲜明，也很少有语言具体描述她们的爱恨情仇。最著名的女神女娲是作为伟大的造物始祖出现的。她做事不会计较个人得失，专注于为人类创造美好的环境，从不显耀自己，处处表现出谦逊的美德。娥皇、女英的声名虽然广为传播，但关于她们的故事却再简单不过：她们得知丈夫舜死去后，哭到泪染斑竹，然后双双投湘水而亡。她们之间有无嫉妒之心、爱意是否深重等都被忽略，中国神话展现的是女性贤良谦让、忠诚等美德。

二、西方神话中的女性以爱情为最高追求，中国神话中的女性将家庭视为重要责任

提及西方神话中的爱情，首先应该请出著名的爱与美的女神阿芙洛狄忒。她生于海中浪花，拥有古希腊女性完美的身段和相貌，象征爱情与女性的美丽，被认为是女性体格美的最高典范。但在西方文化的语境中，典范却与贞洁无关。阿芙洛狄忒本是锻冶工匠之神赫菲斯托斯的妻子，但经常对丈夫不忠。有关她的恋爱传说很多，她和很多神祇育有儿女，包括狄俄尼索斯与阿瑞斯。在阿芙洛狄忒的众多情人中，也许美少年阿多尼斯算得上是她的至爱。阿多尼斯是来自西亚的另一位神祇，是阿芙洛狄忒和冥后普西芬尼争夺的对象。她们为了得到美少年而激烈地争吵，最后天神宙斯不得不出面仲裁，并判决阿多尼斯一生中的三分之一时间属于自己，三分之一属于普西芬尼，另外的三分之一属于阿芙洛狄忒。西方神话中对拥有许多情人的阿芙洛狄忒的美化与喜爱，反映了西方人把爱情看得如生命般重要的思想。

在中国的神话中，美好的女性绝不能每天追求美少年，而应充当一心相夫教子的贤惠表率。嫘祖是黄帝的元妃，她非常贤惠，默默无闻地操持日常事务，以养蚕为业，用心尽妻子的责任。

这其实是中国古代男主外、女主内的社会模式的开始。嫫母是黄帝的次妃。相传嫫母的相貌奇丑无比，“但有德，黄帝纳之，使训后宫”。涂山氏是大禹的妻子，大禹治水时，她就给丈夫煮饭、送饭，平时的主要事务就是管理家务。嫘祖、嫫母和涂山氏可以说是中国传统文化中推崇的贤良淑德的德行楷模，古人认为女子相貌的美丽并非最重要的，道德伦理上的美丽才最受推崇。

三、西方神话中的女性以美为荣，中国神话中的女性以德为尊

西方女神中不乏美得倾国倾城的人物，这些人物以美为荣，以美为傲，以美为资本。除了著名的天神，还有一位不能略过的、因美貌而引发一场旷日持久的著名战争的海伦。相传海伦拥有世间最美的姿容，引来求婚者无数，其父亲怕选出一位女婿会导致杀戮，便以抽签的方式决定海伦嫁给谁。海伦在嫁给墨涅拉俄斯之后，为他生了一个女儿，名叫赫耳弥奥涅。后来特洛伊的王子帕里斯由于“金苹果”事件的缘故，来到海伦的身边，并诱使海伦离开丈夫，跟他同赴特洛伊。海伦的丈夫墨涅拉俄斯求助于他的哥哥阿伽门农，于是希腊各部集结了军队到特洛伊去夺回海伦，一场大战终因海伦而拉开帷幕。十年的战争结束后，海伦的前夫墨涅拉俄斯终于找到了曾经的妻子，却发现自己无法将利剑刺向她那迷人的面孔。墨涅拉俄斯将她轻轻抱起来，他们俩像以前那样相爱，一同消失在遥远的西方。

在中国的神话中，女神中似乎没有多少是以美貌著称的，或者说神话故事中只提及女神的品德，容貌基本不在中国文化的关注之列。如果说偶有提及的话，被奉为楷模的嫫母还是以容貌丑陋著称。而美貌的女性大都是祸水。中国神话故事里最出名的祸水当属妲己。妲己身为殷纣王妃，以美艳著称。虽然其具体故事已不可细考，但是《列女传》明确把妲己定为红颜祸水、女色亡国的典型。史书为了突出妲己之恶，把原本纣王的罪行亦置换到妲己头上。妲己则逐渐被视为负面的形象，是纣王放纵和国家灭亡的罪魁祸首，被视为美色腐化的象征。

总之，中西方向来存在着较大的文化差异。就希腊和中国来说，一个是由海洋文明孕育而出，一个是由农耕文明发展而来。冯友兰先生借用孔子的一段话来形象地比喻希腊与中国，“海洋国家的人是知者，大陆国家的人是仁者”，“知者乐水，仁者乐山；知者动，仁者静；知者乐，仁者寿”。

希腊地处于欧洲南部，地中海东北部，具有典型的开放性海洋环境。海洋文明重冒险、好争斗，生活主要依靠海外贸易。海上的生活具有周期短、频率快、风险大、收获随机的特点，这就造就了他们自由奔放、富于幻想、敢于冒险的性格。同时，悠闲的地中海自然条件优越，有着浪漫的生活气息，这里的人们更重享乐。希腊人以人为主体，赋予诸神人性的种种弱点。由于缺乏道德束缚和宗教的威严，希腊神更像是具有人的情趣、拥有超凡能力的人。

中国半封闭的大陆环境造就了人们重勤劳、好实干的特质。而高山和海洋等不便的外部环境严重阻隔了与其他民族交流的可能性。对自然环境的恐惧和敬畏，形成了对自然的崇尚、顺

服和伦理至上的观念。中国神话中备受尊敬的人物都是德行的楷模，他们在生活中不苟言笑，遇事冷静，威严尊贵，似乎没有常人的七情六欲。人类仰望他们，对这些神顶礼膜拜。东西方的这些差异造就了不同的人物性格倾向。神话中的人物形象正好是这两种文明的体现和承载，成为本民族的形象原型。

VIII. Homework

1. 头脑风暴

在阅读和学习了中西方神话故事中的女性人物之后，你认为她们都是什么样的形象呢？你更喜欢哪一位女性的形象？说出你的理由。

盖娅：大地之母、____________________

潘多拉：好奇心强、____________________

赫拉：嫉妒报复、____________________

雅典娜：智慧、____________________

美狄亚：敢爱敢恨、____________________

阿芙洛狄忒：爱情至上、____________________

海伦：绝世美女、____________________

女娲：勇于牺牲、____________________

观音：心地善良、____________________

娥皇、女英：贤良淑德、____________________

妲己：美艳绝伦、____________________

2. 调研报告

中西方分别塑造了两大美女，即海伦和西施。她们的身世有惊人的相似之处，那就是都与战争或政治纷争有关。她们的美名是建立在历史风云与悲剧命运之上的。她们是历史上最辉煌、最具永恒价值的象征之一。战争是残酷的，导致了战争的“美”同样是残酷的，但必须承认，“美”毕竟也为战争的传说乃至战争本身披上了一层浪漫的底色。同为与战争和权力纠葛相关的女性，但两人却有不同的境遇。海伦获得了众人及丈夫的谅解，而传说中西施却被沉江而死（另一种流传较广的说法是西施与范蠡归隐了）。试着从中西方文化角度探讨两人不同的命运结局。

3. 五分钟演讲

以娥皇、女英和美狄亚为代表的中西方女性对于爱情和婚姻有着不一样的态度和理解，你更支持哪种爱情、婚姻观？假设让你来代言，请大胆地说出你的想法吧。

参考资料

一、书籍

伯恩斯．古希腊罗马神话传说 [M]. 上海：上海世界图书出版公司，2009.

房龙．圣经故事 [M]. 北京：商务印书馆，2016.

施瓦布．希腊神话 [M]. 司马仝，王霹，编译．北京：人民文学出版社，1998.

陶阳，牟钟秀．中国创世神话 [M]. 上海：上海人民出版社，1989.

汉密尔顿．希腊罗马神话全书 [M]. 长沙：湖南文艺出版社，2023.

袁珂．中国神话传说：从盘古到秦始皇 [M]. 北京：世界图书出版公司，2012.

钟健．创世神话 [M]. 北京：中国社会出版社，2006.

Napoli, Donna Jo. Treasury of Greek Mythology: Classic Stories of Gods, Goddesses, Heroes & Monsters[M]. New York: National Geographic Children's Books, 2011.

Giesecke, Annette and Tierney, Jim. Classical Mythology A to Z: An Encyclopedia of Gods & Goddesses, Heroes & Heroines, Nymphs, Spirits, Monsters, and Places[M]. New York: Black Dog & Leventhal, 2020.

Buxton, Richard. The Complete World of Greek Mythology[M]. London: Thames & Hudson, 2004.

二、影视作品

电影：《特洛伊》《奥德修斯》《诸神之战》《诸神之怒》《大力神》《潘神的迷宫》《宙斯之子：赫拉克勒斯》

电视剧、评书：《封神榜》《西游记》

Chapter Two

The Contrast of Chinese and Western Ways of Thinking

课前成果检测

中西方思维方式阅读测试题

一、查一查，说一说

1. 存在就是被感知
2. 亚里士多德关于“第一哲学”的定义
3. 启蒙运动
4. 卢梭的《社会契约论》
5. “奥卡姆剃刀”准则
6. 解释下图

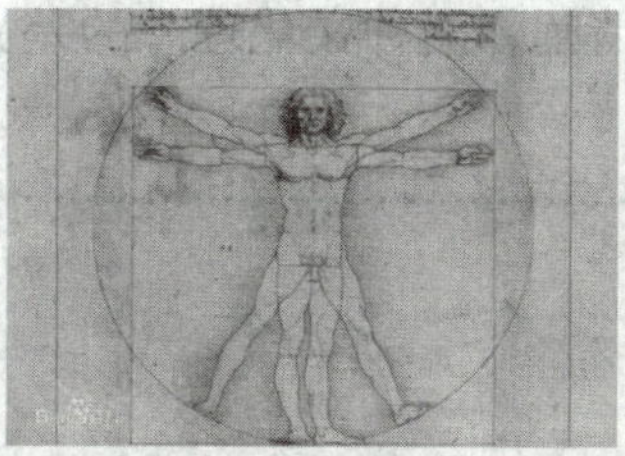

7. 孔子说："天何言哉？四时行焉，百物生焉，天何言哉？"

孟子说："万物皆备于我矣。反身而诚，乐莫大焉。"

老子说："王法地，地法天，天法道，道法自然。"

这些话表达的是同一种文化理念，请问具体是怎样的文化理念呢？

二、生活常识大搜索

1. 你和家人有过接受中医治疗的经历吗？你对中医的看法是怎样的？

2. "身心健康"中的"心"指的是哪个器官？中西医发展史中对器官的认识有什么差异？

3. 中药组方讲求"君臣佐使"的配伍原则，这背后有什么哲学意义吗？

4. 中国现代科技发展迅速，你能列举出在世界范围内享有盛誉的国产技术或品牌吗？

5. 商人在中西方历史上都是不可或缺的角色，你能列举出中西方历史中的商业名人吗？他们的经商之道有什么差异吗？

三、思考题

1. 西方在18世纪60年代掀起了第一次工业革命，进而改变了全世界的发展进程，对比中国同时期的科技发展，你是怎么理解这一现象的？

2. 在西方，商业传统贯穿整个欧洲文明史，商人阶层对社会发展的推动作用也是不容忽视的。而在古代中国，商业长期属于"末业"，属于被压抑、被边缘化的行业。这种对待商业活动的不同态度是基于怎样的文化理念呢？请阐释两种文化理念的差异及其他表现方式。

Section One
The Contrast of Chinese and Western Philosophies

I. Learning Objectives

1. To study the characteristics of the Western and Chinese philosophies
2. To fathom the reasons of the differences between Western and Chinese philosophies

II. Key Points and Difficult Points

1. To get a grip of the development of Western philosophy
2. To understand and summarize Chinese philosophy
3. To compare and contrast the ways of development of Chinese and Western philosophies

III. Lead-in Questions

1. Can you name some famous Chinese and Western philosophers?
2. In what way does the origin of Chinese philosophy differ from Western philosophy?
3. Would you please give us some key words of Chinese philosophical ideas?
4. Can you give examples to illustrate philosophical ideas of life in China and Western countries?

IV. Learning Contents

1. *Sophie's World*

Here I am again, Sophie. Today you are going to hear about the last of the great natural philosophers. His name is Democritus (c.460 BCE–c.370 BCE) and he was from the little town of Abdera on the northern Aegean coast.

If you were able to answer the question about Lego blocks without difficulty, you should have no problem understanding what this philosopher's project was.

Democritus agreed with his predecessors that transformations in nature could not be due to the fact that anything actually "changed". He therefore assumed that everything was built up of tiny invisible blocks, each of which was eternal and immutable. Democritus called these smallest units atoms.

The word "a-tom" means "un-cuttable". For Democritus it was all-important to establish that the constituent parts that everything else was composed of could not be divided indefinitely into smaller parts. If this were possible, they could not be used as blocks. If atoms could eternally be broken down into ever smaller parts, nature would begin to dissolve like constantly diluted soup.

Moreover, nature's blocks had to be eternal—because nothing can come from nothing. In this, he agreed with Parmenides and the Eleatics. Also, he believed that all atoms were firm and solid. But they could not all be the same. If all atoms were identical, there would still be no satisfactory explanation of how they could combine to form everything from poppies and olive trees to goatskin and human hair.

Democritus believed that nature consisted of an unlimited number and variety of atoms. Some were round and smooth, others were irregular and jagged. And precisely because they were so different they could join together into all kinds of different bodies. But however infinite they might be in number and shape, they were all eternal, immutable, and indivisible.

When a body—a tree or an animal, for instance—died and disintegrated, the atoms dispersed and could be used again in new bodies. Atoms moved around in space, but because they had "hooks" and "barbs", they could join together to form all the things we see around us.

So now you see what I meant about Lego blocks. They have more or less the same properties as those which Democritus ascribed to atoms. And that is what makes them so much fun to build with. They are first and foremost indivisible. Then they have different shapes and sizes. They are solid and impermeable. They also have "hooks" and "barbs" so that they can be connected to form every conceivable figure. These connections can later be broken again so that new figures can be constructed from the same blocks.

Today we can establish that Democritus' atom theory was more or less correct. Nature really is built up of different "atoms" that join and separate again. A hydrogen atom in a cell at the end of my nose was once part of an elephant's trunk. A carbon atom in my cardiac muscle was once in the tail of a dinosaur.

But what about the "soul", then? Surely that could not consist of atoms, of material things? Indeed it could. Democritus believed that the soul was made up of special round, smooth "soul atoms". When a human being died, the soul atoms flew in all directions, and could then become part of a new soul formation.

This meant that human beings had no immortal soul, another belief that many people share today. They believe, like Democritus, that "soul" is connected with brain, and that we cannot have any form of consciousness once the brain disintegrates.（节选自《苏菲的世界》，有删节）

雅典学院

单词表

Democritus	*n.*	德谟克里特，古希腊伟大的哲学家之一
Aegean	*adj.*	爱琴海的
Lego	*n.*	乐高（玩具品牌，以拼插玩具著称）
immutable	*adj.*	不变的
constituent	*adj.*	构成的，成分的
Parmenides	*n.*	巴门尼德（古希腊哲学家）
Eleatics	*n.*	埃利亚学派（古希腊哲学中的哲学学派，巴门尼德是此学派的代表之一）
poppy	*n.*	罂粟

disintegrate	*v.*	分解；碎裂；衰变
disperse	*v.*	分散
impermeable	*adj.*	无法渗透的
hydrogen	*n.*	氢
dinosaur	*n.*	恐龙

2. *The Spirit of the Chinese People*（《中国人的精神》）

Now in China because we Chinese have the religion of good citizenship a man does not feel the need of using physical force to protect himself; he has seldom the need even to call in and use the physical force of the policeman, of the State to protect him. A man in China is protected by the sense of justice of his neighbour; he is protected by the readiness of his fellow men to obey the sense of moral obligation. In fact, a man in China does not feel the need of using physical force to protect himself because he is sure that right and justice is recognised by everybody as a force higher than physical force and moral obligation is recognised by every body as something which must be obeyed…

Now the fundamental unsoundness of the civilization of Europe today, it seems to me, lies in its wrong conception of human nature; its conception that human nature is evil and because of this wrong conception, the whole structure of society in Europe has always rested upon force. The two things which the people of Europe have depended upon to maintain civil order are Religion and Law. In other words, the population of Europe has been kept in order by the fear of God and the fear of the Law. Fear implies the use of force. Therefore in order to keep up the fear of God, the people of Europe had at first to maintain a large number of expensive idle persons called priests. That, to speak of nothing else, meant so much expense, that it at last became an unbearable burden upon the people. In fact in the thirty years war of the Reformation, the people of Europe tried to get rid of the priest. After having got rid of the priests who kept the population in order by the fear of God, the people of Europe tried to maintain civil order by the fear of the Law. But to keep up the fear of the Law, the people of Europe have had to maintain another class of still more expensive idle persons called policemen and soldiers. Now the people of Europe are beginning to find out that the maintenance of policemen and soldiers to keep civil order, is still more ruinously expensive than even the maintenance of priests. In fact, as in the thirty years war of the Reformation, the people of Europe wanted to get rid of the priest, so in this present war, what the people of Europe really want, is to get rid of the soldier. But the alternatives before the people of Europe if they want to get rid of the policeman and soldier, is either to call back the priest to keep up the fear of God or to find something else which, like the fear of God and the fear of the Law, will help them to maintain civil order. That, to put the question broadly, I think, everybody will admit, is the great problem of civilization before the people of Europe after this war.（摘自辜鸿铭《中国人的精神》）

和为贵

单词表

sense of justice		正义感
readiness	*n.*	乐意，满意
obligation	*n.*	职责，责任
unsoundness	*n.*	缺陷，缺点
conception	*n.*	理念，观念
imply	*v.*	意味着
idle	*adj.*	闲散的，无所作为的
maintenance	*n.*	维持，维护
ruinously	*adv.*	极其地，非常地（尤指负面情况）
alternative	*n.*	可供选择的事物；替代品

V. Story Links

1. Francis Bacon and "knowledge is power"

As a talented boy, Francis Bacon entered the Trinity College, Cambridge at the age of twelve. He learned himself into a lawyer, and eventually was appointed as the Lord Chancellor. Soon after, he was trapped in a scandal which ended his political career. From then on, Bacon devoted himself to philosophy and science. Francis Bacon's fame rose years after his death. During the 18th-century French Enlightenment, his non-metaphysical approach to science became so influential that Voltaire introduced him to a French audience as the "father" of the scientific method. Bacon's philosophy is displayed in the vast and varied writings he left and he has been reputed as the "Father of Experimental Philosophy". His words "knowledge is power" are thus universally known.

2. 儒商和新儒商文化

儒商，即“儒”与“商”的结合体，既有儒者的道德和才智，又有商人的财富和成功。儒商之祖当推孔子最著名的门徒之一子贡。他按照“人弃我取，人取我予”的原则，不与人抗衡，善于把握时机，以成巨富。他性格豁达、能言善辩，忠实追随孔子，在经济上、精神上资助、扶助孔子，成为儒学传播的重要人物。又如充满传奇色彩的范蠡，既是出色的政治家、军事家，后期更是成为一名蜚声四方的实业家，被称为一代“商圣”。其经商目光远大，善于发现商机，更晓“积著之理”，参透物价涨跌规律，贱进贵出，最终“累十九年三致金，财聚巨万”。相比经商才能，范蠡更是以“富好行其德”的敦厚诚信的从商理念闻名天下。欲从商，先为人，诚信为本、勇于决断、待人接物、规矩方圆，这些不仅仅是为人的品德，更是商人成功的秘诀，亦成为后世儒商的经营之道。

VI. Did You Know?

1. 孔子《论语》摘录

（1）子游曰：“事君数，斯辱矣。朋友数，斯疏矣。”

——语出《论语·里仁》

A disciple of Confucius remarked, "In the service of your prince, if you keep constantly pointing out his errors it will lead to your disgrace; if you act in the same way to your friends it will estrange them."（辜鸿铭译）

（2）季文子三思而后行。子闻之，曰：“再，斯可矣。”

——语出《论语·公冶长》

It was remarked of a public character of the time that he always reflected thrice over every time before he acted. When Confucius heard of the remark, he observed, "Think twice—that is sufficient."（辜鸿铭译）

（3）子曰：“中庸之为德也，其至矣乎！民鲜久矣。”

——语出《论语·雍也》

Confucius remarked, “The use of the moral sentiment, well balanced and kept in perfect equilibrium—that is the true state of human perfection. It is seldom found long so kept up amongst man.”（辜鸿铭译）

2. 亚里士多德名言摘录

（1）Plato is dear to me, but dearer still is truth. 吾爱吾师，吾更爱真理。

（2）Love is composed of a single soul inhabiting two bodies. 爱是栖息在两个身体中的一个灵魂。

（3）It is possible to fail in many ways...while to succeed is possible only in one way. 失败有许多种可能，而成功却只有一种方式。

（4）He who is to be a good ruler must have first been ruled. 想成为一名优秀的统治者，必须先学会被统治。

（5）The high-minded man must care more for the truth than for what people think. 高尚的人应更关心真理，而不是人们的看法。

VII. Cultural Reflection

凡论及哲学，必有人认为它是无趣无用的，是空中楼阁，是独属于“老夫子”书斋里的脑力游戏，进而推断哲学思想、哲学著作必是佶屈聱牙，是我等常人所无法企及和领悟的。究其根源，恐怕是人们把哲学的概念压缩了，范围被圈定在我们个体的经验世界内，在哲学家的所思所想、哲学著作的字里行间，所有的误解、畏惧、退缩也便由此产生。那么到底什么是哲学呢？哲学与人类到底是怎样的关系？中西方对哲学的认识是否有差异呢？

一、什么是哲学？哲学是从哪里来的？

哲学在老子那里是“道可道，非常道；名可名，非常名”。“道”就是万物运转的方式和规律，是不可名状的，与世界上一切可以用某种属性来界定的物质和精神是不同的。而中国哲学的起始便源于这种不可名状的“虚无”。哲学在西方人那里被解读为“对智慧的热爱”（love of wisdom），是一切知识——形而上的、物理的、伦理的、宗教的、美学的、逻辑的、心理的，凡此种种的总和。在他们眼里，哲学的主要任务是对世界——既包括外在世界也包括人类的内在世界进行最根本的、科学性的探究和反思。西方哲学起源于古希腊文明，在那里，哲学是切实的，是可以名状的。正如笛卡尔所说：哲学作为一个整体就像一棵树，这棵树的根部是形而上学，树干是物理学，从树干中长出来的分枝是所有其他科学，可以归结为三个主要部分：医学、力学和伦理学——我是指更高一级和最为完善的道德科学。这一科学预设了对其他科学的完全知识，是最高级的智慧。（出自笛卡尔所著《哲学原理》）作为源起背景与发展脉络截然不同的两种文化，中西文化对哲学的理解在表达、内涵外延和方法论上是有出入的；但对其任务的理解却是共通的，即探讨经验世界背后的真理。这个经验世界是不应该有地域、文化限制的，是适用于全人类的。

如果按照西方哲学的认识，把哲学比作一棵枝叶繁茂的大树，那么种子是从哪里来的呢？蛮荒世界中的原始人类之所以区别于动物，本质上就在于他们会思考。然其最初思考的主要对象恐怕与动物相去不远，也就是如何求生，这还称不上思想。但当人们开始主动地认识世界，有意识地给予世界属性时，思想也便产生了。老子是这样描述这一行为的："无，名天地之始；有，名万物之母。"道，也就是万物按照规律运转，是自在的，不以人的意志为转移。但当人类开始为万物命名，亦即赋予万物于意义的时候，认识世界的活动便开始了，思想也随之产生。"道生一，一生二，二生三，三生万物。"（语出《道德经》）正是在这由无到有、由少到多、由消极认识到主动改造、由零散到系统的进化过程中，哲学也便形成了。

人类最早的哲学思考反映在各自文化中的便是众多的远古神话。神话的源起是人类面对苍茫大地时产生的困惑，为了解决这个困惑，各民族便结合自己的经验世界创造了神话。作为人类首次对世界所做的哲学思考，神话暂时性地为"世界是从哪里来的？人是从哪里来的？"提供了答案。但此时这种思考还被牢牢地限定在经验世界里，于是便产生了诸如化生型、神创型、自然演化型等特征迥异的创世神话。从这种意义上讲，几乎每种文化都有各自的哲学传统，但并不是所有拥有神话的民族都形成了哲学。大多数文明的哲学传统都停留或断裂在神话阶段了。西方文化中的希腊，东方的中国、埃及、印度、波斯等成了其中的幸存者。在这些文化之中，由简单的神话开端，最终发展到复杂全面的体系，哲学也就诞生了。

二、西方哲学核心是什么？经历了怎样的发展历程？

西方哲学指的是西方的哲学思想和哲学著作的总和，发轫并繁盛于古希腊哲学，几经继承、补充、思辨、变革，最终辐射范围超出了欧洲，进而被世界大部分地区所普遍接受。如果将西方哲学比作一棵参天大树，那么现如今这棵大树早已枝繁叶茂，想要找出核心主干，必得循着脉络追根溯源下去，方能窥之一二。

西方哲学史在发展上经历了古希腊哲学、中世纪哲学（经院哲学）和近代哲学三个时期。古希腊文明由最初的神话阶段开始，后来逐渐产生了真正的哲学。希腊人不仅为后来所有的西方思想体系奠定了基础，更几乎为其后两千多年的所有西方哲学研究和文化研究问题提供了答案。更有人认为之后的欧洲文明研究不过是在对希腊哲学做补充和注脚而已。总之，希腊哲学被称为欧洲文明的摇篮是最贴切不过的了。最早的哲学形式是与宗教、科学融为一体的，古希腊的神话既是人们对自然的解读，又是古希腊人的宗教信仰。他们的宗教几乎没有高度集中化的形式，而是将对奥林匹斯诸神的信仰体现在戏剧、文学、诗歌等形式上。这些艺术活动中无论是荷马史诗还是古希腊悲剧，都贯穿着命运决定一切的理念。有哲学家认为正是这种神和人一同受制于命运的精神成为第一批希腊哲学。哲学自此脱离（但并未远离）了宗教，逐渐独立并丰满起来。古希腊哲学经过几百年的发展，在数学、天文学、逻辑学、形而上学、认识论、政治学等方方面面进行了深刻而系统化的思考。柏拉图最终将这些思考发展成了全面而广泛的唯心主义哲学体系。亚里士多德继续向前推进，将哲学与科学区分开来。哲学和科学都是经过理性思考得来的知识，研究事物的最终或第一原因的科学和哲学被亚里士多德称为第一哲学，也就是形而上学；具体科学或哲学（如伦理学、心理学、政治学等）被称为第二哲学。这种将知识划分科目或学科的方法一直沿用至今。

文艺复兴时期和宗教改革运动使得人们的思想冲破了桎梏，人们的视线从超自然的上帝转向了尘世，自然科学、人文主义成为关注点。进入 17 世纪之后，哲学开启了近代化的大门。神学逐渐退位，理性在哲学上取得了权威地位。在理性的大旗下，继文艺复兴时期“人的发现”之后，自然大发现、地理大发现推动着人的发展，各种思潮如百花齐放，呈井喷之势。大批为我们所熟知的巨人纷纷涌现。达·芬奇（Leonardo da Vinci）、哥白尼（Copernicus）、伽利略（Galileo）、布鲁诺（Bruno）、开普勒（Kepler）、牛顿（Newton）等人成为自然哲学的代言人；马基雅弗利（Machiavelli）的政治学论著、哥伦布（Columbus）等人的地理“大发现”改变了人类对世界的认识，为思想的革命提供了契机。近代哲学经历了早期的经验论和唯理论，18 世纪的启蒙运动，乃至 19 世纪“思想体系时代”，德国古典哲学自康德（Kant）起，开始了对整个西方哲学的总结。最终黑格尔成为集大成者，使得哲学成为科学中的科学。哲学家们重新思考哲学的性质，从各个方面对哲学进行了变革性的思考、探索和尝试。

纵观整个西方哲学史，不难发现西方哲学虽几经变迁、迂回甚至停滞，但“科学”和“理性”却贯穿始终。这也是西方哲学区别于其他哲学的精髓所在。

三、中国到底有没有“哲学”？中国的哲学是怎样的？

黑格尔（2013：135）在最早提到中国思想时，认为包括中国哲学在内的东方哲学都不是真正的哲学，“我们所以要提到它，只是为了表明何以我们不多讲它，以及它对思想，对于真正的哲学有何种关系。”也就是说，中国哲学思想与西方哲学是不同的，是相背离的。《西方哲学史》的作者梯利也曾指出：包括中国在内的东方民族并没有超越神话阶段，他们的理论并不是完整的思辨思想体系，是由神话和伦理学构成的。因此，他的著作虽有《哲学史》（*A History of*

Philosophy）之名，却并不包括除却西方哲学以外的哲学体系。这一观点不仅仅限于西方，即使在中国也有不少拥趸。他们认为中国的哲学思想是不系统、不科学的，只是一般东方人的宗教思想方式，属于宗教哲学、道德哲学，唯独不属于“哲学”。

中国的哲学传统并非从一开始就遵循西方的“抽象”思维模式。中国哲学的起源与发展深受其历史文化、社会结构和儒道佛三教思想的影响。中国哲学的传统任务不是为了对客观实际增加知识，而是为了提高人们的心智，为了探讨人与自然的关系。如果从哲学的根本任务——研究人类的一切知识和智慧来看哲学的内涵的话，那么中国的先秦诸子、老庄的“道家”、孔孟的“儒家”、墨家、法家、后期的禅宗抑或是新儒学，不正是在天道、人生之道、德行之道上进行着上下几千年孜孜不倦的追寻吗？

在中国哲学中，思辨活动与生活实践、伦理道德、政治理想和社会责任紧密结合，强调“道”“德”“天人合一”的理念，更多地关注人类如何与自然、社会和他人和谐相处，如何通过自我修养实现个人的道德完善与社会的和谐发展。

中国哲学自古以来分为多个重要流派，其中最具代表性的当属儒家、道家和佛家。儒家是中国传统哲学的核心流派，始于孔子，发扬光大于孟子、荀子等学者。儒家哲学重视伦理道德，提倡“仁爱”“礼义”“中庸”“孝悌”等概念，强调个体的修身齐家治国平天下的责任。儒家思想强调“人性本善”和“道德自觉”，认为人的本性是善良的，教育与修养能够使人达到理想的道德境界。儒家不仅是中国古代政治和社会秩序的基础，也是中国文化认同和精神家园的重要支柱。道家以老子和庄子为代表，其思想强调“道”的观念，提倡顺应自然、无为而治。道家哲学看重个体的内在自由，反对过度的社会约束，提倡“无为而治”与“天人合一”的思想。佛教的传入使得中国哲学体系更加丰富多彩。佛教强调“四谛”“八正道”等教义，提出“空”“无常”“无我”的概念，注重个人的内心修养和对苦难的超越。

中国哲学的伟大之处在于其强调“天人合一”和“和谐”的理念。在儒家、道家和佛家的思想体系中，人与自然、人与社会、人与他人之间的和谐共处被视为理想的状态。中国哲学并不追求独立的个体主义，而是强调个体与集体、个体与环境之间的和谐统一。这种思想不仅体现在个人的道德修养中，也渗透到政治治理和社会秩序中。中国哲学的“天人合一”“和谐共生”理念为现代的环境危机和社会矛盾提供了宝贵的思想资源。

中国哲学并非仅仅是历史的遗产，它更是一种活的思想传统，指引着人们在现代化进程中寻找文化根基，探索人类与自然、社会、他人之间的和谐关系。中国哲学在全球化背景下的再思考，不仅提升了中国的文化软实力，也为世界提供了不同于西方的思想视角和解决方案。

四、中西方哲学的主要差异点在哪里？

中西方都产生了具有各自特征的哲学，并且在长达几千年的历史长河中相互独立，互无交集。

两种哲学体系各自生发的地理环境和成长时社会环境的不同造就了各自在关注的领域、哲学语言性质和表达形式、哲学目的上都有着明显的差异。

（一）内省式与外向型

首先，中国地理环境的广袤与自然的悠久变化，使得中国文化对自然规律的尊重与顺应成为其哲学的核心。中国传统哲学，尤其是儒家、道家思想，强调“天人合一”，即人与自然的和谐共生。在这一框架下，思想并非完全依赖外在的逻辑推演，而更多依赖内心的直觉与感悟。道家思想中的“无为而治”和儒家的“中庸之道”便是内省式哲学的典型代表。中国哲学所提倡的“非常道”“非常名”的“道”与“名”，以及“过犹不及”的中庸理念，均反映了中国思想对宇宙、社会、家庭的整体把握与内省反思。与此形成鲜明对比的是，西方哲学则深受古希腊文明的影响，希腊的海洋文化造就了西方的外向性和探索精神。古希腊人通过海上贸易与征服，将世界看作可以被理解、控制与征服的领域。在这一过程中，西方哲学开始强调理性与逻辑，希腊哲学家如柏拉图、亚里士多德通过推理与逻辑的方式探索宇宙与人类存在的本质。特别是在希腊的市民社会中，商人与士族的互动培养了重视辩证与推理的思维方式，形成了与东方哲学截然不同的“外向型”哲学取向。中国文化的内省式哲学体现了对自我修养和社会伦理的高度重视，这种深厚的文化传统在现代社会中依然具有强大的生命力与指导意义，尤其是在全球化进程中，强调和谐、平衡与道德责任的中国哲学为解决当代世界的伦理问题提供了独特的视角与方案。

（二）直觉思维与逻辑思维

中国哲学更加注重生命的体悟，而西方哲学则更注重对自然的探索。正如牟宗三（2010）所指出的，中国哲学的核心关注点是生命的意义与存在，而西方哲学则着重通过理性推理和科学手段来理解自然界的规律。中国哲学，尤其是儒家和道家思想，更多地强调“无为”的智慧和“中庸”的哲理，其思想方法在本质上是开放的、直觉的，并不刻意追求精确的逻辑推导或固定的结论。

在这一背景下，语言的作用显得尤为重要。西方哲学的语言表达往往强调语法的严密性和逻辑的清晰性。这种语言结构非常适合表达哲学理论中的严谨推理，因为西方语言（如古希腊语和拉丁语）自古以来便具备完整的语法体系，为系统化的哲学论述提供了基础。相反，汉语，尤其是古汉语，虽然没有严格的语法结构，文字也源自象形文字系统，这让它看似不适合用于逻辑化的学术表述。然而，正是这种“无语法”的特点，使得汉语更适合表达中国哲学中“直觉思维”和“不可言说”的精神内涵。

辜鸿铭曾指出，汉语是一种没有语格、时态和复杂语法规则的语言，它也没有西方语言中那种严密的规则和不规则动词体系，甚至可以说，汉语本身似乎缺乏语法。然而，正是这种看似简化的结构，使得汉语在表达哲学思想时展现出极大的灵活性和开放性。汉语不拘泥于形式上的复杂规则，而更注重情感的传递和思想的体悟，这与西方语言的逻辑性形成了鲜明对比。汉语的表达方式依赖于直觉和意象，而非单纯的逻辑推理，这使得它能够更好地容纳“道”的无形与含蓄。汉语作为一种表达哲学思想的语言，凭借其简洁、灵活和富于直觉的特点，为中国哲学提供了独特的表达方式。汉语的“无规则性”与“直觉性”使得它能够更加自由地表达那些复杂的、无法言说的哲学体悟，成为中国文化自信的象征。

在文化的演进中，中西哲学的差异不仅限于形式与内容的对比，更在深层次上反映了两者在文化背景和社会历史中的不同发展轨迹。中国的哲学体系在几千年的历史中积淀了丰富的智慧，而西方哲学则经历了从古希腊到现代的变革与进化。现代人进行中西方哲学对比时，往往容易忽略两者所处的历史维度差异。因此，简单地评判哪一方“优于”另一方往往缺乏意义。正如“关公战秦琼”，两者的历史背景和文化土壤不同，无法用同一个标准来衡量。

五、中西哲学之争到哪里去？对抗抑或是对话？

古代中国与西方的联系虽可以追溯到汉代之前，但彼时这种联系主要是以商品输出和阶段性的文化交流为主。直至明清时期，基督教传入中国，以利玛窦为代表的传道士将世界地图展现给中国皇帝的时候，中西方哲学真正意义上的交流和碰撞才刚刚开始。这一时期更多的是中国“发现”西方的时期。中西方哲学交流的第二个时期是鸦片战争打开了中国大门之后，从19世纪末期直到五四运动开启的新文化运动及至20世纪40年代。这一时期是中西方互相“发现”的时期。中国的有识之士为西方的坚船利炮、工业革命的成就所震撼，开始接触并如饥似渴地吸收西方的哲学思想，试图为困境中的中国找到新的出路。然而很快人们就发现，纯粹地照搬西方思想并不能解决中国的问题，反倒陷入了“唯西方论”的误区。“西方中心论”不仅否定了中国几千年的传统，更摧毁了中国人的立足之本，矛盾和争议也便产生了。进入21世纪，全球化过程加快，中西方文明之间发生前所未有的碰撞。在这场史上规模最大的文化交流过程中，几乎没有哪个文明能够独善其身，更没有哪种哲学体系能够套用到所有文明身上。曾经借助发达的物质成就横扫大半个地球的西方文明，如今在经济全球化、文化多元化的大背景下，却陷入了生存困境和价值危机，成为精神上的“荒原”。西方哲学在战争、恐怖主义等现实问题的拷问下疲于应对。中西方哲学交流中同样面临着诸如利益与道德、自由与人权、平等与效率、公正与和谐等基本价值观的碰撞。中国在这场大变革中，只有从哲学的价值观入手，区分中国化和西方化的内容，判断哪些是合理的并加以吸纳，哪些是错误的要提高警惕，才能在“求同存异”的同时，更好地以文化自信立足于世界。

VIII. Homework

1. 头脑风暴

列举一些习语或俗语，以体现中庸思想在中国政治、经济及日常社会生活中的表现。

2. 趣味问答

（1）我们普遍认为西方社会遵循“契约”原则，而中国则看重个人信誉，亦即秉持“君子一言，驷马难追”的交际原则。这两种处事原则矛盾吗？各自体现了怎样的世界观？

（2）中西方文化中都对道德高尚、富有操守的人持肯定和尊重的态度。中国“君子”的道德标准是什么？西方文化中有无与“君子”相对应的概念？西方“君子”的概念和内涵与中国的“君子”有什么异同点？

（3）中国人视“修身、齐家、治国、平天下”为人生格言，认为个人的内在修为是第一位的，也是惠及家人和国家的前提条件，你怎么解读这句话？

3. 调查与研究

中西方在历史上、现实生活中对待宗教的态度是有很多差异的。请结合史实分析不同宗教观的表现，探索其背后的哲学原因。

4. 文化万花筒

（1）全球化浪潮下，中西方在经济技术、商业贸易、文化交流等方面的接触已经成为生活的常态。以商业谈判为例，哪些是职场或谈判桌上的行为禁忌呢？

（2）请找出 10 句《论语》中关于君子和小人的句子以及至少两种相关的英文翻译，请将这些翻译进行对比，并就此对中国文化中的君子概念进行总结，梳理中国文化中君子的品质。

Section Two

The Contrast of Chinese and Western Medicine

I. Learning Objectives

1. To compare and contrast the ways of getting to know the human body
2. To fathom the reasons of divergence of Western and Chinese Medicine

II. Key Points and Difficult Points

1. To study the essence of Chinese medicine
2. To research the relationship between Chinese philosophy and traditional Chinese medicine
3. To summarize the development of Western medicine
4. To study the relationship between Western philosophy and Western medicine

III. Lead-in Questions

1. Can you name some famous doctors in Ancient China and the West and their contributions?
2. How did ancient Chinese people understand human body? And are those understandings different from the Western medicine?
3. Do you know some terms of Traditional Chinese Medicine skills?
4. How do you understand the strength and weakness of Traditional Chinese Medicine?

IV. Learning Contents

1. News on medical— "Smoking Can Lead to Artery Disease in Legs"

Now there's one more reason to stop smoking.

Everyone knows that smoking causes cancer. But what smokers might not realize is that it also causes hardening of the arteries in legs.

This life-threatening condition is known as peripheral vascular disease, or PVD, and it's caused by atherosclerosis, which is often due to smoking. Atherosclerosis is a gradual process in which cholesterol and scar tissue build up, forming a substance called plaque that clogs the blood vessels.

The hardened arteries restrict blood flow to the legs, which can lead to painful cramping in the legs or hips, particularly when a person is walking. The pain typically goes away when the muscles are rested. This pain associated with PVD is an early warning sign of blocked arteries throughout the body that can lead to stroke or heart attack. Untreated peripheral vascular disease also can result in gangrene or amputation.

Ten-million Americans, including five percent of the over-50 crowd, suffer from PVD, but diagnosis is simple. Physicians can perform a pain-free screening known as ankle brachial index, which compares the blood pressure in the arm to that in the ankle. People at risk also can be diagnosed with contrast X-rays that highlight blocked arteries.

Available treatments for PVD include drugs to prevent blood-clotting, non-surgical angioplasty and stent implants to dilate narrowed arteries, and surgery to bypass the diseased part of the artery.

The best prevention, of course, is to not smoke, and to maintain a healthy lifestyle.

单词表

artery	*n.*	动脉
condition	*n.*	（尤指健康）状况，症状
peripheral vascular disease		周围血管疾病
atherosclerosis	*n.*	动脉硬化
cholesterol	*n.*	胆固醇

scar tissue		疤痕组织
plaque	*n.*	斑块
cramp	*v.*	抽筋
gangrene	*n.*	坏疽
amputation	*n.*	截肢；切断术
angioplasty	*n.*	血管成形术
dilate	*v.*	扩张，扩大

2. Chinese Acupuncture and Moxibustion

Acupuncture-moxibustion therapy, which mainly consists of both acupuncture and moxibustion, is a unique approach to medical care in China and is also an indispensable component of Chinese medicine. The acupuncture treatment is the insertion of different fine needles on the body's surface according to a certain point, to stimulate certain parts of the body and use various methods to evoke the channels as well as the vital energy of human body, in order to adjust physiological functioning of the body so to cure diseases. Moxibustion is the burning of moxa on or near a person's skin as a counterirritant. For a long time, acupuncture and moxibustion treatment are often combined together in clinical practice application, therefore we collectively referred to them as Acupuncture-moxibustion therapy.

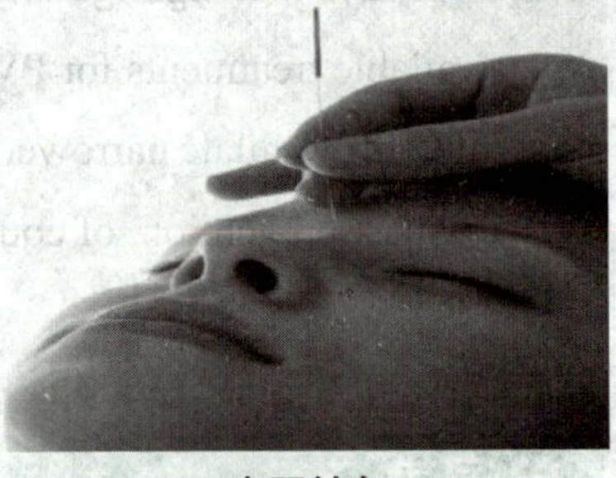
中医针灸

The earliest written record that is available about acupuncture is *Yellow Emperor's Classic of Internal Medicine*, which suggests acupuncture originated in China and would explain why it is most commonly associated with Traditional Chinese Medicine.

An acupuncturist usually pays due attention to the basic techniques including the way the needle is inserted rapidly or slowly, the depth of insertion, the length of time the needle should be left in the body, and the number of needles required to the treatment.

（资料来源：http://www.foreignercn.com/）

单词表

acupuncture	*n.*	针灸
moxibustion	*n.*	艾灸
point	*n.*	点，此处指中医所称的穴位
channel	*n.*	通道，渠道，此处指经络
vital energy		中医中的气
moxa	*n.*	艾绒，艾条
counterirritant	*n.*	抗刺激剂；敷于皮肤上激起痛楚以减轻深部组织炎症的药物
Yellow Emperor's Classic of Internal Medicine		《黄帝内经》

V. Story Links

1. 扁鹊三兄弟的故事

《鹖冠子·卷下·世贤第十六》中记载，魏文王问扁鹊曰："子昆弟三人其孰最善为医？"扁鹊曰："长兄最善，中兄次之，扁鹊最为下。"魏文王曰："可得闻邪？"扁鹊曰："长兄于病视神，未有形而除之，故名不出于家。中兄治病，其在毫毛，故名不出于闾。若扁鹊者，镵血脉，投毒药，副肌肤间，而名出闻于诸侯。"

2. The Hippocratic Oath

I swear by Apollo Healer, by Asclepius, by Hygieia, by Panacea, and by all the gods and goddesses, making them my witnesses, that I will carry out, according to my ability and judgment, this oath and this indenture.

To hold my teacher in this art equal to my own parents; to make him partner in my livelihood; when he is in need of money to share mine with him; to consider his family as my own brothers, and to teach them this art, if they want to learn it, without fee or indenture; to impart precept, oral instruction, and all other instruction to my own sons, the sons of my teacher, and to indentured pupils who have taken the Healer's oath, but to nobody else.

I will use those dietary regimens which will benefit my patients according to my greatest ability and judgment, and I will do no harm or injustice to them. Neither will I administer a poison to anybody when asked to do so, nor will I suggest such a course. Similarly I will not give to a woman a pessary to cause abortion. But I will keep pure and holy both my life and my art. I will not use the knife, not even, verily, on sufferers from stone, but I will give place to such as are craftsmen therein.

Into whatsoever houses I enter, I will enter to help the sick, and I will abstain from all intentional wrong-doing and harm, especially from abusing the bodies of man or woman, bond or free. And whatsoever I shall see or hear in the course of my profession, as well as outside my profession in my intercourse with men, if it be what should not be published abroad, I will never divulge, holding such things to be holy secrets.

Now if I carry out this oath, and break it not, may I gain for ever reputation among all men for my life and for my art; but if I break it and forswear myself, may the opposite befall me.

VI. Did You Know?

1. 中医四诊

四诊是中医诊察疾病基本方法的合称，包括望诊（Observation）、闻诊（Auscultation and Olfaction）、问诊（Inquiry）、切诊（Pulse Feeling and Palpation），即“望、闻、问、切”。望是观察病人的身体状况，包括面色、舌苔等；闻是听病人的说话、咳嗽、呼吸，并嗅其口中或身上是否有异味；问是询问病人症状以及患病史等；切是用手把脉或按腹部诊察是否有异常。通过四诊，诊察疾病显现在各方面的症状和体征，以了解疾病的病因、性质及其与内脏的联系，从而为治疗疾病提供充分的依据。望、闻、问、切各有独特的作用，它们之间互相联系，互相补充，不能相互取代。临床必须结合运用，互相参证，才能全面系统地了解病情，称为“四诊合参”。

中医把脉

2. 西方养生俗语

（1）Leave off with an appetite. 吃得七分饱，就该离餐桌。

（2）Study sickness while you are well. 无病应思有病时。

（3）Go to bed with the lamb and rise with the lark. 早睡早起。（随羔羊就寝，与云雀同起。）

（4）Diseases are the price of ill pleasure. 疾病是纵欲的代价。

（5）A good surgeon must have an eagle's eye, a lion's heart, and a lady's hand. 优秀的外科医生应具有鹰眼、狮心和女性般灵巧的手。

VII. Cultural Reflection

人类史上医药的起源已经不可考了，神创论、圣人论、医巫同源说、动物说、劳动说各有依据，又各有所偏。但这并不妨碍我们认为医药是人类智慧的结晶，是综合多种因素不断发展的结果，其缘起甚至早于人类社会活动和规范。中西医学不仅是两种医学技术体系，更是两种不同文明中人们对人类自身、对人类与世界的关系所进行的认识和反思，是两种世界观的科学体现。对中西医的认知和对比，也不应限于两种技术的对比，中西医更是对中西方世界观、人生观的梳理和检阅。

一、中西医比较的两个前提性问题

对中西医学进行对比反思首先应当明确两个前提性问题：比较的对象是什么？可否用一种标准——西方的科学标准来评价中西医学？

（一）比较的对象是什么？

在近现代医学产生之前，世界早已存在独立发展起来的多种医疗知识体系，其中大多属于传统医学。根据世界卫生组织的定义，传统医学是“利用基于植物、动物、矿物的药物、精神疗法、肢体疗法，和实践中的一种或多种方法来进行治疗、诊断和防止疾病或者维持健康的医学”。中医属于传统医学的范畴，也是我们与西医做对比的对象。西方的医学“科学化”可以追溯到16世纪，但是在17世纪逐步成熟，成为现代西医的基础。因此我们以17世纪近现代的开启为时间节点，纵览这两种医学体系的发展脉络，研究中西方对人体、对人与自然的理解变迁。

（二）传统中医是否属于科学？

鸦片战争后，随着西方学术思想的传入，中国开始了广泛的“西学东渐”和新文化运动，传统中医首次与近现代西医进行直接对比。西医的科学化特点使得中医的理论与实践逐渐暴露出其相对的短板。在当时，一些信奉西方科学的知识分子视传统中医为“旧世界”的产物，试图将其废除，并通过妖魔化中医来促进西方医学的推广。时至今日，这种文化冲突和科学辩论的影响依然存在，甚至影响了现代社会对中医的认知。

中医虽然不同于西医在实验和实证上的发展路径，但它作为一个拥有几千年历史的医学体系，其深厚的理论基础和实践成果同样具有科学价值。中医的学术体系，不仅在治疗方法和药物应用方面取得了长足进展，其理论体系在人体学、病理学、养生学等领域也做出了显著贡献。中医的独特之处在于其哲学背景,尤其是"天人合一"理念的应用。中医强调人与自然的和谐统一、疾病的预防与调理，体现了一种动态的、整体的健康观。这种有机论的思想，与西方医学中的局部化治疗和疾病应对方式形成了鲜明对比。正因如此，传统中医的价值不应仅通过西方科学标准来衡量。虽然中医与西医在科学方法、实验验证等方面存在差异，但这种差异并不妨碍中医在中国乃至世界范围内的实际效果与价值。

此外，传统中医的悠久历史以及它在中国几千年文明进程中的作用，也证明了中医作为一种文化遗产的科学性和实用性。中医虽然不完全符合西方现代科学的框架，但它的理论体系和治疗方法是人类智慧的结晶，具有独特的哲学思想和实际应用价值。基于此，我们不能仅以现代西医的标准来评判中医是否属于科学，而应从更加宽广的视野出发，理解中医在中华民族文化中的地位，以及它在当今世界发挥的巨大作用。

二、中西方医学发展的阶段比较

人类对自身的认识是与对世界的认知和探索同步的，都经历过从无到有，从简单到复杂的发展过程。

（一）差异萌发期

早期的古希腊医学与中国古代医学，以及几乎所有民族的医学起源都相似，都是在生产实践中产生的，并与神话、巫术、宗教有先天性的密切关系。中国古人将医者视作圣人，体现在"神农尝百草""伏羲制九针"等神话传说中。古希腊人认为疾病是神迁怒于人的证据，如荷马史诗中就有因神发怒而降下瘟疫的情节。古希腊医学在这一时期，在病因探究和疗法上也以祭神（如古希腊医药神阿斯克勒庇俄斯 Asclepios）、按摩、敷药膏为主。中医最初也是与巫术有关，如商周时代巫医盛行。

古希腊哲学重逻辑、重理性的特点也反映在对医学的认知上。德谟克里特（Democritus）的原子论认为世间万物都是由微小的原子组成的，而且是在不断运动变化着的。人体作为客观世界的一部分，是可以被研究和认识的对象，这成为古希腊医学理论的立足点。希波克拉底通过实体解剖，获得了许多关于人体结构的知识，提出"四体液"理论，从根本上推翻了神怒是疾病原因的谬论。他根据行医实践制定的"希波克拉底誓言"（The Hippocratic Oath）为后世西方医学从业者的行业行为和医德标准设立了标杆，是西方医学迈向科学化的重要一步。

中国在春秋战国时期，阴阳说、五行说被用于解释人体脏腑器官的运行和联系，成为中国传统医学的理论基础。如《黄帝内经》这部医学巨著采用了阴阳五行学说，强调了整体观念，对病因、病机、诊法、治疗、预防、养生等内容也有大量阐述，可以作为中医学术体系形成的标志。东汉时期名医张仲景在《伤寒杂病论》等著作中，提出了辨证论治的理论，尤其在药物的使用上，记载和创制了多种方剂，"君臣佐使"配伍的中药组方原则也在此时被提出。

这一时期虽然中西方医学发展相对缓慢，但医学理念的差异已经悄然萌发。古希腊医学将人体看作由部分组成的整体，进而用解剖法实证了部分的病变是疾病的原因；古代中医则是通过"取象类比"，用阴阳转化和五行相生相克来比拟内脏器官的运行，认为人体本身是不可分割的整体，牵一发而动全身。运转和谐则身康体泰，否则就会横生疾病。而医生的任务就是恢复这种和谐与平衡，并借助养生来加以维持。在药物的配置上"君臣佐使配伍"的组方原则注意主次平衡，同样是这种和谐论、整体论的体现。这两种整体论有本质上的不同，为各自医学的发展差异与深化埋下了伏笔。

（二）差异扩大期

古希腊医学知识被罗马人继承。罗马人注重公共保健和卫生，设立专门的饮用水道和下水道、公共浴室、公厕等设施防止大规模疾病的传播。盖伦通过实验证实了神经和呼吸等的假设。他受制于不能解剖人体的禁令，利用近似于人体的灵长类动物做解剖，对人体构造有了新的认识。然而进入中世纪后，由于受宗教的钳制，疾病被认为是上帝对作恶者的惩罚，医学研究陷入停顿甚至倒退的状态。

相对应的，中国隋唐宋时期则见证了中国医药学的辉煌。这一时期，系统总结医学技术成就和药学发展的专著大量涌现，如孙思邈的《千金要方》——中国医学史上最早的医学百科全书，反映了实践医学在这一时期得到了长足发展。至宋元时代，哲学思想进入一个新的活跃期，与之密不可分的医学理论也得以进一步完善。

（三）差异深化期

中世纪，黑死病席卷整个欧洲，改变了西方人对疾病乃至人生价值的认识。文艺复兴时期，对古希腊和阿拉伯文化的吸收以及大学的萌芽重新点燃了研究医学的热情。达·芬奇进行人体解剖，用以研究肌肉和骨骼。维萨里通过实体解剖，推翻了盖伦的错误认识，创立了科学的人体解剖学，将古代西方医学研究推向了高峰。进入近现代后，西方医学继续了实证研究的传统，借助同时发展起来的科学技术，发展速度呈突飞猛进的态势。英国生理学家哈维（Harvey）发现了血液循环；伽利略（Galileo Galilei）发明的显微镜被应用于医学发现；临床医学、病理解剖学、接种预防天花等重要成就成为 18 世纪医学的特征。进入 19 世纪，工业革命改变了世界的面貌，大机器时代加快了人类发展的进程。被归为自然科学的医学也得到了质的飞跃，最终形成了当今的西学，也主宰了西方人对自身的认识。

明清时期，中医总结并完善了辨证论治的理论体系，最终走向成熟。然而这种发展态势终究没有逃过西方坚船利炮的冲击。在中西方文化的碰撞下，这两种截然不同但都已经发展成熟的医学体系开始了旷日持久的遭遇战。

三、困境与出路

西医重实验，重数据。中医一旦被置于西方科学这个放大镜下，曾经被视作中国文化成就的中医理论 —— 病理说、药理学、诊断法、治疗法等则饱受诟病。20 世纪初期起，批判中医的浪潮迭起,但仍有一股力量在试图通过倡导中医“科学化”来保存传统中医学。近代著名医学家、改革家施今墨提出中西医要融会贯通。“科学化”就是以现代科学的思维、方法和技术来改造、发展中医。具体来说就是将中医客观化、规范化、标准化。这种中西合璧的尝试确实有利于弥补中医缺乏实证、效果难以客观量化的短板，为传统中医的继续发展指明了出路。

西医的发展似乎也陷入了某种怪圈。西医病理学诊断上通过精确测定人体发病部位，从器官组织、物质成分的角度弄清发病原因，并因病施治。这种诊断方法虽然有利于精确判断病症部位，监控病情进展，进而快速有效地施以治疗，但实践中却不免陷入实际意义上的“头痛医头、脚痛医脚”，即只顾部分而忽视整体的误区。更多更深层的问题如今也已经初现端倪，例如抗生素的滥用导致新的病毒出现、西药副作用显著等问题已然引发了人们的担忧。很多西方人已经把目光投向了中国传统医学。如何在两者的差异中找到平衡、取长补短、实现共赢是当今中西方医学都应当思考的问题。2015 年，屠呦呦团队凭借“青蒿素”对治疗疟疾方面的重大贡献而获得了诺贝尔生理学或医学奖。其灵感很有可能来源于东晋葛洪所著的《肘后备急方》中使用青蒿的一个验方，利用西式科学化的技术手段将青蒿素以分子式的形式提炼出来。这一发现使得青蒿素可以被制成治疗疟疾的药物，成功挽救了上百万人的性命。可以说这一成就是中西医合璧的绝好证据，也在某种程度上启发了人们对传统中医药学的重新认识。

VIII. Homework

1. 查一查，说一说

天下之人之身

克隆与伦理

阴阳调和

2. 文化万花筒

中国人对养生学情有独钟，认为“养”是“医”的有益补充。日常生活中，人们总结了很多养生秘诀和生活禁忌，诸如少食多餐、阴阳调和、“贴秋膘”、孕产妇禁忌、“春捂秋冻”等。你的家乡有哪些养生秘诀或生活禁忌呢？这些秘诀和禁忌可以用西医的“科学论”来解释吗？

3. 调查与研究

公共卫生建设是反映一个国家发展程度的标准之一。中国和欧洲在历史上有哪些公共卫生方面的建设和成就？这些对世界文明的延续起到了怎样的作用？

Section Three

The Contrast of Chinese and Western Science

I. Learning Objectives

1. To reflect on the relationship between philosophy and development of science and technology

2. To study and fathom out the forms of scientific and technological development in ancient China and the West

II. Key Points and Difficult Points

1. To know the history of science and technology in ancient China and the West

2. To study the reasons of different paces of development of science and technology in ancient China and the West

3. To compare and contrast the different forms and driving forces of science and technology development

III. Lead-in Questions

1. Can you list some outstanding achievements of science and technology in ancient China?

2. What are the differences in the interpretations of the world in ancient China and the West?

3. In what aspects did the world change impressively via the development of science and technology in human history?

4. Have you heard of the "Needham Problem"? What's your opinion on this problem?

IV. Learning Contents

1. Darwin and *On the Origin of Species*

Darwin was particularly influenced by the works of men of science like astronomer Sir John Herschel, traveler Alexander von Humboldt and geologist Charles Lyell. Lyell's new book, *Principles of Geology* (1830–1833), profoundly influenced Darwin. Lyell offered not just a new geology but a new way of understanding nature. Lyell showed how tiny, slow, gradual and cumulative change over immense periods of time could produce large changes. Natural, visible, non-miraculous causes should be sought to explain natural phenomenon. Darwin had the opportunity to witness all of these forces, such as erosion, earthquakes and volcanoes, during the *Beagle* voyage and he became convinced that Lyell's views were correct. Darwin made several very important discoveries about the geology of South America, volcanic islands and the origins of coral reefs by building on Lyell's ideas. Darwin later wrote in the 2nd edition of his *Journal of Researches*:

Where on the face of the earth can we find a spot, on which close investigation will not discover signs of that endless cycle of change, to which this earth has been, is, and will be subjected?

Darwin also collected organisms of all sorts which he recorded in his specimen lists and zoology notes. These formed the basis of the five volume series he edited and superintended after returning home *The Zoology of the Voyage of H.M.S. Beagle* (1838–1843).

人类进化示意图

Darwin also unearthed many fossil creatures in South America. He wondered why the fossils resembled the present inhabitants of that continent more than any other species. Where had the new species come from? In fact, why was the world covered with so many different kinds of living things? Why were some very similar to one another and others vastly different? If species were somehow created to fit their environments, as was then believed, why were jungle species different in Asia, Africa and South America despite the similarity of climate?

（资料来源：http://darwin-online.org.uk/darwin.html）

单词表

geologist	*n.*	地质学家
cumulative	*adj.*	堆积的，累积的
non-miraculous	*adj.*	非奇迹的
erosion	*n.*	侵蚀，腐蚀
volcano	*n.*	火山
coral reef		珊瑚礁
subject	*v.*	使臣服，使遭受
organism	*n.*	有机物
superintend	*v.*	监督，管理
fossil	*n.*	化石

2. 中国古代世界起源论

（1）五行说

中国古代先民将无法理解和控制的自然现象归诸主宰万物的超自然力。商代（前 1600—前 1046）有类似“上帝”的观念，通常指一种至高无上的神明或超自然的力量，周代改为“天”，而所谓的“天子”则受天之命来统治人间。从周代（前 1046—前 256）起，人们对天地、自然现象和物质分类有了思考和探讨，诸如阴阳、五德、天命等。春秋战国时正式提出“五行”理论。最早的“五行说”可追溯到《淮南子》等文献中。“五行说”（金、木、水、火、土）与阴阳说相结合，便形成成熟的体系。

（2）精气说

战国（前 475—前 221）中期，宋钘、尹文两位哲学家提出“精气”学说，以无法直接感受的精微原始物质“元气”解释世界。元气看不见、摸不着，但存在于任何地方，聚集起来即可成万物。三国时期（220—280），哲学家杨泉更进一步认为，天是由元气构成的，银河众星也是由元气精华构成的。

（3）混沌阴阳说

战国时期，认为天和地是在混沌中阴阳作用下而诞生的见解已经存在。而最早明确论述天地和日月星辰起源和演化的，应推溯至西汉时期（前206—公元25）淮南王刘安等人写成的《淮南子》。

书中解释道：天和地的精气融合起来产生了阴阳二气，阴阳二气的精华融合集中产生春秋冬夏四季，四季各自的精气分散产生万物。阳气中的热气积聚便产生了火，而火气的精华部分形成太阳；阴气中的寒气积聚便产生了水，而水气的精华部分形成月亮。太阳、月亮溢出之气的精华散逸为星辰。天空容纳着日月星辰，大地承载着水潦尘埃。

V. Story Links

1. 工业革命的辉煌——伦敦万国博览会

万国工业博览会（Great Exhibition of the Works of Industry of All Nations）于1851年5月1日在伦敦水晶宫开幕，历时五个多月，主要内容是展示世界文化与工业科技，是第一场世界博览会。这次盛会由维多利亚女王的丈夫阿尔伯特亲王主办，著名工程师布鲁诺尔（Brunel）等参与筹办。博览会受到了举国人民的欢迎，参观者超过六百万人次，展品超过一万三千种，诸如轨道蒸汽牵引机、高速汽轮船、起重机以及来自美国的收割机等。这次又被称为“水晶宫博览会”的万国工业博览会正是英国维多利亚女王辉煌时代的代表，向世人展示了一个工业、军事、经济高度发展的英国。

2. Zhang Heng and Seismograph

During the Eastern Han period, earthquakes occurred frequently. Contrary to the popular belief at that time, Zhang Heng maintained that earthquakes were not signs of Heaven's anger but natural disasters. As a result of careful observations of earthquakes, he invented a seismograph in the then national capital of Luoyang in 132 CE, which was the world's first instrument to identify and ascertain the direction of earthquakes. The seismograph was made of fine copper, and was ingeniously constructed. Inside, there was a balanced post and eight rods. Outside, it was cast with eight dragons on the surface, whose heads pointed in eight directions—east, south, west, north, southeast, northeast, southwest, and northwest, and each dragon had a copper ball in the mouth. On the ground below the dragons there were eight copper toads raising their heads and opening their mouths opposite the dragons' mouths. When an earthquake occurred, the balanced post would tilt in the direction of the quake and push a rod. The dragon facing that direction would open its mouth, and the ball would fall into the mouth of the toad below, automatically indicating the direction of the earthquake. One day in 138 CE, the dragon in the west expelled its ball. As expelled, an earthquake had occurred that day in Longxi, a thousand kilometers away. It was the first time that mankind had used an instrument to detect an earthquake. It was over 1,700 years later that a similar instrument was invented in Europe.

VI. Did You Know?

中国历法的二十四节气及英译

二十四节气的名称分别是：立春、雨水、惊蛰、春分、清明、谷雨、立夏、小满、芒种、夏至、小暑、大暑、立秋、处暑、白露、秋分、寒露、霜降、立冬、小雪、大雪、冬至、小寒、大寒。

The names for the 24 solar terms are: Beginning of Spring, Rain Water, Waking of Insects, Vernal Equinox, Pure Brightness, Grain Rain, Beginning of Summer, Grain Budding, Grain in Ear, Summer Solstice, Slight Heat, Great Heat, Beginning of Autumn, Limit of Heat, White Dew, Autumnal Equinox, Cold Dew, Frost's Descent, Beginning of Winter, Slight Snow, Great Snow, Winter Solstice, Slight Cold, and Great Cold, respectively.

VII. Cultural Reflection

科学门类庞杂，具体到机械制造、数学、物理学、建筑学、地理学、水力学、天文学、人体学等；抽象来说又涉及科学思维、科学观念和科学传统。不分对象、混淆阶段，笼统地谈中西方的科学差异是不可取的。按照世界史的划分规则，我们将 17 世纪作为分界点。17 世纪之前的科学发展统称为古代科学，而这之后直到 21 世纪这短短几百年内的科学成就称为近现代科学。

一、古代中西科学对比

（一）不同的哲学观造就了不同的科学观

自超越了神话阶段起，古希腊文明便与科学密不可分。在古希腊哲学家那里，形而上学与自然科学是不分家的。早期的自然哲学派便是首先从认识客观世界中的本质着手，进而探讨形而上的命题。他们提出"构成世界的基础性物质是什么"这一实体性的问题。米利都学派认为"气"是世界的本源，按照气的凝聚、疏散、转换来理解宇宙生成的内在机理。毕达哥拉斯派则认为"数"是事物的本质也是事物的最终原因，这一理解对物理学和天文学研究影响巨大，更是西方数学传统的源头。柏拉图甚至在学院的门楣上刻上"不懂几何者不得入此门"，对数学的重视程度可见一斑。德谟克里特的原子论认为世间万物都是由原子构成的，是最小的单位，不可分割，而且总是处在运动当中。这一理论是当时对世界本质所做的最为科学的推论，对之后西方所有的哲学家、科学家都有着深远的影响。

秦汉之前的中国古代对世界本质的认识分为"五行说"和"精气说"两种。"五行说"认为宇宙万物是由水、火、木、金、土五种基本物质构成，这五种物质按照一定的规律运转、变动，导致了宇宙和社会甚至人体的发展和变化。战国时期的宋钘、尹文提出了"精气"学说，之后，这一学说逐渐演变成"阴阳说"。阴阳冲突便产生了运动，进而产生了变化。因此世间万物是变化着的，寒来暑往，奔腾不息，这些都对中国人的思维方式产生了重要影响。

古希腊时期和古代中国的哲学理念有许多表面上的相似之处，例如世界起源的"气"说、元素说，以及对形而上的思考，可以说这两种相互独立的文明有着"异曲同工"的妙趣。

（二）不同的科学观造成了迥异的科学传统和成果

从古希腊时期起，西方的科学传统便开始形成，且这一过程自上而下地得到政府和统治阶级的支持。古希腊哲学家柏拉图开创的学院，成为西方思辨与科学教育的源头。公元前 385 年到公元 529 年，柏拉图学院培养了大批逻辑思维严谨的哲学家，为后来的西方科学思想奠定了坚实的基础。继柏拉图之后，毕达哥拉斯、欧几里得、阿基米德等伟大的科学家，凭借数学和逻辑的理论框架，推动了几何学、力学等学科的系统化发展。这一时期的西方科学探索更多的是从形而上的哲学思辨出发，继而通过实验与数学推导对自然世界进行解析，形成了强烈的理论与实践相结合的科学观。

与西方科学注重分析、实验和推理的思维方式不同，中国古代的科学观则更多地体现在对自然的整体性理解上。古代中国的哲学始终强调人与自然的和谐共生，认为人类是自然界的一部分，而非与自然对立的独立存在。这一思想不仅深刻影响了中国的文化发展，也决定了中国科学传统的独特走向。中国的哲学体系，无论是道家的"无为而治"还是儒家的"仁政"，注重的都是顺应自然的规律，而非从对自然的控制与改造出发。因此，中国古代哲学所体现的自然观是整体性的、动态的，而非线性、单向的。在这种思想背景下，中国的科学研究更多地侧重于与自然的和谐共处，强调适应和优化，而非通过实验和反复验证去追求抽象的理论突破。

然而，这并不意味着中国古代没有推动科学发展的动力。实际上，儒家、墨家和法家等学派的思想中蕴含着深刻的科学思想，尤其是墨家学派。墨子不仅在光学、力学方面有所建树，且在实践中注重技术发明与应用，例如与公输盘的虚拟战争便展示了墨子在军事工程和机械技术方面的创新。遗憾的是，墨家和法家的政治理念最终未能得到统治阶级的广泛接受和支持，这在一定程度上限制了他们思想的进一步发展和影响力。

虽然古代中国的科学研究在体制上并未像西方那样系统化和独立化，但这并不意味着中国古代缺乏科学成就。实际上，中国的数学、天文学、医学等学科，虽然更多地服务于实际社会需求，但也取得了显著的成果。特别是在数学领域，中国古代在历法的计算、天文观测、实用算法等方面展现了非凡的智慧。诸如《九章算术》，不仅给出了计算圆周率的科学方法，还为后来的数学研究提供了宝贵的经验。这些数学成就，虽然不完全符合西方科学对理论和实验的严格要求，但它们在中国古代社会中发挥了重要作用，服务于农业、天文等领域，为国家治理和社会安定提供了有效支持。

（三）民间智慧是推动科技发展的强大力量

古希腊是一个海洋之国，农业资源的匮乏促使人们很早就进行海上贸易。商业成为希腊各城邦的立国之本。为了扩大海外市场，发展航海技术成为迫切的需求，进而带动了天文、数学、机械等相关学科的发展。这些知识将人们的活动范围扩大到令后人吃惊的广度，进而开启了西方的商业传统。

中国疆域辽阔，农业是主要的经济形态。从春秋战国时期起，为了提高生产力，古代工匠从直观经验出发，重视实用价值，新发明与新技术纷纷涌现。例如铸铁冶炼技术领先了西方将近两千年，建筑技术、水利设施、制瓷业、造纸业、制盐业、纺织业、造船技术等实用技术都远超同时期的西方，成为中国科技史最为辉煌的成就。

二、近现代科学对比与“李约瑟难题”

自 17 世纪起，在度过了一段漫长的黑暗时期之后，获得自由的西方在众多领域取得了革命性的进步。首先是知识的爆发，文艺复兴时期，人们“重拾”了古希腊的科学成就和传统，中断了几百年的科学得到了延续；欧洲私立大学纷纷涌现，高等教育脱离了政府和贵族的赞助，极大地促进了科学和教育的推广，反过来又促进了科学的发展。紧随其后的是军事力量上的革命。由中国发明的火药辗转传到欧洲后，欧洲借助冶炼技术的进步，把它们制造成威力巨大的火枪、火炮，骑士以及弓箭退出了历史舞台。军事力量的强大也直接促成了“地理大发现”，从此开启了欧洲的资本主义殖民历程。然后是科学的革命，旧有的亚里士多德式科学观被抛弃，以科学实证为特征的“新科学”——近现代科学诞生了。1543 年，维萨里通过实体解剖刷新了人们对身体的认识；同一年，哥白尼发表了“日心说”，之后伽利略首次在观察、实验的基础上经过推理和计算证明了科学推论，开创了科学理性与科学实验相结合的科学传统。牛顿提出了万有引力和三大运动定律，重塑了人们的宇宙观，为接下来三个多世纪的物理世界提供了框架。长达两千多年的科学成就和思想积累最终在 19 世纪以工业大革命的形式爆发出了前所未有的力量，创造了人类物质文明的辉煌，并迅速将整个世界卷了进去。

正当西方在科学技术的道路上大步前进的时候，中国科学技术的发展却“急踩刹车”，甚至出现了倒退。汉学家李约瑟（Joseph Needham，1900—1995）最早对这种逆转提出了质疑：“尽管中国古代对人类科技发展做出了很多重要贡献，但为什么科学和工业革命没有在近代的中国发生？”这一问题被称为“李约瑟难题”（the “Needham Problem”），包括李约瑟本人在内，人们纷纷从各种角度给予分析和猜想，不断地否定他人，又不断地自我否定，始终无法形成定论。但对以下几个观点却是普遍认可的。

一是中国“天人合一”的哲学观。中国是一个早熟的民族。在其他民族还在嗷嗷待哺的时候，中国就已经有了成熟的哲学思想以及完善的社会体系。中国人“天人合一”的整体观引导人们以合乎自然、顺应规律为人生之道。既然人本身就是自然世界的一部分，道的要义在于内省，又何谈以研究和改造客观世界为人生要义呢？

二是“农本位”成为科技发展的绊脚石。商业、技术等被视为末业，受制于“学而优则仕”的主流思想的影响，商业活动受到压抑，自然也就缺乏自由竞争精神，发展科学的动力也趋于消弭了。然而，作为以农耕文明为内核的中华文化，如果几千年来不在肥沃广袤的土地上发展农业，则必然是违背天道，也是绝不可能的。注重农业发展，形成热爱土地、依恋故土、向往稳定和谐的生活是中华文明的必然之路。

三是中华文化所反映的中国式思维不利于西方式科学推断的逻辑性和客观性。例如象形文字、缺乏语法规范的语言、重写意轻写实的山水画、只能意会不可言传的哲理等文化表现都是中国人重类比式推理或联想思维的证据。这与重逻辑、重实验、重推理的科学语言有着本质上的差异。

四是中国的地理环境使得中国长久以来处在相对独立的环境里。在这里，中华文明可以在几千年的时间里不受外来力量的侵扰。即使偶有曲折，也会很快凭借自身的强大精神力量将对方纳入自己的麾下。

虽说历史不可能重演，对这一问题的研究永远只能停留在猜想的阶段。但这些分析和猜想却为研究中西方近代的社会结构、思维方式差异提供了新的角度，同时或许有利于启发未来。但我们也应该谨防其中的“西方本位”思想作祟。东西方科学文化同属人类精神财富，短短几百年不过是历史长河中须臾一瞬，岂足以搏出优劣？若以近现代几百年间科技发展的成果为基准，西方的科学观确实暂时地占据了上风。丰富的物质成果使人类获得了实实在在的益处。然而“福兮祸之所倚”，长期把人凌驾于自然之上的后果便是遭受自然的报复，环境危机便是其中一例。同时精神和物质发展速度的不对等，使人类在丰盛的物质文明面前感到了前所未有的精神危机。中国作为世界上唯一没有中断过的古老文明，其存在和发展正是遵循自然规律的结果。中国哲学中“天人合一”的整体观、有机论不失为一种解决之道。因此以西方的立场质疑中国为什么没有出现西方式的工业革命本身就是一个伪命题。

VIII. Homework

1. 解释以下名词

唯科学论　　科学主义　　天人合一　　万物有灵论

2. 查一查，说一说

（1）你能列举出日常生活中哪些行为或观念属于“伪科学”吗？

（2）分别研究一位中西科学家的生平和贡献，分析他们对于各自文化背景下的科学发展的影响，探讨他们的思想和方法如何融合了中西科学的特点。

3. 头脑风暴

（1）你能想象一下五十年后的科技世界吗？哪些想法现在已经初露端倪了？

（2）学习 TED Talk “Can a Computer Write Poetry?”（电脑能写诗吗？），就此展开对 DeepSeek 的探讨。你认为 DeepSeek 在哪些方面能够取代人？ DeepSeek 未来发展会怎样？它会给人类带来危险吗？

参考资料

一、书籍

凯恩．西医的故事 [M]. 北京：商务印书馆，2015.

梁漱溟．中国文化要义 [M]. 上海：上海人民出版社，2003.

费孝通．美国人的性格 [M]. 北京：文化发展出版社，2018.

林语堂．吾国与吾民 [M]. 北京：外语教学与研究出版社，2009.

罗素．西方哲学简史 [M]. 西安：陕西师范大学出版社，2010.

冯友兰．中国哲学简史 [M]. 北京：世界图书出版公司，2011.

冯泽永．中西医学比较 [M]. 北京：科学出版社，2001.

牟宗三．中国哲学十九讲 [M]. 长春：吉林出版集团有限责任公司，2010.

黑格尔．哲学史讲演录：第 1 卷 [M]. 贺麟，王太庆，译．北京：商务印书馆，2013.

胡适．中国哲学史大纲 [M]. 北京：商务印书馆，2011.

皇甫慈．中西医学比较的哲学基础 [M]. 北京：高等教育出版社，2011.

梯利．西方哲学史 [M]. 北京：光明日报出版社，2014.

笛卡尔．哲学原理 [M]. 北京：商务印书馆，2023.

McClellan, James E. III, and Dorn, Harold. Science and Technology in World History: An Introduction[M]. Baltimore and London: The Johns Hopkins University Press, 2015.

McNeill, William Hardy. A World History[M]. Oxford: Oxford University Press, 1998.

Buck, Pearl Sydenstricker. The Good Earth[M]. New York: Washington Square Press, 2020.

Gaarder, Jostein. Sophie's World: A Novel about the History of Philosophy[M]. New York: Farrar, Straus and Giroux, 2007.

二、网站

http://darwin-online.org.uk/darwin.html (Darwin Online)

三、影视作品

《蒸汽男孩》《豪斯医生》《急诊室的故事》《美丽心灵》《这个男人来自地球》

Chapter Three

The Contrast of Chinese and Western Literature

课前成果检测

中西方文学阅读测试题

一、单选题

1. 在英国伊丽莎白时期，盛行哪一种文体？（　　）

A. 小说　　B. 随笔　　C. 史诗　　D. 戏剧

2. 以下哪一位作家不是浪漫主义时期的作家？（　　）

A. 济慈　　B. 雪莱　　C. 华兹华斯　　D. 笛福

3. 以下哪位作家的作品以讽刺著称？（　　）

A. 瓦尔特・斯各特　　B. 乔纳森・斯威夫特

C. 丹尼尔・笛福　　D. 简・奥斯汀

4. 以下哪部小说不是勃朗特姐妹的作品？（　　）

A.《傲慢与偏见》　　B.《阿格尼斯・格雷》

C.《呼啸山庄》　　D.《简・爱》

5. 埃米莉·狄金森是（　　）世纪美国新英格兰著名诗人。

A. 17　　B. 18　　C. 19　　D. 20

6. 斯威夫特的写作特点是（　　）。

A. 犀利的讽刺　　B. 优美的文笔　　C. 随意的语气　　D. 复杂的句式

7. “今宵酒醒何处？杨柳岸，晓风残月。”这是（　　）《雨霖铃》中的名句。

A. 秦观　　B. 白居易　　C. 柳永　　D. 苏轼

8. 杜丽娘是（　　）中的人物。

A.《汉宫秋》　　B.《牡丹亭》　　C.《梧桐雨》　　D.《西厢记》

二、连线题（请将作品和其作者相连）

作品：	作家：
1.《金银岛》	a. 孔尚任
2.《德伯家的苔丝》	b. 老舍
3.《美国的悲剧》	c. 马克·吐温
4.《哈克贝利·芬历险记》	d. 曹禺
5.《复乐园》	e. 托马斯·哈代
6.《日出》	f. 罗伯特·史蒂文森
7.《桃花扇》	g. 莫言
8.《红高粱家族》	h. 西奥多·德莱赛
9.《聊斋志异》	i. 约翰·弥尔顿
10.《茶馆》	j. 蒲松龄

三、思考题

1. 回忆你之前读过的中外诗歌、剧本、小说，这些文学作品从哪些方面影响了你的思维方式或对人生的态度？

2. 有人说，伟大的作品反映的都是人性，那么中西方诗人、剧作家、小说家对于人性的反思在内容与形式上有何不同？

3. “历史除了人名外都是假的，小说除了人名外都是真的。”你如何理解这句话？

Section One

The Contrast of Chinese and Western Poetry

I. Learning Objectives

1. To know the characteristics of Chinese and Western poetry

2. To summarize the differences between Chinese and Western poetry from perspectives of content and form (e.g. diction, image, rhyme, length, etc.)

II. Key Points and Difficult Points

1. To summarize the main characteristics of Chinese and Western poetry

2. To contrast and compare Chinese and Western poetry

III. Lead-in Questions

1. What are your favorite Chinese poems? Why do you like them?

2. Have you read any Western poems in their original language? If so, share your understanding of one of these poems in English. If not, find some online and try to understand them.

3. What are the differences between Chinese and Western poetry? Try to compare them from the perspectives of themes, logic, images, symbols, diction, length, rhyme, etc.

IV. Learning Contents

1. Western and Chinese Nature Poems

Wordsworth, a Worshipper of Nature

William Wordsworth is regarded as "a worshipper of nature" because he can penetrate to the core of things and give the readers the very life of nature. He wrote many poems to reveal his genuine love for the natural beauty which can release him out of the solitude and sorrow when he is sad or empty-minded, as is expressed in *I Wandered Lonely as a Cloud*. Beyond the pleasures, the poems lay a moral awareness as he is aware of his own sublime communion with all things. Nature has become an inspiring force of rapture and a power that reveals the working of the soul. To Wordsworth, nature acts as a substitute for imaginative and intellectual engagement with the development of embodied human beings in their diverse circumstance. It's nature that gives him "strength and knowledge full of peace".

I Wandered Lonely as a Cloud (William Wordsworth, 1770–1850)

I wandered lonely as a cloud
That floats on high o'er vales and hills,
When all at once I saw a crowd,
A host, of golden daffodils;
Beside the lake, beneath the trees,
Fluttering and dancing in the breeze.

Continuous as the stars that shine
And twinkle on the milky way,
They stretched in never-ending line
Along the margin of a bay:
Ten thousand saw I at a glance,
Tossing their heads in sprightly dance.

The waves beside them danced; but they
Out-did the sparkling waves in glee;
A poet could not but be gay,
In such a jocund company;

I gazed—and gazed—but little thought
What wealth the show to me had brought:

For oft, when on my couch I lie
In vacant or in pensive mood,
They flash upon that inward eye
Which is the bliss of solitude;
And then my heart with pleasure fills,
And dances with the daffodils.

单词表

rapture	*n.*	狂喜，欢天喜地，兴高采烈
daffodil	*n.*	黄水仙
flutter	*v.*	飘动，挥动
toss	*v.*	摇摆，挥动；甩头
sprightly	*adj.*	精力充沛的
jocund	*adj.*	高兴的，欢乐的，愉快的
oft	*adv.*	时常，经常
pensive	*adj.*	沉思默想的
inward cyc		心灵；脑海
bliss	*n.*	极乐

Tao Yuanming (陶渊明，365—427)

Tao Yuanming, original name Tao Qian (陶潜), is a great poet of reclusion in Eastern Jin (东晋). He once served as a minor official in local government but retreated not long afterwards from government which he thought to be extremely corrupt and chose to live in accord with nature and the true self in the country. During his retirement, Tao supported his family by farming and wrote many famous poems about a quiet way of existence such as drinking, cultivating his land, enjoying natural beauty, and rustic life among friends and family. The vivid and beautiful description of pastoral landscape established him as the creator of the pastoral poetry.

饮酒（其五）

结庐在人境，而无车马喧。
问君何能尔？心远地自偏。
采菊东篱下，悠然见南山。
山气日夕佳，飞鸟相与还。
此中有真意，欲辨已忘言。

单词表

reclusion	*n.*	隐居（a poet of reclusion 指隐逸派诗人）
pastoral	*adj.*	田园的，乡村生活的

2. Western and Chinese Love Poems

Song to Celia (Ben Jonson, 1572–1637)

Drink to me only with thine eyes,
And I will pledge with mine;
Or leave a kiss but in the cup,
And I'll not look for wine.
The thirst that from the soul doth rise
Doth ask a drink divine;
But might I of Jove's nectar sup,
I would not change for thine.

I sent thee late a rosy wreath,
Not so much honouring thee
As giving it a hope, that there
It could not withered be.
But thou thereon didst only breathe,
And sent'st it back to me;
Since when it grows, and smells, I swear,

Not of itself, but thee.

单词表

thine	*pron.*	你的
pledge	*v.*	这里指祝酒，干杯
doth	*v.*	does
Jove's nectar		天神的美酒。Jove 即朱庇特，罗马神话中的主神。
thee	*pron.*	你（古英语 thou 的宾格）
late	*adv.*	这里指 lately，不久前
wreath	*n.*	花环
wither	*v.*	干枯
thou	*pron.*	你（主格）
thereon	*adv.*	以……为依据，由……而产生
didst	*v.*	did
sent'st	*v.*	sent

夜雨寄北（李商隐，813—858）

君问归期未有期，巴山夜雨涨秋池。

何当共剪西窗烛，却话巴山夜雨时。

V. Story Links

1. 叶芝的爱情故事

威廉·巴特勒·叶芝（William Butler Yeats, 1865—1939）是爱尔兰诗人和剧作家，24 岁时认识了女演员、爱尔兰争取民族自治运动领导人之一的莫德·岗（Maud Gonne）并爱上了她，却被拒绝。五年后，叶芝写出著名的 *When You Are Old*。莫德在 1903 年嫁给了爱尔兰军官布莱德少校，十年后，布莱德少校去世，叶芝再度向莫德求婚却再一次遭到拒绝。1917 年，52 岁的叶芝终于与另一女子结婚。至此，他用一生中最宝贵的二十多个春秋实践了自己诗中的表白。

When You Are Old

When you are old and gray and full of sleep
And nodding by the fire, take down this book,
And slowly read, and dream of the soft look
Your eyes had once, and of their shadows deep;

How many loved your moments of glad grace,
And loved your beauty with love false or true;
But one man loved the pilgrim soul in you,
And loved the sorrows of your changing face;

And bending down beside the glowing bars,
Murmur, a little sadly, how love fled
And paced upon the mountains overhead,
And bid his face amid a crowd of stars.

这首诗被中国音乐人赵照改写成著名歌曲《当你老了》，用来表达对母亲的感情。

当你老了

当你老了，头发白了，睡意昏沉；
当你老了，走不动了，炉火旁打盹，回忆青春。
多少人曾爱你青春欢畅的时辰，
爱慕你的美丽，假意或真心；
只有一个人还爱你虔诚的灵魂，
爱你苍老的脸上的皱纹。
当你老了，眼眉低垂，灯火昏黄不定；
风吹过来，你的消息，这就是我心里的歌。
多少人曾爱你青春欢畅的时辰，
爱慕你的美丽，假意或真心；
只有一个人还爱你虔诚的灵魂，
爱你苍老的脸上的皱纹。
当你老了，眼眉低垂，灯火昏黄不定；
当我老了，我真希望，这首歌是唱给你的。

2. 美食家苏轼

苏轼（1037—1101）是个美食家，宋人笔记小说有许多关于苏轼发明美食的记载。苏轼在杭州时，元祐五年五六月间，浙西大雨，太湖泛滥。苏轼指挥疏浚西湖，筑苏堤。杭州百姓感谢他，过年时大家抬猪担酒来给他拜年。苏轼指点家人将猪肉切成大块，烧得红酥，然后送给大家吃，这就是东坡肉的由来。《曲洧旧闻》又有记载：苏东坡与客论食次，取纸一幅，书以示客云："烂蒸同州羊羔，灌以杏酪，食之以匕不以箸。南都麦心面，作槐芽温淘，粉襄邑抹猪，炊共城香梗，荐以蒸子鹅，吴兴庖人斫松江鲙。既饱，以庐山康王谷帘泉烹曾坑斗品茶。少焉，解衣仰卧，使人诵东坡先生《赤壁前后赋》，亦足以一笑也。"

VI. Did You Know?

1. 谐趣诗一首

并非所有诗歌都高雅、严肃，下面这首小诗就很有趣：

The Pig

It was an evening in November,
As I very well remember,
I was strolling down the street in drunken pride,
But my knees were all aflutter,
And I landed in the gutter
And a pig came up and lay down by my side.

Yes, I lay there in the gutter
Thinking thoughts I could not utter,
When a colleen passing by did softly say,
"You can tell a man who boozes
By the company he chooses."
And the pig got up and slowly walked away.

2. 中国趣诗——拆字诗

拆字诗是根据汉字的特点，将合体字拆成独体字，或拆成相关的部件（偏旁加独体字），敷衍成篇。举个有趣的例子：苏东坡有一侍女，名叫朝云，非常聪明。她有一次去桥下淘米，被一个无赖秀才纠缠，秀才道：

有木便为桥，无木也念乔。去木添个女，添女便为娇。阿娇休避我，我最爱阿娇。

朝云轻篾地一笑，当即对答：

有米便为粮，无米也念良。去米添个女，添女便是娘。老娘虽爱子，子不敬老娘。

VII. Cultural Reflection

中西方诗歌之间的差异与中西方文化其他方面的差异一脉相承。由于中西方思维方式不同、诗歌理论的发展不同、诗歌受宗教影响的程度不同，以及人们对待爱情和事业的看法不同，中西方各类诗歌都表现出不同的特征。

一、西方诗歌重逻辑阐释，中国诗歌重情感表达

西方诗歌受亚里士多德三段论的影响，强调诗歌内在的逻辑，注重事物与诗人之间理性的统一；而中国诗歌注重意境与诗人心境的统一，偏感性。由于西方诗人注重诗歌的逻辑性，而中国诗歌注重表达某一刻的感受，因此西方多长诗，而中国长诗较少，没有类似于荷马史诗（*The Homer Epic*）、《失乐园》（*Paradise Lost*）那样的长篇巨著。另外，长篇诗歌多为叙事诗，短篇诗歌则大多抒情，由此也可以看出诗歌这种体裁在中西方作用的不同：中国诗歌多用于抒情，而西方诗歌则兼用于抒情与叙事。

二、西方许多诗人在创作的同时研究诗歌理论，并依据自己的诗歌理论进行创作

威廉·华兹华斯（William Wordsworth）即依照自己的诗歌理论来作诗，比如他认为诗歌表现的是"不由自主产生的、强烈的情感"，但这种情感要经过时间的沉淀，经年之后在平静中回忆起来，才成为诗歌。以本节 Learning Contents 部分所选的 *I Wandered Lonely as a Cloud* 为例，诗人于 1802 年 4 月的某天散步时，突然发现了湖边有一大片黄水仙，深受震撼。诗歌创作于 1804 年，即诗人用了两年多的时间来积淀、追忆、咀嚼，最后创作成诗。除此之外，西方诗人常常在自然诗中表达哲学思想，如对于美以及真理的思考。华兹华斯在诗中表达的是，人的一生不应该失去与大自然的联系，在自然中能随时感受到脱俗的喜悦之情。与西方诗人形成对比的是，中国诗人大多不研究诗歌理论，在创作时有借景自由抒情的意味。

三、西方诗歌受宗教影响明显，具有神秘色彩；而中国诗歌与之相比，具有现实性

当西方诗人置身自然时，会不由自主地察觉到一种神秘的力量在支配万物，这便是上帝的力量。几乎所有西方诗人的诗歌都或多或少受基督教的影响，诗歌中与基督教相关的意象也较为常见。而道教、佛教虽然在一定程度上影响中国诗歌，但与基督教对西方诗歌的影响相比则非常不明显。许多诗人借诗歌表达自己的处世哲学。例如陶渊明是在政治理想无法实现时，才回归田园，求得内心平静。从此意义上讲，诗人表面上写的是田园，实际写的是自己。中国文学史上这种现象很常见，孟浩然、王维、李白等诗人都写过许多歌颂自然的名篇，但这些诗篇都反映出他们在仕途上的挫折。

四、在抒情方面，西方诗歌往往直抒胸臆，而中国诗歌多用以咏志，情态表达含蓄内敛

西方男子在事业与爱情发生矛盾时，常常会以爱情为重，因此西方表现对女性倾慕的诗歌俯拾皆是。西方爱情诗中比较著名的是中世纪的骑士抒情诗。为了讨贵妇人的欢心，骑士们甘愿冒险或作战。骑士抒情诗对后来的爱情诗影响很大，在后来的爱情诗中，诗人直白地表达出对异性的爱慕，诗中男女的感情可以不指向婚姻，而仅仅是精神上的伴侣。诗人对于情人的赞美十分直白，许多诗歌都大胆地直接称赞恋人的美，似乎认为美可以征服一切。对美的推崇可以追溯到荷马史诗，海伦的美导致了长达十年的特洛伊战争。除体貌美之外，心灵美也经常受到歌颂，心灵和体貌的美相互依存，融为一体，构成诗人心中理想女性的最高标准。

与西方不同的是，中国男子往往以事业为重，爱情绝对没有与之抗衡的分量。由于夫婿赶考或为国远赴沙场，夫妻两地分居现象较为普遍，所以中国爱情诗中表现出的离愁别绪较多。另外，在中国传统观念中，爱情与婚姻应当合一，非婚姻的男女感情是不被接受的。《诗经》中的诗篇表达的男女感情比较直白，之后由于中国进入长达两千多年的封建社会，人的感情受到压抑，因此这种直白的抒情诗大幅度减少。即使是相对直接的感情抒发，也是借助他物来抒情，而不会出现西方诗歌“你是那么美 / 漂亮的姑娘 / 我爱你那么深切”这种直抒胸臆式的表达。中国诗人若论及爱情，需要利用一系列意象，将爱情比作他物，比如“比翼鸟”“连理枝”等，间接歌颂爱情，给人一种“只可意会，不可言传”的感觉。例如，李商隐在《夜雨寄北》中表达了对妻子的深切思念，但全诗中并没有提到“思念”“忧愁”这样的词，他的强烈情感是通过“巴山夜雨”等意象表达的。另外，中国爱情诗许多时候描写的不是真正的爱情，而是表面写美好的女子，实际暗指君主，即以男女之情来譬喻君臣之谊，这种现象在西方并没有出现。

VIII. Homework

1. 我来翻译

请将 Did You Know? 部分中的 *The Pig* 译成中文，将《夜雨寄北》译成英文，注意兼顾“意”与“神”，之后与同学讨论并再次修改，最后上交译文。

2. 跨越时空的对话

从西方诗人与中国诗人中各找出一位善于写相似题材的诗人，例如李商隐与罗伯特·彭斯（Robert Burns），想象他们之间的交流，以“当诗人 A 遇见诗人 B（When A Meets B）”为话题写一篇 200 字左右的英文文章。

3. 阅读邀请

利用网络或图书馆，选一首中国古诗的英文译本，邀请一位外教、外国留学生或外国朋友阅读，之后请他（她）谈一下感受，尤其谈一下这首诗使他（她）非常赞叹、惊讶、不理解之处，做好记录，并在下次上课时与同学交流。

Section Two

The Contrast of Chinese and Western Drama

I. Learning Objectives

1. To learn about Chinese and Western outstanding playwrights and their works
2. To summarize the characteristics of Chinese and Western drama
3. To compare the similarities and differences between Chinese and Western drama

II. Key Points and Difficult Points

1. To summarize the influential factors of Chinese and Western playwrights and their works
2. To contrast and compare Chinese drama and Western drama

III. Lead-in Questions

1. Talk about the Chinese and Western plays you have watched or the scripts you have read. Which one do you like best? Why?

2. What are the differences between Chinese and Western drama? Try to compare them from the perspectives of plot, characters, themes, diction, music, spectacle, etc.

IV. Learning Contents

1. *Oedipus the King* (Sophocles, c. 496 BCE–406 BCE)

Oedipus the King vows to find the murderer of their former King, Laius, and curses the murderer for causing the plague ravaging Thebes. He summons the blind prophet Tiresias for help. When Tiresias arrives Oedipus is enraged by Tiresias' refusal to speak. Outraged, Tiresias tells the king that Oedipus himself is the murderer. Oedipus mocks Tiresias' lack of sight, and Tiresias in turn tells Oedipus that he himself is blind. Eventually Tiresias leaves, muttering darkly that when the murderer is discovered he shall be a native citizen of Thebes, brother and father to his own children, and son and husband to his own mother.

Jocasta enters and attempts to comfort Oedipus, telling him about an incident in which she and Laius received an oracle which never came true. The prophecy stated that Laius would be killed by his own son; however, Jocasta reassures Oedipus that Laius was killed by bandits at a crossroads on the way to Delphi. Oedipus suddenly becomes worried that Tiresias's accusations were true. It turns out that, years ago, Oedipus was given a prophecy that he would one day murder his father and sleep with his mother. Upon hearing this he resolved to leave Corinth and never return. While traveling he came to the very crossroads where Laius was killed, and encountered a carriage which attempted to drive him off the road. An argument ensued and Oedipus killed the travelers, including a man who matches Jocasta's description of Laius. Everything is at last revealed, and Oedipus curses himself and fate. The chorus laments how even a great man can be tripped by fate. Jocasta runs to the palace bedroom and hangs herself. Shortly afterward, Oedipus enters, takes her down and removes the long gold pins that held her dress together, before plunging them into his own eyes in despair. A blind Oedipus now exits the palace and begs to be exiled as soon as possible. On an empty stage the chorus repeats the common Greek maxim that no man should be considered fortunate until he is dead.

单词表

ravage	*v.*	毁坏，严重损害
oracle	*n.*	神谕，神示
bandit	*n.*	土匪
maxim	*n.*	格言，箴言

俄狄浦斯王

2. *The Palace of Eternal Youth*（《长生殿》）by Hong Sheng（洪昇，1645–1704）

When Lady Yang (杨贵妃) becomes the Emperor's favorite consort, he gives her as love tokens a gold hairpin and a casket adorned with gold-leaf flowers. Her older brother Yang Guozhong (杨国忠) becomes Chancellor of the Right. A frontier geneal, An Lushan (安禄山), is sent to the capital for an offense, but Yang Guozhong obtains a pardon for him, and he wins a promotion and a princely title for himself. A military man, Guo Ziyi (郭子仪), comes to the capital and is appointed a powerful military commissioner.

After challenging the power of Yang Guozhong, An Lushan stirs up a rebellion, and Guo Ziyi trains his troops to counter the imminent rising. Oblivious of this situation, Emperor Xuanzong (唐玄宗) and Lady Yang bathe together and vow eternal love for each other. When An Lushan's forces menace the capital, Xuanzong departs with his entourage toward the relative safety of Sichuan. On the way, his mutinous troops, blaming the Yangs for their plight, kill Yang Guozhong and demand Lady Yang's death. Helpless, Xuanzong forces her to hang herself, and she is provisionally buried there. An Lushan usurps the imperial throne, and takes over the capital. Xuanzong, grieving for Lady Yang, on reaching Sichuan places a portrait of her in a temple. Meanwhile, moved by the plight of Lady Yang's forlorn soul, the Spinning Damsel (织女) persuades the Jade Emperor of Heaven (玉皇大帝) to permit Lady Yang to become an immortal in the paradise of Penglai (蓬莱). Later, aided by the Spinning Damsel, the Taoist necromancer Yang Tongyou (杨通幽) reaches Penglai, where Lady Yang gives him half the gold hairpin and part of the casket to take to Xuanzong as tokens of renewed love. On the appointed date, Yang Tongyou sets up a fairy bridge to the Moon Palace (月宫) and sends Xuanzong alone on it to the moon. There the two lovers are blissfully reunited, match the halves of the hairpin and the casket, and are commanded by the Jade Emperor to dwell forever as man and wife in paradise.

单词表

consort	*n.*	（统治者的）配偶
casket	*n.*	（尤指旧时存放珠宝等贵重物品的）精致的小盒子，装饰精美的小箱子
commissioner	*n.*	首长，长官
imminent	*adj.*	（尤指不愉快的事）即将发生的，临近的
oblivious	*adj.*	未注意的，未察觉的
entourage	*n.*	（统称）随行人员，随从
mutinous	*adj.*	不驯服的，桀骜不驯的，有意反抗的
plight	*n.*	苦难，困境，苦境
provisionally	*adv.*	临时地，暂时地
usurp	*v.*	篡夺，侵权
forlorn	*adj.*	孤苦伶仃的，孤独凄凉的
necromancer	*n.*	通灵者，巫师
blissfully	*adv.*	极乐地，幸福地

V. Story Links

1. *Othello* (William Shakespeare, 1564–1616)

Othello, a Moorish general in the Venetian army, and Desdemona, the daughter of a Senator, have got married secretly. Iago hates Othello for promoting a younger man named Cassio above him, and he plans to use Othello for his own advantage. Iago persuades Othello to be suspicious of Cassio and Desdemona. Iago finds a handkerchief dropped by Desdemona (the first gift given to her by Othello), and plants the handkerchief in Cassio's lodgings, then tells Othello to watch Cassio's reactions while Iago questions him. Iago goads Cassio on to talk about his affair with Bianca, a local courtesan, but whispers her name so quietly that Othello believes they are talking about Desdemona. Later, Iago convinces him that Cassio received the handkerchief from Desdemona. Enraged and hurt, Othello confronts Desdemona, and then strangles her to death in their bed. In the end, realizing Desdemona's innocence, Othello commits suicide.

2.《窦娥冤》(关汉卿，约 1230—约 1300)

书生窦天章因无力偿还蔡婆的高利贷，把七岁的女儿窦娥送给蔡婆当童养媳来抵债。窦娥长大后与蔡婆儿子成婚，婚后两年蔡婆儿子病死。张驴儿要蔡婆将窦娥许配给他不成，便将毒药下在汤中要毒死蔡婆，结果误毒死了自己的父亲。张驴儿反而诬告窦娥毒死了其父，昏官桃杌最后做成冤案将窦娥处斩，窦娥临终发下"血染白绫、天降大雪、大旱三年"的誓愿。窦天章最后科场中第荣任高官，听闻此事，为窦娥平反昭雪。

VI. Did You Know?

1. 俄狄浦斯情结（Oedipus complex）

俄狄浦斯情结也称"恋母情结"，这一词在心理学和文学批评中常用。《牛津高阶英汉双解词典（第 8 版）》是这样解释这一术语的：feelings of sexual desire that a boy has for his mother and the jealous feelings towards his father that this causes. It originates from the Greek story of **Oedipus**, whose father Laius had been told by the oracle that his son would kill him. Laius left Oedipus on a mountain to die, but a shepherd rescued him. Oedipus returned home many years later but did not recognize his parents. He killed his father and married his mother Jocasta.

2. 古希腊三大悲剧作家及三大悲剧

古希腊三大悲剧作家：埃斯库罗斯（Aeschylus）、索福克勒斯（Sophocles）和欧里庇得斯（Euripides）。

古希腊三大悲剧：《被缚的普罗米修斯》(*Prometheus Bound*)、《俄狄浦斯王》(*Oedipus the King*) 和《美狄亚》(*Medea*)。

VII. Cultural Reflection

中西方戏剧的历史都非常悠久，都有令人荡气回肠的著名戏剧。戏剧艺术的共同特性是依托于舞台的表现艺术，然而在具体的表现形式上，中西方戏剧却又表现出极大的差异。《美狄亚》和《西厢记》带给观众的美学享受与艺术想象截然不同。这些区别绝不仅仅是不同风格的服装、不同内涵的台词或者不同风格的演绎所能阐释清楚的，最重要的差异是不同文化背景的内在差异，主要表现在创作依据与内容两个方面。

一、中西方戏剧的差异首先体现在创作依据上

西方戏剧创作遵循一系列的戏剧创作理论。早在古希腊时期，西方就形成了一套戏剧范式，以冲突律、明确的悲喜属性以及严谨的闭锁式结构为特征。亚里士多德在其《诗学》（*On the Art of Poetry*）中系统地阐述了这一戏剧理论。虽然这种戏剧创作的范式自 20 世纪以来不断受到挑战和反叛，但它从来没有被完全倾覆。另外，西方传统艺术重写实，戏剧也是如此，强调舞台演出的真实性，故事的情节和具体的细节在剧作中都用写实性的手法表现。中国戏剧源于歌舞，因此自古以来中国戏剧都带有娱乐性，其故事脚本大多来自民间。传统中国戏曲的文学成就以宋元杂剧、南戏和明清传奇为代表，其相应的理论自成体系，不同于西方有完整的理论贯穿戏剧发展史。自宋元起，有不少思想家对戏剧文学的本质有独到的理解，例如明代的汤显祖，清代的李渔、孔尚任等。

二、中西方戏剧在内容上呈现出鲜明差异

中西方悲剧内容的差异反映的是中西方对人生、命运的态度差异。亚里士多德把悲剧定义为“对一个严肃的、完整的、有一定长度的行动的模仿”，“借引起怜悯与恐惧来使这种情感得到净化和宣泄”。因此，西方的悲剧自古以来重在表现矛盾和冲突，而且往往是重要人物性格内部的冲突，或人与命运的冲突。《俄狄浦斯王》作为古希腊悲剧的代表，叙述伟人的故事，俄狄浦斯王确实建立了丰功伟绩，且与命运斗争，然而最终还是受到命运这种强大力量的摆布，发生悲剧。因此，俄狄浦斯既是西方悲剧中常出现的“智者受难”的典型，又象征着每个普通的人。莎士比亚是文艺复兴时期的剧作家代表，其作品之所以经久不衰，是因为其表现的是亘古不变的人性。悲剧的发生都是由于主人公性格中的某种缺陷，体现了莎士比亚对人性的反思。与西方悲剧相比，中国悲剧较少关注人性、命运，而是关注人与他人、整个社会，甚至与整个国家的关系。例如，《赵氏孤儿》中表现的更多的是忠于君主及维护皇家传统，反映了以“血亲”关系为主的文化认同。剧中人物若要实现愿望、改变命运、获得幸福，无法依靠自己的力量，而是必须依赖他者。许多作品中还体现了轮回思想，例如《长生殿》中的杨贵妃在现世中没有与爱人相依相守，死后灵魂满足了其生前的愿望。从这点上看，中国戏剧作家对于个人是否可以

掌握自己的命运是持悲观态度的，并没有西方人普遍带有的反抗精神。从另一个方面讲，中国戏剧也反映出在封建社会的背景下，个体的无能为力。

中西方喜剧的不同主要表现在西方喜剧所表现的更多的是乐观精神，而中国的喜剧相对于西方喜剧而言更带有讽刺性。在西方喜剧发展史上，剧作家时而针砭时弊，但是并不否定制度本身。这一现象与西方传统的喜剧观相联系，亚里士多德在《诗学》中指出，喜剧应当描写“比我们今天的人坏的人”，即反映的是“丑”，而不是“恶”。中国喜剧以讽刺喜剧为主，与现实和民众生活结合，具有平民性。传统喜剧往往表达讽刺、批判意义，因为封建社会中人与人的关系多为从属、依附关系，服从、忍耐的成分较多。中国剧作家在当时大多地位低下，受封建专制社会制度的制约，经常有机会接近普通百姓，同情人民，因此愿用更多笔墨讽刺权势。另外，在中国喜剧中，利用某一人物“逗趣”的现象较为普遍，例如《西厢记》著名的“拷红”一折中，除对老夫人的讽刺之外，喜剧效果还通过红娘这一人物的语言、动作明确地表现出来。这种专门利用某一人物表现喜剧特色的现象在西方喜剧中并不多见。

VIII. Homework

1. 五分钟演讲（从以下两个话题中任选一个话题）

（1）你所读过或看过的悲剧中，哪种（部）悲剧最能触动你？为什么？

（2）你所读过或看过的喜剧中，哪种（部）喜剧让你印象最深刻？为什么？

2. 思考与讨论

（1）中西方剧作家对于死亡的看法有什么不同？

（2）戏剧的目的是否仅为反映现实？如果是，那么举例说明戏剧如何反映现实；如果不是，说明戏剧创作的其他目的。

3. 欣赏与写作

利用网络资源，观看相同时期的中英文戏剧各一部，并写一篇 200 字左右的英文观后感，比较两者在创作背景、主题、人物塑造、舞台表现等方面的差异。

Section Three

The Contrast of Chinese and Western Fiction

I. Learning Objectives

1. To learn about the plot, characters, and themes of famous Chinese and Western fiction

2. To summarize the characteristics of Chinese and Western travel fiction, love fiction, and war fiction

3. To compare the similarities and differences between Chinese and Western fiction

II. Key Points and Difficult Points

1. To understand the influential Chinese and Western fiction

2. To contrast and compare Chinese and Western fiction

III. Lead-in Questions

1. Talk about the Chinese and Western novels you have read. Which one, or what kind of novels, do you like best? Why?

2. What are the differences between Chinese and Western fiction? Try to compare them from the perspectives of plot, characters, themes, narrating techniques, etc.

IV. Learning Contents

1. Travel Fiction

Robinson Crusoe (Daniel Defoe, 1660–1731)

Robinson Crusoe by Daniel Defoe was published in the year 1719. It is the first person narrative of a fictionalized character who, after his initial journeys to the sea and South America, finds himself washed up on the shore of a deserted island near the mouth of the Orinoco River. Through his resourcefulness he finds ways to survive and even thrive, especially in the areas of farming and raising goats. He spends decades on the island, tending to his houses and crops, and avoiding the "savages" who occasionally land on his island. It's the portrayal of these natives, as well as Crusoe's and the author's attitudes towards them, that most relates to the study of colonial and post-colonial literature.

Journey to the West（《西游记》）by Wu Cheng'en（吴承恩，约 1500—约 1582）

Journey to the West by Wu Cheng'en is an outstanding romantic work full of fantastic tales. It is generally recognized as a masterpiece about deities and spirits. The novel tells of the Tang-dynasty monk, Xuanzang (唐玄奘), overcoming 81 adversities and defeating various monsters and demons before finally reaching India, assisted by his three disciples: the Monkey King (孙悟空), the Eight-Commandment Pig (猪八戒), and Monk Sha (沙僧). Wu Cheng'en illuminated the intelligence, bravery, and loyalty of the Monkey King, the piety of Monk Xuanzang, the straightforwardness and good nature of the Eight-Commandment Pig, and the kindness of Monk Sha. Through telling tales of deities and spirits, Wu Cheng'en exposed the darkness and corruption of feudal society, criticized social realities, and implicitly expressed people's different forms of resistance.

As far as artistic expression is concerned, the most striking features of the book are its eerie imagination and bald exaggeration by which the writer created a grotesque, gaudy, fanciful and magical world which broke the boundary between time and space, life and death, humans and deities. The book is thus permeated with an intense romantic flavor. The book provides the reader with a varied and colorful art gallery of deities and ghosts. Even to this day, their images remain familiar to every household and to both the old and the young.

单词表

deity	*n.*	神仙
adversity	*n.*	苦难
disciple	*n.*	徒弟，门徒
piety	*n.*	虔诚
feudal	*adj.*	封建的
implicitly	*adv.*	含蓄地
eerie	*adj.*	怪异的，神秘的
grotesque	*adj.*	怪诞的，荒唐的，荒谬的
gaudy	*adj.*	花哨的
permeate	*v.*	弥漫，渗透，扩散

2. Love Fiction

Wuthering Heights (Emily Brontë, 1818–1848)

The story of *Wuthering Heights* is concerned with two symmetrical families and an intruding stranger. The Earnshaws, rough in manner, include Mr. Earnshaws, his son Hindley, and his daughter Catherine. They live in their old house, Wuthering Heights, up in the folds of the moor. The Linton family, richer and more genteel, includes Mr. Linton, his wife, his son Edgar, and his daughter Isabella, and they live down in a neighboring valley at Thrushcross Grange. One day Mr. Earnshaw brings home a Gypsy looking little boy he has found in the streets of Liverpool. He calls the boy Heathcliff. The children grow up together. Catherine loves Heathcliff, while Hindley hates him, being jealous of his father's fondness for the stranger.

After the death of Mr. Earnshaw, Hindley degrades Heathcliff in every way he can. Heathcliff grows brutal and sullen, and Catherine turns from him to the mild Edgar Linton. Heathcliff runs away and returns when Catherine has become Edgar's wife. Heathcliff is now rich and is determined to take revenge on Hindley and the Lintons. Between Heathcliff and Edgar, Catherine becomes distracted. She gives birth to Edgar's daughter and dies. Heathcliff turns Hindley into a drunkard and gambler and wins all his possessions so that Hindley's son Hareton becomes a pauper in his house. Moreover, he contrives to marry Edgar Linton's vain and silly sister Isabella, and marry Linton's daughter, the young Catherine, to his own peevish ailing son, Linton Heathcliff. But all his revenge is foiled by Catherine and Hareton, who love each other. Heathcliff dies a defeated man. After his death people see the ghosts of Heathcliff and Catherine Earnshaw roam on the moor.

单词表

symmetrical	*adj.*	对应的，相似的，相仿的
intruding	*adj.*	闯入的，侵入的，不受欢迎的
moor	*n.*	荒原，旷野，荒野
genteel	*adj.*	显得彬彬有礼的，装体面的，上流社会的
Gypsy	*n.*	吉卜赛人
degrade	*v.*	降低……的身份，侮辱……的人格
sullen	*adj.*	闷闷不乐的，郁郁寡欢的，面色阴郁的
pauper	*n,*	穷人，贫民，乞丐
peevish	*adj.*	爱生气的，易怒的，脾气坏的
ailing	*adj.*	有病的，体弱的

《呼啸山庄》

A Dream of the Red Mansions（《红楼梦》）by Cao Xueqin（曹雪芹，约 1715 或 1721—约 1764）

A Dream of the Red Mansions has long been acknowledged as one of the greatest novel in Chinese literature. This novel describes the prosperity and decline of a large feudal family. The central thread of the novel is the tragic love story between Jia Baoyu (贾宝玉) and Lin Daiyu (林黛玉). Instead of just

telling the love story, it taps the social origins of the tragedy through probing deeply into the characters' minds and complicated relationships. The book also expounds on the fact that life tragedies are in fact caused by the tragedies of the age, pointing out that all forms of high position and great wealth are nothing but an illusory dream which is bound to end up in a "vast expanse of empty and desolate wilderness". None of the ingenious beauties in the "Grand View Garden" (大观园) is able to escape from her tearful and tragic fate in the end. It indicates a historical awareness that prolonged glory is bound to be followed by ruination and protracted prosperity by decline. In the book, the author also expresses his desolate life experiences coming from his insightful understanding of life. Running through the book is not only a strong sense of fate and destiny but also a clear concept of "vanity" and "void". The plot of the novel is ingeniously arranged. Its narratives use mature colloquial language, plain but elegant, explicit but expressive. The novel is really a panorama of feudal society and has been considered an encyclopedia of Chinese literature.

单词表

desolate	*adj.*	荒凉的
protracted	*adj.*	延长的，持久的
ingeniously	*adv.*	独具匠心地
panorama	*n.*	全景画

3. War Fiction

A Farewell to Arms (Ernest Hemingway, 1899–1961)

A Farewell to Arms is a Shakespearean tragic romance between an American Lieutenant, Frederic Henry, and a British army nurse, Catherine Barkley, which unfolds along the Italian front during World War Ⅰ. Falling in deep love with Catherine, Henry deserts from the retreating Italian front with her. Having escaped to Switzerland, they live in harmony until the tragic end of her pregnancy, during which both she and the child die. It is a semi-autobiographical novel which is inspired by Hemingway's own experiences in World War Ⅰ and his relationship with Agnes von Kurowsky. Below the surface, the novel is about World War Ⅰ and individual tragedy within the larger picture of greater tragedy.

单词表

lieutenant	*n.*	中尉

Romance of the Three Kingdoms (《三国演义》) by Luo Guanzhong (罗贯中，约1330—约1400)

Romance of the Three Kingdoms is recognized as the earliest chapter-by-chapter historical novel in China. Based on history books and folk legends, the book describes the rise and fall of the three kingdoms of Wei (魏), Shu (蜀) and Wu (吴), and the complex political, military, and diplomatic struggles during that period. It also manifests the miseries and disasters suffered by the people and expresses their strong desire to fight against war and separation and their longing for peace and unification. The basic expressive technique of *Romance of the Three Kingdoms* is realism, but the plot arrangement and the portrayal of historical figures are full of romantic color. One main theme the writer wants to advocate is brotherhood. By praising Liu Bei (刘备) and depreciating Cao Cao (曹操), the book reveals the writer's political ideal for "benevolent government". Besides, it advocates "personal loyalty", canonizes wisdom and favors talented people, thus creating a lot of artistic images with distinct individualities, such as Guan Yu (关羽), "the incarnation of personal loyalty" and Zhuge Liang (诸葛亮), "the embodiment of wisdom". The skillful description of war is an outstanding characteristic of *Romance of the Three Kingdoms*. Its language is featured by "moderate profundity and temperate vulgarity"; it is a mixture of vernacular and classical Chinese that suits both the refined and the popular tastes.

单词表

depreciate	*v.*	贬低
canonize	*v.*	推崇，褒扬，将……列为圣品

incarnation	*n.*	化身
profundity	*n.*	深刻性
vernacular	*n.*	方言

V. Story Links

1. *The Great Gatsby* (Francis Scott Key Fitzgerald, 1896–1940)

Gatsby is a poor youth from the Midwest. He falls in love with Daisy, a wealthy girl, but is too poor to marry her. The girl is then married to a rich young man, Tom Buchanan. Determined to win his lost love back, Gatsby engages himself in bootlegging and other "shady" activities, thus earning enough money to buy a magnificent imitation French villa. There he spreads dazzling parties every weekend in the hope of alluring the Buchanans to come. They finally come and Gatsby meets Daisy again, only to find that the woman before him is not quite the ideal love of his dreams. A sense of loss and disillusionment comes over him. Then Daisy kills a woman in an accident, and plots with Tom to shift the blame on Gatsby. So Gatsby is shot and the Buchanans escape.（资料来源：《美国文学简史》）

2.《镜花缘》（李汝珍，约 1763—约 1830）

《镜花缘》是一部带有浓厚神话色彩的长篇小说。该书前半部分描写了唐敖、多九公等人乘船在海外游历的故事，包括他们在女儿国、君子国、无肠国、黑齿国、白民国、淑士国、两面国、犬封国等见识的各种奇人异事、奇风异俗，并结识由十二名花仙转世的女子的故事。后半部分描述了武则天科举选才女，由百花仙子托生的唐小山及其他各花仙子托生的一百位才女考中，并在朝中有所作为的故事。

VI. Did You Know?

1.《老人与海》中的名句

形容海明威为"硬汉"的经典句子：But man is not made for defeat. A man can be destroyed but not defeated. 这句话出自《老人与海》（*The Old Man and the Sea*）。同一自然段中的后面几句话同样富有哲理：I am sorry that I killed the fish though, he thought. Now the bad time is coming and I do not even have the harpoon (鱼叉). The dentuso (登多索鲨) is cruel and able and strong and intelligent. But I was more intelligent than he was. Perhaps not, he thought. Perhaps I was only better armed.

2. 华裔文学作品对中西文化碰撞的关注

许多华裔文学作品都较充分地表现了中西文化碰撞，例如谭恩美（Amy Tan）的《喜福会》(*The Joy Luck Club*)。该小说讲述20世纪50年代移民圣弗朗西斯科的四位中国女性的故事。她们建立了一个麻将俱乐部“喜福会”，由此寄托她们对美好生活的向往。她们各自有一个女儿，然而由于文化背景的不同，作为中国母亲的她们与在美国出生的女儿以及女儿的爱人、朋友之间的沟通困难重重。

VII. Cultural Reflection

中西方小说中反映的文化差异表现在许多方面，这里仅以游记小说、爱情小说、战争小说为例进行简要分析。需要说明的是，这里分析的是小说中表现出的文化差异，而不是中西方小说本身的差异。

一、游记小说

西方游记小说的代表是《鲁滨孙漂流记》和《格列佛游记》(*Gulliver's Travels*)。《鲁滨孙漂流记》是以真实事件为基础创作的小说，其中体现了理性、科学的思想，情感因素较少。鲁滨孙即使被困荒岛，也非常冷静、乐观，对自身处境的分析极具条理性，体现了理性时代的精神。小说中也表现出较强的征服、殖民意识，具有外向性，例如鲁滨孙教给星期五的第一个英文单词是“master”。这些都与作者生活的时代的殖民精神相契合。《格列佛游记》是一部针砭时弊的作品，作者通过想象的游记故事，反思人性中的贪婪、敌对，他创作“不是为了提供娱乐而是为了激怒这个世界”。西方传统文学、艺术重写实，小说作者有意增加故事的亲历感、真实感，因此西方游记小说往往以第一人称叙述。

西方许多游记小说的主人公是主动出行，表现出对既定状态的不满足和积极冒险、勇于探索的精神。而中国许多小说的主人公是处于危机而被迫离家，或者身负重任上路，例如《西游记》中主人公远行的目的不是征服而是取经，即交流、学习，之后教化国民，体现出深刻的家国情怀。中国小说脱胎于史学，许多故事基于历史改编，作者有意增加故事的历史感，因此中国古典游记小说往往以第三人称叙述。此外，《西游记》四位主人公象征着成功所需的多元品质。唐僧象征坚定不移的目标和信念，孙悟空象征非凡的能力与智慧，猪八戒代表人性中轻松乐观的心态，而沙僧则代表任劳任怨的品格，这部小说本质上展现的是中华文化中的集体主义精神。

二、爱情小说

西方小说中以描写爱情为主的小说占大多数。由于西方自古以来对于爱情、自我感受的重视，西方爱情小说中往往会出现大段的、细腻的心理感受描写。另外，西方爱情小说的作者普遍赞扬了爱情中的抗争，例如《傲慢与偏见》中敢于反抗以物质财产衡量人价值的伊丽莎白，以及《德伯家的苔丝》中为了自己的真爱与命运抗争到最后的苔丝，都是作者称颂的对象。哈代对于苔丝的复仇精神持肯定态度，结合小说情节和副标题——“一个纯洁的女人”即可看出。

《红楼梦》是一部百科全书式的小说，以宝玉、黛玉之间的爱情纠葛为主线，这里只就这部小说中爱情这一方面进行分析。中国自古的封建伦理秩序决定了人们不像西方人那样关注个体的心理感受，因此在爱情小说中外部描写居多，例如黛玉进贾府时，重点表现的是人物的语言和动作。《红楼梦》中人物的心理描写往往通过诗歌来表现，例如黛玉通过著名的《葬花吟》，表达了心中的悲切。这种在小说中以诗抒情的形式，西方较少见。中国爱情小说里的主人公面对命运一般采取顺从的态度，例如黛玉虽然在浊世中保持清净，但她面对爱情、命运的悲观态度以及她的早逝都暗示了她并不像西方爱情小说主人公那样具有抗争精神。

三、战争小说

西方多战争，自古希腊时期起便战争不断。仔细阅读西方小说可以发现，字里行间都表现出西方人对于抗争精神和冒险精神的推崇，例如海明威的《老人与海》以及其“人可以被毁灭，但不可以被打败”等名言，均表明此意。西方战争往往是以一方消灭另一方为目的。然而，自20世纪以来，尤其是两次世界大战之后，西方小说家开始对战争进行反思，因此反战小说涌现。海明威在赞许抗争精神的同时，也是一位反战作家，他的许多小说都以此为主题，小说中的主人公是战争中的普通人，海明威通过他们揭露战争的残酷性。西方好以小人物的经历大做文章，这与西方人（尤其是美国人）重视发展人的个性，注重个体的价值、能力相联系。

中国古代战争远没有西方战争那样残酷，中国古代战争的结局往往是改朝换代，并不是以消灭为目的。战争的双方或几方文化根基相同，体现出中华文化的一致性、延续性，以及自古以来中国坚持的“和谐”传统。中国古典小说与历史关联紧密，小说的主人公往往是关键时刻决定历史发展的大人物，写到的事件往往是历史上的大事件。这是因为，中华文化的连续性使中国的史学非常发达，历史记载较为完备，在小说发展还处在萌芽阶段时，史学著作的写作已经取得了辉煌的成就，这些史学著作对于文学作品具有很大的影响力。

除此之外，中西方小说还有其他方面的不同之处。第一，西方小说的叙述顺序较为多样，许多小说利用倒叙的手法展开叙述，例如《茶花女》（*The Lady of the Camellias*）。中国除当代小说之外，往往以时间顺序为叙述顺序；中国古典小说在正式叙述故事之前，都会有较长的铺陈，往往占一回的篇幅，详细交代主人公的生活背景以及故事背景，例如《红楼梦》在正式开始叙述贾府的故事之前，用了两回的篇幅将背景交代清楚。第二，西方小说中往往渗透着哲学思想，甚至有些小说家将自己的哲学、美学思想融入小说，例如王尔德在其小说《道林·格雷的画像》（*The Picture of Dorian Gray*）中提出“艺术无用”的美学主张；而传统的中国小说家一般不会在作品中论及哲学问题，由于中国自古深受儒家思想的影响，小说家关注的往往是道德、伦理层面的问题，更注重行为的规范与道德的完善。

VIII. Homework

1. 思考与讨论

（1）有人说中国的古代战争小说更像武侠小说。你怎么看？西方小说中是否有对应的题材？

（2）吉尔伯特·基思·切斯特顿（Gilbert Keith Chesterton）有一句名言：A good novel tells us the truth about its hero; but a bad novel tells us the truth about its author. 你是否同意这一说法？为什么？

2. 好书大家读

为你喜欢的一部小说写一篇 100 词左右的英文介绍，将这本书推荐给同学们。

3. 我来预言

思考一下“经典”的含义，然后尝试预言：在过去 100 年内诞生的作品中，哪些作品在 100 年之后还会被人铭记？为什么？

参考资料

一、书籍

曹萌．英美文学简史及文学要略 [M]. 北京：光明日报出版社，2016.

茅于美．中西诗歌比较研究 [M]. 北京：中国人民大学出版社，1987.

辜正坤．中西诗比较鉴赏与翻译理论 [M]. 北京：清华大学出版社，2010.

曹顺庆．中西比较诗学 [M]. 北京：中国人民大学出版社，2010.

张健．中西小说理论要义 [M]. 北京：文史哲出版社，2004.

杨星映．中西小说文体比较 [M]. 北京：中国社会科学出版社，2008.

陈家宁．中西小说艺术谈 [M]. 北京：北京师范学院出版社，1990.

庞希云．“人心自悟”与“灵魂拯救”[M]. 北京：中国社会出版社，2007.

蓝凡．中西戏剧比较论 [M]. 上海：学林出版社，2008.

胡健生．中西戏剧名家名作探幽 [M]. 北京：中央编译出版社，2012.

Greenblatt, Stephen, et al. The Norton Anthology of English Literature[M]. New York: W. W. Norton & Company, 2018.

Foster, Michael. The Norton Anthology of World Literature[M]. New York: W. W. Norton & Company, 2012.

Damrosch, David. What Is World Literature?[M]. Princeton: Princeton University Press, 2003.

Abrams, M. H. The Norton Anthology of English Literature: Volume 1[M]. New York: W. W. Norton & Company, 2000.

Pound, Ezra. The Cantos of Ezra Pound[M]. New York: New Directions, 1997.

Levenson, Joseph R. Confucianism and the Chinese Experience[M]. Cambridge: Harvard University Press, 1966.

Bloom, Harold. The Western Canon[M]. New York: Riverhead Books, 1994.

Said, Edward W. Culture and Imperialism[M]. New York: Alfred A. Knopf, 1993.

二、网站

http://foreignliterature.cass.cn/（中国外国文学网）

http://novel.tingroom.com/（英文小说网）

https://www.douban.com/note/433201999/（25 个国外著名英语文学网站链接）

http://www.zggdwx.com/（中国古典文学网）

http://www.zgwenxue.com/forum.php（中国文学网）

三、影视作品

电影：《明亮的星》《飘》《莎翁情史》《成为简·奥斯汀》《花木兰》《死亡诗社》（以及文中提到的其他作品改编的电影）

电视剧：20 世纪 80 年代和 90 年代中国四大名著改编的电视剧

Chapter Four

The Contrast of Chinese and Western Arts

课前成果检测

中西方艺术阅读测试题

一、填空题

1. 中国画的构成首先在于 ________ 的运用，其次是 ________ 的变化，它们构成了艺术表现的基本要素。

2. 在中国，建筑是 ________ 的诗篇；在西方，建筑是 ________ 的史书。

3. ________ 被称为“凝固的音乐”。

4. 中国古代屋顶色彩级别最高的是 ________ 色，级别最低的是 ________ 色。

5. 中国古代乐器按其制作材料的不同一般分为八类，俗称“八音”，它们是 ________、________、________、________、________、________、________ 和 ________。

6. 中国古代将收集民歌的活动称为 ________。

二、单选题

1. 东晋顾恺之的代表作品是（　　）。

A.《游春图》　B.《潇湘图》　C.《洛神赋图》　D.《人物御龙图》

2.《清明上河图》的作者是（　　）。

A. 马远　B. 夏珪　C. 黄公望　D. 张择端

3.《日出印象》是（　　）的作品。

A. 毕加索　B. 凡・高　C. 莫奈　D. 马奈

4. 意大利的米兰大教堂属于（　　）。

A. 罗马建筑　B. 拜占庭建筑　C. 哥特式建筑　D. 希腊建筑

5. 佛宫寺木塔属于（　　）。

A. 印度建筑　B. 中国建筑　C. 伊斯兰建筑　D. 缅甸建筑

6. 可与故宫相媲美的、欧洲宫殿建筑的第一典范是（　　）。

A. 克里姆林宫　B. 凡尔赛宫　C. 阿兰布拉国王行宫　D. 卢浮宫

7. "建筑是石头的史书" 反映了建筑的（　　）。

A. 科学性　B. 实用性　C. 文化性　D. 艺术性

8. 下列哪些建筑体现了西方建筑中无限向上升腾的强烈效果和中国建筑中向四方无限扩展的秩序空间？（　　）

A. 巴黎埃菲尔铁塔和中国的长城

B. 法国的沃・勒・维贡特府邸花园和苏州园林

C. 德国科隆大教堂和北京故宫

D. 欧洲北部的住宅和北京民居

9. 下列哪位属于浪漫主义时期的作曲家？（　　）。

A. 海顿　B. 舒伯特　C. 莫扎特　D. 亨德尔

10. 我国国歌的作曲者是（　　）。

A. 冼星海　B. 聂耳　C. 沈心工　D. 刘天华

三、简答题

1. 试述西方绘画的透视方法。

2. 花鸟画的分类有哪些？试述中国画的意境说。

3. 一个国家的建筑风格是由哪些因素决定的？

4. 中西方的音乐风格有哪些差异？

Section One

The Contrast of Chinese and Western Paintings

I. Learning Objectives

1. To learn about the characteristics of Chinese and Western paintings

2. To understand the impressionistic style of Chinese paintings and the realistic style of Western paintings

II. Key Points and Difficult Points

1. To compare and contrast Chinese and Western paintings
2. To understand the development of Chinese and Western paintings
3. To understand the relation between philosophy and paintings

III. Lead-in Questions

1. Can you list some famous Chinese and Western paintings?
2. What is the most striking difference between Chinese and Western paintings?
3. How do you understand the influence of integrated thinking mode on Chinese paintings?
4. How do you understand the influence of analytical thinking mode on Western paintings?

IV. Learning Contents

1. *Last Supper*

Leonardo da Vinci began working on *Last Supper* in 1495, and finished it in 1498. This is worth noting, as Leonardo was a known procrastinator with a marked tendency to leave projects unfinished.

The painting is huge, really 460 cm × 880 cm. It covers an entire large wall, very unlike reproductions sized to hang neatly behind one's sofa.

As an image, *Last Supper* is the most reproduced religious painting of all time and has been put on everything from mirrors, to mouse pads, to musical pillows. If Leonardo were still around, he'd be earning billions of dollars on licensing fees alone.

Firstly, *Last Supper* is remarkable because the disciples are all displaying very human, identifiable emotions. The biblical scene had certainly been painted before. Leonardo's version, though, was the first to depict real people acting like real people. Secondly, and of major importance—the technical perspective in *Last Supper* is incredible. You can see that every single element of the painting directs one's attention straight to the midpoint of the composition, Christ's head. It's arguably the greatest example of one point perspective ever created.

Last Supper is Leonardo's visual interpretation of an event chronicled in all four of the Gospels (books in the Christian New Testament). The evening before Christ was betrayed by one of his disciples; he gathered them together to eat, tell them he knew what was coming, and wash their feet (a gesture symbolizing that all were equal under the eyes of the Lord). As they ate and drank together, Christ gave the disciples explicit instructions on how to eat and drink in the future, in remembrance of him. It was the first celebration of the Eucharist, a ritual still performed.

Specifically, *Last Supper* depicts the next few seconds in this story after Christ dropped the bombshell that one disciple would betray him before sunrise, and all 12 reacted to the news with different degrees of horror, anger, and shock.

Why is the painting falling apart? Leonardo, always the inventor, tried using new materials for *Last Supper*. Instead of using tempera on wet plaster, he thought he'd give using dry plaster a whirl. His experiment resulted in a more varied palette, which was his intent. What he hadn't taken into account was that this method wasn't at all durable. The painted plaster began to flake off the wall almost immediately, and people have been attempting to restore it ever since.

单词表

procrastinator	*n.*	拖延者
chronicle	*v.*	记录，载入编年史
Gospel	*n.*	福音书
remembrance	*n.*	回想，回忆，纪念
tempera	*n.*	蛋彩画，蛋彩画法
palette	*n.*	调色板，颜料

2. Court Lady Paintings（仕女图）

Throughout history, painters have never tired of featuring beautiful and tender female figures as the main subject in their work. Among ancient Chinese court paintings, there is a sort of painting with noble women as the theme, called "court lady paintings". These paintings often provide information unavailable from written texts. Many paintings are especially interesting to historians because they help us understand what life looked like in the earlier periods of the imperial palace.

Spring Morning in the Han Palace, a work of the famous Ming painter Qiu Ying held in the Taipei Palace Museum has long been cherished by Chinese art lovers as one of the top 10 masterpieces in traditional Chinese painting. The long handscroll depicts a variety of activities on a spring morning in the imperial palace of Han Dynasty (206 BCE–220 CE), though some of the objects and textile patterns apparently belonged to the painter's own time.

《汉宫春晓图》

In the painting, there are altogether 115 figures, including court ladies, maids, eunuchs, painters and children. In an idyllic atmosphere, some of them are unhurriedly sweeping the yards, watering flowers or carrying things about, others are playing Chinese musical instruments, appreciating paintings, playing chess, reading books, chasing a butterfly or dancing and chatting.

One of the major scenes in the painting portrays a group of court ladies and maids watching an imperial palace artist paint the portrait of another court lady, which was common practice during that time as emperors usually depended upon portraits to pick the court ladies. So, the ladies always bribed the artists to paint them prettier than they really were.

From right to left, the usual way of appreciating almost all traditional Chinese handscroll paintings, one will find that scenes in this artwork are very well arranged in an intricate and rather sophisticated composition. The brush works here are crisp and refined and the colors are bright and elegant.

Qiu's court ladies and maids in this painting are so well portrayed that the artwork soon became a paradigm of belle painting or traditional Chinese painting of beautiful women for Chinese artists in the following centuries.

单词表

handscroll	*n.*	手卷
eunuch	*n.*	太监；阉人
intricate	*adj.*	错综复杂的
paradigm	*n.*	范例

V. Story Links

1. *Mona Lisa's Smile*

One of the charms of the world's famous painting is that she appears radiant one moment and then serious and sardonic the next. Now scientists claim to have come up with an answer to her changing moods: our eyes are sending mixed signals to the brain.

They believe Mona Lisa's smile depends on what cells in the retina pick up the image and what channel the image is transmitted through in the brain. Sometimes one channel wins over the other, and you see the smile, sometimes others take over and you do not see the smile.

Different cells in the eye are designed to pick up different colors, contrasts, backgrounds and foregrounds. Some deal with central vision while others with peripheral.

（资料来源：http://www.telegraph.co.uk/news/science/science-news/6453526/The-secret-behind-Mona-Lisas-enigmatic-smile.html）

《蒙娜丽莎的微笑》

2.《洛神赋图》的背景故事

《洛神赋图》是东晋画家顾恺之根据曹植的《洛神赋》创作的，画的内容是曹植和他的随从在岸上遥望水上飘逸美丽的洛神和各种神仙怪物，《洛神赋图》将《洛神赋》中的人物心境栩栩如生地表达了出来。《洛神赋》是曹植于魏文帝黄初四年创作的作品，是曹植所有文章中比较著名的浪漫主义名篇。

《洛神赋图》

据《文昭甄皇后传》载：甄氏乃中山无极人，上蔡令甄逸之女。建安年间，她嫁给袁绍的儿子袁熙。东汉献帝七年，官渡之战，袁绍兵败病死。曹操乘机出兵，甄氏成了曹军的俘虏，继而嫁曹丕为妻。当时曹操三子曹植因年纪尚小，又生性不喜争战，遂得以与甄妃朝夕相处，进而生出一段情意。曹操死后，曹丕登上帝位，甄氏被封为妃，因为郭后的挑拨甄氏最后惨死。甄妃死的那年，曹植到洛阳朝见哥哥，想起甄妃之死，心中酸楚无比。曹植在返回封地时，夜宿舟中，恍惚之间，遥见甄妃凌波御风而来，曹植一惊而醒，原来是南柯一梦。回到鄄城，曹植脑海里还在翻腾着与甄妃洛水相遇的情景，于是文思激荡，写了一篇《感甄赋》。大约三年后（公元 236 年），明帝曹叡继位，因觉原赋名字不雅，遂改为《洛神赋》。

VI. Did You Know?

1. 中国绘画之源：伏羲画八卦

伏羲画卦是中国古代神话传说故事。相传八卦是伏羲画的。伏羲时常盘坐山巅，苦思宇宙的奥秘。他仰观日月星辰的变化，俯察山川风物的法则，不断反省自己。也许是他的精诚感动了天地，有一天，他的眼前出现了一派美妙的幻境，一声炸响之后，渭河对岸的龙马山豁然中开，但见龙马振翼飞出，悠悠然顺河而下，直落河心分心石上，通体分明，闪闪发光。这时分心石亦幻化成为立体太极，阴阳缠绕，光辉四射。此情此景骤然震撼了伏羲的心胸，太极神图深切映入他的意识之中，他顿时目光如炬，彻底洞穿了天人合一的密码；原来天地竟是如此的简单明了——唯阴阳而已。为了让人们世世代代享受大自然的恩泽，他便将神圣的思想化作最为简单的符号，以“—”表示阳，以“--”表示阴，按四面八方排列而成了八卦。

2. *American Gothic*（《美国哥特人》）

American Gothic is a painting by the American artist Grant Wood, created in 1930. It depicts a serious-looking farmer and a woman standing in front of their house. Wood enjoyed painting faces he knew well. For the grave farmer, he used his dentist, a sour-looking man, as the model. For the woman standing alongside him, the artist chose his sister, Nan. Wood painted the house along with the people who he imagined might live there.The house actually exists in Eldon, Iowa. Wood saw it while traveling through the Iowa landscape in the summer of 1930, and he was greatly inspired. Some people believed that Grant Wood was making fun of small-town folk. The house had an unusual window, with a design based on Gothic architecture originally from Europe, which was quite different from the typical American farmhouse. Wood was strongly influenced by medieval artists and inspired by the Gothic window of this old farmhouse, but it was the faces in his composition that captured the world's attention.

《美国哥特人》

VII. Cultural Reflection

绘画不仅是艺术家对外界事物的临摹，而且是抒发个人内在情感的一种艺术形式。这种艺术形式是艺术家个人精神世界的呈现，却又并非纯粹的个人行为，它与各民族的思维模式息息相关。中西绘画的差异可以从以下几个方面进行探讨：

一、中西绘画艺术背后的宇宙观：天人合一与天人二分

中国绘画，从伏羲画八卦开始，已经有数千年的历史，发展到近现代时期，为了与西洋绘画相区分，被简称为中国画或者国画。而以老子、庄子为代表的道家思想则是中国传统绘画的思想根基。道家的核心思想是“道”，老子曾言：“人法地，地法天，天法道，道法自然。”道的运行又是以自然为法则的。换言之，道的运作要以宇宙自然的规律为规律。在“道法自然”思想的影响之下，中国画描绘的物象多取材于自然，并且追求“以形写神”的妙趣。再谈庄子的“天人合一”。庄子说：“有人，天也；有天，亦天也。”天是自然，人是自然的一部分。而这种“天人合一”的人文精神便构成了中国艺术精神的本体。在绘画过程中，画家不是将自己独立于作品之外，而是将自己的气韵与所描绘的物象贯通，融为一体，在描绘客观物象的同时更为重视物象之外的思想与情感，把审美对象转向内部世界，在客观的事物中融入画家自身的个性与思想，将主体与客体密不可分地联系在了一起。唐代画家张璪就曾以“外师造化，中得心源”八个字来概括画家的创作过程。“造化”指的是大自然，而画家的职责不仅是再现自然，而且是以自然为师，领会大自然的神韵，带着心中的感悟进行创作。在这种思想的影响之下，画得像不像只是其次，而能否画“活”、能否“传神”则是国画艺术的最高标准。

与中国“天人合一”的思维不同，西方传统认识论倾向于把很多概念范畴置于对立的状态，人与自然的关系亦是如此。人独立于自然而存在，认识自然、了解自然、探索自然的终极目的是为了征服自然、为己所用。这种“天人二分”的思维模式正是西方艺术的本质。在这种思维模式的影响下，艺术家与外界物象是彼此隔离，甚至对立的。艺术家在进行绘画创作时希望客观再现这个现实世界的原貌，因此会借助于丰富的色彩以及光影变化等手段来刻画对象。而从敦煌壁画、汉代画像砖等早期中国绘画作品可以看出，中国画家并不以眼前物象的临摹作为绘画目的，而是注重通过画面表达内在的意境和深层的精神体现。如在一幅题为《深山藏古寺》的国画中，虽然画家要画的是一座寺庙，但画中却连寺庙的影子都找不到，画面以一个在溪边汲水的和尚来隐喻曲径通幽处的古老的寺庙，使人产生丰富的联想。

二、中西方绘画：“科学”的绘画与“文学”的绘画

西方绘画艺术的发展离不开艺术解剖学理论。以达·芬奇、米开朗琪罗为代表的许多西方画家都曾进行过解剖实验，借此来了解人体的骨骼筋肉及其形状的种种变化，以求掌握更精准

的绘画技法，将人物形象实实在在地搬到画纸上。中国画则不然，为了追求神韵，有时会不在意各部分的比例关系，甚至与现实相差甚远，比例失调到夸张的程度。尤其是国画中的人物画，有时为了凸显女子的羸弱，便以“削肩细腰”的形象展现人物，有时为了塑造男子的雄伟气概，人物身首不称，五大三粗。画家在塑造人物时，往往把人物的性情体现在其外形中，以象征的手法来创造强烈的印象，给人以活灵活现的生动感，从而取得“神似”“传神”的效果。

西方画家在创作时，还会遵照色彩、构图、线条、明暗、透视等手段进行构图，分析对象的比例大小，追求色彩的冷暖厚薄以及深浅浓淡，强调对象的体积质感以及空间效果，以一种相对科学和理性的态度进行分析和创作。几何透视法产生于数学原理，把几何透视运用到绘画艺术表现之中，正是西方绘画具有科学性的一种表现。画家借助近大远小的透视现象来表现物体的立体感，将物象与周围环境的位置关系在画中体现了出来。中国画则不同。中国画家作画时如行云流水般浑然天成，并不受透视法的束缚。

中国绘画与文学密不可分。首先，中国画与书法同源异体。唐代张彦远在《历代名画记》中就提到了书画同源的问题；苏东坡也提出“诗画本一律”，即书法和绘画虽是两种不同的艺术形式，但二者同质异体。宗白华在《论中西画法的渊源与基础》中写道：“中国画以书法为骨干，以诗境为灵魂，诗、书、画同属于一境界。”从书画共性的角度深刻阐明了中国书画互相衬映、互相彰显的特性。因此，中国画本身就带有强烈的书法趣味，国画的线条、墨韵，处处都透露着抽象之美，它有着独立的审美价值。也就是说即使离开了物象，单独地欣赏一笔一画、一点一块，都使人怡然有得、心醉神迷。其次，中国画具有诗趣。从中国画家身份来看，古代的国画大家多是文人骚客，无不通晓诗词歌赋。文人作画自然不求形似，而是旨在意味深长。而且，古人品画绝非独立地赏析画面内容，而是从“诗、书、画”三个方面来评断，一幅上好的画作不仅要画得好，画上题的诗也要绝，画上写的字亦不可马虎。就像郑板桥笔下的竹子，寥寥数笔就能使竹子的形态跃然于纸上，再题上“咬定青山不放松，立根原在破岩中。千磨万击还坚劲，任尔东西南北风”的诗句，竹子的宁折不屈与艺术家的一身傲骨便栩栩如生了。“诗、书、画”互为一体，诗趣与画趣彼此交融，方可成就诗情画意，而这也正是中国绘画具有文学性的一个佐证。

VIII. Homework

1. 找找看：找找现存最早的中西方绘画作品，并比较其特点。
2. 老外看国画：邀请一个外国朋友欣赏国画，了解他的感受。
3. 谈谈中西方绘画有无融合之势。

Section Two
The Contrast of Chinese and Western Architectures

I. Learning Objectives

1. To learn about the characteristics of Chinese and Western architectures

2. To understand the differences between Chinese and Western architectures in terms of aesthetics, philosophical backgrounds, construction materials and ornaments

II. Key Points and Difficult Points

1. To describe the unique characteristics of Chinese architectures

2. To describe the unique characteristics of Western architectures

III. Lead-in Questions

1. Do you know the following architectures?

2. Can you list some other world-famous architectures?

3. Can you tell the differences between Chinese architectures and Western architectures?

4. What factors may lead to the differences between Chinese architectures and Western architectures?

IV. Learning Contents

1. The Palace Museum

Located in the center of Beijing, the Palace Museum, historically and artistically one of the most comprehensive museums in China, was established on the basis of the Forbidden City, a palace of the Ming and Qing dynasties (1368–1911), and their collection of treasures.

The Forbidden City used to be the imperial palace of the Ming and Qing dynasties. It is nearly 600 years old, with construction started in 1406 and completed in 1420. The rectangular palace covers an area of some 720,000 square kilometers, 961 meters in length and 753 meters in width.

故宫

The Forbidden City is China's largest and most intact ancient building complex. It is laid out symmetrically along a north-south axial line. The well-designed palace appears magnificent, solemn and harmonious, representing the long cultural tradition of China and its outstanding architectural accomplishments five centuries ago. It is a truly superb masterpiece in every sense.

The Palace Museum in the Forbidden City has the country's largest collection of ancient art works, some of which are invaluable national treasures. Art works in the museum's collection total 1,863,404 (Dec. 25, 2024), including paintings, pottery, bronze wares, inscribed wares, toys, clocks and court documents.

The palace grounds are divided into two parts: the Front Palace (Qianchao) to the south and the Inner Palace (Neiting) to the north. In the Front Palace, important ceremonies, such as the accession of a new emperor to the throne and the emperor's birthday and wedding, were held. The Inner Palace mainly includes the Palace of Heavenly Purity (Qianqinggong), the Hall of Prosperity (Jiaotaidian) and the Palace of Earthly Tranquility (Kunninggong), where emperors and empresses lived. Behind them is the Imperial Garden. On each side of the inner three great halls are six eastern palaces and six western palaces, respectively, which were used as residences for concubines.

Since yellow is the symbol of the royal family, it is the dominant color in the Forbidden City. Roofs are built with yellow glazed tiles; decorations in the palace are painted yellow; even the bricks on the ground are made yellow in special process. However, there is one exception. Wenyuange, the royal library, has a black roof. The reason is that it was believed black represented water then and could extinguish fire.

故宫

单词表

symmetrically	*adv.*	对称地，平衡地，匀称地
axial	*adj.*	轴的，轴向的
accession	*n.*	增加，就职，到达
concubine	*n.*	妾，妃子

tile	*n.*	瓷砖，瓦片

2. Palace of Versailles

The Palace of Versailles is the central part of a complex that housed the French government, most notably its royalty, during the reigns of Louis XIV (France's famed "Sun King"), Louis XV and Louis XVI. After the French Revolution in 1789, it ceased to be a permanent royal residence.

The palace that we recognize today was largely completed by the death of Louis XIV in 1715. The eastern facing palace has a U-shaped layout, with the corps de logis (an architectural term referring to the principal block of a large, usually classical, mansion or palace) and symmetrical advancing secondary wings terminating with the Dufour Pavilion on the south, and the Gabriel Pavilion to the north, creating an expansive courtyard known as the Royal Court. Flanking the Royal Court are two enormous a symmetrical wings that result in a facade of 1,319 feet in length. Encompassing 721,182 square feet the palace has 700 rooms, more than 2,000 windows, 1,250 fireplaces and 67 staircases.

凡尔赛宫

Located about 10 miles (16 kilometers) southwest of Paris, it is beside the settlement of Versailles. Before the construction of the palace by Louis XIV, this settlement was little more than a hamlet but by the time of the revolution it had a population of more than 60,000 people, making it one of the largest urban centers in France.

Before the revolution, the Versailles complex included the palace, gardens, a walled-in royal hunting ground, a smaller palatial structure known as the Grand (or Marble) Trianon and an estate used by Marie Antoinette, Louis XVI's queen. Between the palace and the town there are also buildings that housed the war and foreign affairs ministries, residences for those not entitled to live in the palace,

凡尔赛宫

stables and a kennel, among other structures.

The palace was chock full of paintings and sculptures, ornately designed rooms (like the "Hall of Mirrors") and even technological innovations, such as pressurized water fountains in its gardens that jetted water into the air, and an opera house with a mechanical device that allowed the orchestra pit to rise up to the stage, allowing it to be turned into a dance or banqueting hall.

Overall, the palace was built to impress. "Versailles is a mirage, a sumptuous and theatrical entertainment. It is also a manifestation of glory and power imposed to a great extent by art, luxury, and magnificence," writes Valérie Bajou, a modern-day curator at Versailles, in her book *Versailles*.

单词表

Dufour Pavilion		杜福尔馆
Gabriel Pavilion		加布里埃尔馆
facade	*n.*	正面，表面，外观
hamlet	*n.*	小村庄
palatial	*adj.*	宫殿似的，宏伟的，壮丽的
chock	*adv.*	满满地
pressurized	*adj.*	加压的，受压的
jet	*v.*	射出
curator	*n.*	馆长，监护人，管理者

V. Story Links

1. 阿房宫

阿房宫号称"秦川第一宫"。"阿房"二字，是"近旁"的意思。秦始皇的建宫计划是以阿房宫为中心，建造众多的离宫别院。前殿筑于秦始皇三十五年（公元前 212 年），全部工程至秦亡时犹未完成，故未正式命名。《汉书·贾山传》记载整个阿房宫的规模：东西五里，南北千步。由此可见阿房宫宫殿之多，建筑面积之广，规模之宏大。

后人复制的阿房宫

2. Palace of Persepolis

With an extravagant hall measuring almost 70 square meters and supported by 100 stone columns, this palace formed one of two principal reception areas in Persepolis. Built during the reigns of Xerxes and Artaxerxes Ⅰ, some believe it was used to receive the military elite upon whom the empire's security rested. Today, enough of the broken columns remain to give an idea of the palace's former grandeur, and fine reliefs show a king, soldiers and representatives of 28 subject nations.

波斯波利斯宫遗址

Only a little remains of the adjacent Hall of 32 columns, which was built at the end of the Achaemenid period. The arrival of Alexander and his armies brought an end to work on a larger version of the Xerxes' Gateway (Gate of All Nations) in the wide courtyard in front of the Palace of 100

Column; the unfinished gate still stands—a commentary on the city's sudden demise.

（资料来源：https://www.lonelyplanet.com/iran/persepolis/attractions/palace-of-100-columns/a/poi-sig/1444255/361015）

VI. Did You Know?

1. Milan Cathedral

Milan Cathedral is the cathedral church of Milan, Italy. Dedicated to St. Mary of the Nativity, it is the seat of the Archbishop of Milan, currently Cardinal Angelo Scola. The Gothic cathedral took nearly six centuries to complete. It is a famous church in Italy and one of the five largest churches in the world.

米兰大教堂

The American writer Mark Twain visited Milan in the summer of 1867. He describes the Duomo as follows: "What a wonder it is! So grand, so solemn, so vast! And yet so delicate, so airy, so graceful! A very world of solid weight, and yet it seems... a delusion of frostwork that might vanish with a breath!... They say that the Cathedral of Milan is second only to St. Peter's at Rome. I cannot understand how it can be second to anything made by human hands."

2. 成语里的建筑艺术

升堂入室，也作登堂入室，比喻学问或技能由浅入深，循序渐进，达到更高的水平。《论语·先进》："由也升堂矣，未入于室也。"意思是仲由学业有成，但还没有达到最高境界。由此我们知道了中国古代建筑中的堂与室的布局情况，即堂前室后。在古代，堂屋一般待客用。故李白的《将进酒》中才有这样的说法："高堂明镜悲白发，朝如青丝暮成雪。"而室一般指内室，做卧室用，是不轻易让外人进入的。若有人不怀好意看一下，往往被称为窥室。

（资料来源：http://www.360doc.com/content/13/0906/19/709425_312692411.shtml）

VII. Cultural Reflection

虽然建筑风格受制于自然环境、经济发展、地理位置等多方面因素的制约，但无论是中国还是西方，建筑的最初目的都是为人提供遮风避雨的场所。既然是为人所用的艺术，不同民族的建筑风格和建筑文化必然会体现该民族人们的精神特质，对比中西方建筑可窥见中西方民族个性之迥异。

一、中西方建筑体现了逻辑思维与写意思维的差异

逻辑思维即人运用概念、判断、推理等思维类型反映事物的本质与规律。混沌思维是一种模糊地认识事物、打破固有秩序的整体思维模式，它的主要特征在于重直觉与体验，注重对认识对象的意会、领悟和直观的把握，而不太关心概念的确定性和明晰性。混沌思维与逻辑思维相对立，如果说逻辑思维是左脑型的、意识型的，那么混沌思维就是右脑型的、潜意识型的。

法国著名文学家维克多·雨果曾阐释过东西方艺术之间的根本差别，“艺术有两种渊源：一为理念——从中产生了欧洲艺术；一为幻想——从中产生了东方艺术”。这在建筑艺术上也有体现。西方人在建筑中看重各部分之间的比例关系，关注外部造型的几何图案，他们依靠严密的逻辑关系和推理论证等手段来绘图，在面与体之间寻找最和谐的比例。西方人这种科学的、理性的、富有逻辑性的思维方式使得西方建筑在造型方面具有雕刻艺术的特征。

而中国人在设计建筑的时候不仅会考虑一些基本的构建原理，还会考虑人在建筑中的主观感受，因此好的建筑作品应该是能产生令人愉悦的意境和“步移景异”的空间感受的。这种建筑的理念正是受混沌思维的影响，处处以人为本，不仅关注人的理性要求，而且重视人的情感寄托。

二、中西方建筑体现了群体意识与个体意识的差异

从“东西五百步，南北五十丈”的阿房宫到“大小宫殿七十多座，房屋九千余间”的紫禁城，纵观中国古代的宫殿园林和城池庙宇，它们大多雄伟壮观。但若是把其中的每一个房间或是宫阙当作个体来研究，陈设、布局等又是大同小异，缺少个性。皇室住宅如此，民宅亦是如此。若干年前，从京城上方俯瞰下去，胡同巷子之间尽是成片的四合院，每个四合院的格局也都是基本相似的。一般而言，中式建筑以“间”为单位构成单座建筑，再以单座建筑组成“庭院”，进而以庭院为单元，重重院落相套组成各种形式的建筑群。由此可见，中国传统建筑以群体组合见长，精巧的平面布局使得整个建筑群富有旋律和韵味。这正是中国传统文化中重群体、轻个体的思维方式的体现，以实现群体的和谐统一。而西方建筑却以表现个性、张扬个性为重。体现在建筑上，即便有些建筑单体突兀孤立，与周遭的建筑风格无法统一，却也能凭借自身特色而流传于世。

三、中西方建筑体现了向内与向外的民族个性差异

从古代中国的地理环境来看，东南为海，西北为山，这些天然的屏障阻隔了中华文明与其他古文明的交流；中华民族是农耕民族，农耕民族的生活正如先秦时期民间流传的《击壤歌》中所写："日出而作，日入而息，凿井而饮，耕田而食。"而农耕文明也造就了人们安土重迁的意识。这些因素在一定程度上促成了中华民族向内的民族个性。从中国传统建筑来看，一个城池修有城墙，一座皇宫筑有宫墙，寻常百姓家有院墙，人们倾向于用墙来创造一个相对封闭的空间，在这封闭的空间里建造花园亭台、山水楼榭，给自己隔出一方天地，不受外界尘世的干扰。不仅如此，中国传统建筑四合院也是"口字形"的闭合结构，一家数口围靠在一起，尽享自己的小日子。再从西方文明的源头古希腊、古罗马来看，地中海地区海陆交错的自然地理环境决定了各城邦、国家之间要通过海路互通有无，而海运的便利性又将古希腊、罗马与其他文明之邦联系起来，造就了其文明的开放性。而且，西方民族很多是游牧民族，居无定所是生活的常态，征服、侵略、扩张是其赖以生存的方式，这也铸就了其向外的民族性格。因此，西方建筑会强调外部空间的利用。

四、中西方建筑体现了"重君"与"重神"的差异

从中西方古典建筑的用途来看，中国经典建筑作品中大多是皇室大大小小的主宫和行宫，即便是修建庙宇祠堂，也是要优先考虑君主的祭祀、朝拜等需求。中国社会经历了几千年的封建君主专制，天子至尊的思想深入人心，处处以天子为先自然是理所当然的事情。而且，从空间角度上来看，中国古典建筑一般是由多个建筑单体铺建而成，在二维空间中给人以辽阔壮观之感，却很少有陡然耸立的造型设计，这其中自然有建筑材料、设计手法等因素的影响，但这也是君主至高无上的地位的体现。西方建筑的经典作品则主要是教堂神殿等与宗教活动有关的场所，如希腊神庙、巴黎圣母院、梵蒂冈广场等。古希腊是西方文明发源地之一。从希腊神话到基督教，希腊人对神的信仰是从未止息过的。一座座的神庙和教堂便是狂热的宗教情绪在建筑上的外在表现。为了表现神性的永恒，人们用不易腐烂、不易被摧毁的石头做材料，花上几十年甚至上百年来建造一座教堂。

建筑是一种积淀，亦是一种影射。这种沉淀让我们在林林总总的建筑体上看到了各个时代的印记；迥然各异的中西方建筑又影射了各自的文化、信仰以及生活方式。值得一提的是，在当今文化交流愈加频繁的时代背景下，设计师们常常在民族特色与异国风情之间游走，呈现出更加饱满多元的建筑风格，而这样的作品正是中西方文化交流的产物。

VIII. Homework

1. 小组作业：分组讨论中国建筑的布局，以 PPT 的形式向全班汇报。
2. 现代建筑作品欣赏：作为一名导游，向外国游客介绍“鸟巢”国家体育场。

Section Three

The Contrast of Chinese and Western Music

I. Learning Objectives

1. To learn about the characteristics of Chinese and Western music
2. To get a general understanding of the origin and development of music
3. To appreciate different music styles

II. Key Points and Difficult Points

1. To probe deeply into the origins of Chinese and Western music
2. To summarize the representative genres of Chinese and Western music
3. To describe the development of Chinese and Western music

III. Lead-in Questions

1. Can you describe your feelings after you listen to the following pieces of music?

   《渔舟唱晚》(*A Fishing Boat Song at Dusk*)

   《第九交响曲》(Beethoven—*Symphony No. 9 in D minor, Op. 125*)

   《二泉映月》(*Erquan Yingyue*)

   《降 E 大调夜曲》(Chopin—*Nocturne in E-flat Major, Op. 9, No. 2*)

   《高山流水》(Chinese Ocarina—*High Mountains and Flowing Water*)

   《小星星变奏曲》(Mozart—*Variations on Twinkle, Twinkle, Little Star*)
2. How many musical instruments do you know? List them.
3. Which music genre do you prefer?

IV. Learning Contents

1. Symphony

A symphony is an extended musical composition in Western classical music, most often written by composers for orchestra. Although the term has had many meanings from its origins in the ancient Greek era, by the late 18th century the word had taken on the meaning common today: a work usually consisting of multiple distinct sections or movements, often four, with the first movement in sonata form. Symphonies are scored for string (violin, viola, cello and double bass), brass, woodwind, and percussion instruments which altogether number about 30–100 musicians. Symphonies are notated in a musical score, which contains all the instrument parts. Orchestral musicians play from parts which contain just the notated music for their instrument.

交响乐演奏

The word "symphony" is derived from a Greek word meaning "agreement or concord of sound" or "a concert of vocal or instrumental music," which is related to the word "harmonious." The word referred to an astonishing variety of different things, before ultimately settling on its current meaning designating a musical form.

In the sense of "sounding together", the word begins to appear in the titles of some works by 16th and 17th century composers. In the 17th century, pieces scored for large instrumental ensemble did not precisely designate which instruments were to play which parts, as is the practice from the 19th century to the current period. When composers in the 17th century wrote their pieces, they expected that these works would be performed by which group of musicians was available.

贝多芬

The Symphony No. 9 is Ludwig van Beethoven's final complete symphony. Completed in 1824, the symphony is one of the best-known works in classical music. Among critics, it is almost universally considered one of Beethoven's greatest works, and many consider it one of the greatest compositions in the western musical canon. The symphony was the first example of a major composer using voices in a symphony (thus making it a choral symphony). The words are sung during the final movement by four vocal soloists and a chorus. They were taken from the *Ode to Joy*, a poem written by Friedrich Schiller in 1785 and revised in 1803, with additions made by the composer. Today, it stands as one of the most performed symphonies in the world.

单词表

orchestra	*n.*	管弦乐队
sonata	*n.*	奏鸣曲
viola	*n.*	中提琴
cello	*n.*	大提琴
double bass		低音提琴
brass	*n.*	铜管乐器
woodwind	*n.*	木管乐器
percussion instrument		打击乐器
ensemble	*n.*	合奏组
canon	*n.*	标准，教规

2. *Erhu* Music

The *Erhu* is a two-stringed instrument played with a bow that is popular not only in China, but in those areas of East Asia where Chinese culture has had particularly great influence. Due to its resemblance in function to a violin, it is occasionally called a Chinese Violin.

It is said that its origin would be dated up to the Tang Dynasty (618–907) and related to the instrument, called *Xiqin* originated from a Mongolian tribe Xi. During Song Dynasty (960–1279), the instrument was introduced to China and was called "*Jiqin*". Soon the second generation of the *Huqin* was among the instruments played at the imperial banquets. During the dynasties of Yuan (1206–1368), Ming (1368–1644) and Qing (1616–1911), the *Erhu* underwent a great development at the time of the golden age of the local operas. The *Erhu* then developed in different "schools". Two famous artists Hua Yanjun (1893–1950) and Liu Tianhua (1895–1932) made an exceptional contribution to the improvement of the *Erhu*, and it was indeed due to the latter that the *Erhu*, an instrument mainly for accompaniment in an opera, becomes a solo instrument. After the founding of the People's Republic of China (1949), the manufacture of the *Erhu*, the playing techniques, the repertoire as well as the musical education of this instrument have undergone an unprecedented development. The repertoire has grown rapidly in the genres of solo, with ensemble as well as concerti with symphony orchestra. *Erhu* now has become one of the most popular instruments in China.

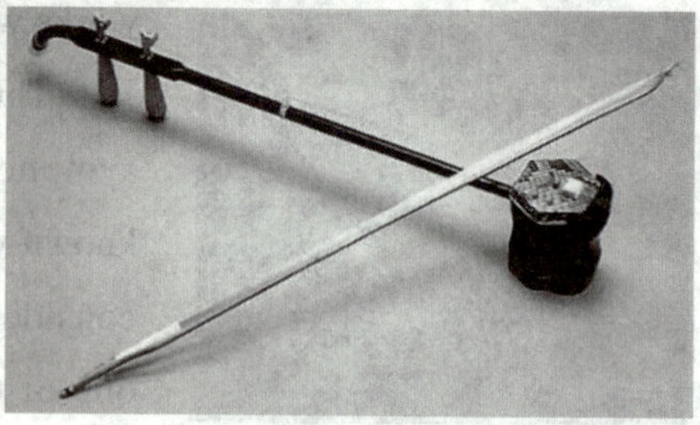

二胡

The instrument is particularly unique, especially when compared to other stringed instruments from the West. It lacks a fingerboard, so instead of pressing the strings to the wood to stop their vibration, the player instead simply presses his/her finger against the wood. Additionally, it is not the vibration of the strings themselves that cause the noise, but instead a piece of python skin that is adjacent to the strings and vibrates when they move. As a result of the incredible popularity of the *Erhu* in China, the Chinese government has taken steps to ensure that any python skin used in an *Erhu* comes from farm-grown pythons, and has limited the number of *Erhu* that may be exported.

阿炳

Erquan Ying Yue means "Two Springs Reflecting the Moon". It was written by Hua Yanjun (also known as A Bing), a blind artist living between 1893 and 1950. It is perhaps the most famous *Erhu* tune.

单词表

solo	*n.*	独奏，独唱，独奏曲
repertoire	*n.*	保留剧目，常备剧目
concerti	*n.*	协奏曲
python	*n.*	巨蟒，大蟒

V. Story Links

1. 与音乐相关的成语故事

（1）高山流水

释义：比喻知音难遇或乐曲高妙。俞伯牙和钟子期的知音故事千百年来一直感动着人们，人们不是羡慕俞伯牙的高超琴艺，而是羡慕他遇到了一个能听懂他的琴声的人——钟子期。

出处：《吕氏春秋·本味》。伯牙善鼓琴，钟子期善听。伯牙鼓琴，方鼓琴而志在太山，钟子期曰："善哉乎鼓琴，巍巍乎若太山！"少选之间，而志在流水，钟子期又曰："善哉乎鼓琴，汤汤乎若流水！"钟子期死，伯牙破琴绝弦，终身不复鼓琴，以为世无足复为鼓琴者。

（2）余音绕梁

释义：歌唱停止后，余音好像还在绕着屋梁回旋，形容歌声或音乐优美，耐人寻味。

出处：《列子·汤问》。昔韩娥东之齐，匮粮，过雍门，鬻歌假食。既去而馀音绕梁欐，三日不绝，左右以其人弗去。过逆旅，逆旅人辱之。韩娥因曼声哀哭，一里老幼悲愁，垂涕相对，三日不食。遽而追之。娥还，复为曼声长歌，一里老幼喜跃抃舞，弗能自禁，忘向之悲也。乃厚赂发之。故雍门之人至今善歌哭，仿娥之遗声。

2. 与音乐有关的英语习语

（1）play second fiddle

我们知道管弦乐队中的小提琴声部有第一小提琴（first fiddle）、第二小提琴（second fiddle）之分。第一小提琴常演奏主旋律，是主角，第二小提琴则多做陪衬。fiddle 是现代小提琴的前身，现在它是 violin 的一个非正式的名称。play second fiddle 相当于 play second violin，只是在习语里不能随意换词，它的意思是“居于次要地位，不起主要作用”，多用于口语中。

如：As the term is drawing to a close and examinations are around the corner, after-class activities should play second fiddle to lessons.

（2）double in brass

19 世纪 80 年代美国的马戏团演员为了多挣钱，除了扮演丑角、表演杂技或马术，还常常在铜管乐队中吹奏乐器。因此 double in brass 成了当时的马戏行话，意思是“吹奏（两种）铜管乐器”。后来此习语被广泛用来表示“能演奏一种以上的乐器；兼职做另一项工作；多才多艺”等，成为常用的美国俚语。

如：The drummer doubles in brass as a violinist.

VI. Did You Know?

1. 为何叫“五音不全”

中国是个文明古国，音乐的发展也有着悠久的历史，但古乐曲是五声音阶，同西方有别。如果与西乐的七个音阶对照一下的话，古中乐的“五音”相当于 Do、Re、Mi、So、La，少去了半音递升的“Fa”和“Ti”。当然，古中乐的五音唱名，不可能同西乐的“Do、Re、Mi、So、La”叫法一样，唐代时用“合、四、乙、尺、工”，更古则用“宫、商、角、徵（读 zhǐ 音）、羽”。所以，如果我们稍加留意，正宗中国古乐曲是没有“Fa”和“Ti”这两个音阶的。

（资料来源：http://baike.so.com/doc/5418239-5656399.html）

2.“桂冠音乐家”的由来

在希腊神话中，太阳神阿波罗爱上了女神达弗涅，但女神不喜欢他，达弗涅请求河神帮助她逃避太阳神阿波罗的追求，河神就施法把达弗涅变成了一棵茂盛的月桂树，阿波罗看到这棵月桂树很伤心，为了安慰自己，就指定这棵茂盛的月桂树为诗人和音乐家们的圣物。它的树叶永不枯萎而美丽，把树的枝叶变成桂冠供艺术家佩戴。直到今天，西方人还把艺术成就卓著的诗人和音乐家称为“桂冠诗人”和“桂冠音乐家”。

VII. Cultural Reflection

音乐是人类呈现内在精神世界的一种形式，是自身感受的一种表达。不同民族对于世界的认识方式不同，自然会有不同的体验和感受，音乐内涵及音乐形式自然千差万别。

一、以气为重与由数而生

在中国传统哲学自然观中存在一个“气”的概念。《周易·系辞上传》指出“精气为物”。《管子·内业》认为，气“下生五谷，上为列星”。《庄子·知北游》提出，“人之生，气之聚也。聚则为生，散则为死”。《论衡·自然篇》里讲：“天地合气，万物自生，犹夫妇合气，子自生矣。”因此，中国传统哲学把“气”看作万物的本源，认为“气”是形成外在世界的基本单位，物质现象以及精神现象都是由“气”构成的。而“至大无外”“至小无内”的“气”是一个柔性的、不定形的概念，这就决定了中国人重直觉、重体验的整体性、混沌式思维，而以“神似”说、“气韵”说为主导的美学信条则贯穿了绘画、建筑、音乐、舞蹈、书法等各种艺术表现形式。具体到音乐上，则提出音乐应该“合生气之和，道五常之行，使之阳而不散，阴而不密，刚气不怒，柔气不慑。四畅交于中而发作于外，皆安其位而不相夺也”的准则。即音乐当合乎“生气”的调和，体现“五常”的关系，使得气质属“阳”的人不散漫，气质属“阴”的人不保守，气质刚强的人不粗暴，气质柔和的人不畏缩，阴、阳、刚、柔四种气质在人的内部畅通地相互作用，同时表现在外部，都有适当的关系，互相补充而不互相克制。这样的音乐在情感上是收敛且不张扬的，讲求意境的深远以及人们内心的平和。从笛子、二胡等中国传统乐器来看，乐器相对简单轻巧，没有西方乐器的厚重。而正是这样简单的乐器才能演奏出清澈悠扬的音乐，才能表现出悠远闲适的意境。

西方传统哲学自然观把“原子”看作世界万物的基本构成单位，而把“几何”和“数”看成宇宙生成的基本方式。“数的原则是一切事物的原则”“整个天体就是一种和谐和一种数”。相比于中国传统哲学中“气”的概念，“原子”是刚性的、定形的。这一概念使得“临摹”“形似”成为可能，而“临摹”“形似”则成为西方艺术的核心内容。几何和数又强调事物之间的逻辑关系，这是重推理、重实证的西方思维方式的根源。例如，西方建筑艺术通过几何原理来塑造作品的造型；古希腊著名数学家、哲学家毕达哥拉斯提出“和谐论”来解释数与音乐的关系。这一观点认为，美是和谐，而音乐的美在于对立因素的和谐统一。他们将比例、尺度和以数的各个组成部分的数学关系的和谐看作音乐中和谐与不变因素的基础。同时，他们找到了宇宙和谐与音乐和谐的共同要素，即“数”。最终，该学派从“数统割一切”的观点出发，认为音乐体现了数的原则，并通过对音程关系的抽象研究来揭示音乐的本质。

二、线性时间性思维与立体空间性思维

之前已经讲过，中国传统文化的内涵是重直觉、重体验的整体性思维方式，这种思维方式具有流动性、混沌性。既然是流动性的，就没有边界可以限制，既然是混沌性的，就不可分解与组合，只能把它看作一个整体，如同时间一样直线发展，看不到尽头。西方思维以“数”为源，宇宙万物皆是“数”和“几何”，因此立体空间性思维便成了西方审美型文化的根基。

无论是绘画、建筑还是音乐，中国传统艺术都呈现出了线性时间性的特点，而西方传统艺术则表现出了立体空间性的特征。在绘画艺术中，中国绘画用线条进行勾勒，不注重物象的立体感，意境、神韵的构建是作品的核心内容；而西方绘画重视明暗透视、色块组合，画家会利用几何知识、光影理论等手段力图将物象凸显在纸上。在建筑作品中，中国传统建筑惯于采用铺建的手法横向发展，作品往往占地面积辽阔，在高度上却很少给人耸立之感；西方建筑则倾向于在有限的占地面积内，将空间不断向上延展，从而造就庞大的体积感。中西方音乐中的线性思维与立体思维则主要体现在以下几个方面：

（1）声部处理。西方音乐体系在处理多声部关系时，特别注重主调旋律与其他声部的和声关系，将乐曲的音响立体化，以浑厚的音响效果来产生汹涌澎湃的气势，给人带来听觉上的震撼。而大部分中国传统乐曲则采用单音部的形式，强调这一个音部在不同时间段的变化或重复，属于横向线性的延展，通过旋律在线形游动时所做的起伏、强弱、虚实等方面的变化所产生的节律感让听者体会到蜿蜒游走之感。

（2）乐器配合。西方音乐擅长以多种乐器合奏的形式来创作音乐作品。以西方经典器乐体裁交响曲为例，“交响乐”的名称源自希腊语，意即“一起响”，通常由弦乐器、木管乐器、铜管乐器和打击乐器等各组乐器组成，十至百余人共同演奏。这种把不同的音乐模块叠加组合在一起的方式正是西方立体空间思维在音乐创作中的另一种体现。相反，中国音乐中很少有大规模的合奏，一般以某一种特色乐器为主，把听者的注意力集中在这一种乐器中，并随之延展，形成线性的流动起伏。

（3）通过中西方绘画、建筑、音乐的对比可以看出，无论是哪一种艺术表现形式，在分析其特征与内涵的同时都避免不了对该民族文化精神的理解和分析，都要去探究造就民族文化精神的哲学根源。固然，艺术依托情感，哲学讲求理性。但无论是艺术还是哲学，都是对特定环境下人们现实生活的折射。

VIII. Homework

1. 辩论：日本指挥家小泽征尔来我国演出，听了《二泉映月》后流泪不止。我们是否可以说音乐无国界？

2. 调研报告：对比《中国好声音》与《美国偶像》这两档音乐节目，发掘中西方当代音乐的特点。

参考资料

一、书籍

龚云表 . 中国绘画这棵树 [M]. 上海：上海书店出版社，2004.

李磊 . 西方绘画这棵树 [M]. 上海：上海书店出版社，2004.

刘天华 . 凝固的旋律：中西建筑艺术比较 [M]. 上海：上海古籍出版社，2005.

刘月 . 中西建筑美学比较论纲 [M]. 上海：复旦大学出版社，2008.

葛姝亚 . 中外音乐赏析 [M]. 成都：四川大学出版社，2009.

二、网站

http://cul.china.com.cn/（文化中国 - 中国网）

http://www.co188.com/special/difference/（中西方建筑风格差异之缘由 _ 土木在线专题）

Chapter Five

The Contrast of Chinese and Western Language

课前成果检测

中西方语言阅读测试题

一、填空题

1. 中国文字的演变，大致经历了 ____________ 等几个阶段。

2. 甲骨文是刻在 ________ 和 ________ 上的文字。

3. 英语造句主要采用形合法，汉语造句主要采用 ________。

4. 英文的 26 个字母最早起源于 ________。

5. 汉语一般更习惯 ________ 的表达，尤其是主语，能施行动作或有生命的物体为主语首选。

6. 英语有一种少用动词或使用其他手段表示动作意义的自然倾向，而汉语往往大量采用兼语式或连动式的说法。所以说英语是 ________，而汉语是动态语言。

二、单选题

1. 许慎在《说文解字》中系统地阐述了汉字的造字规律——（　　）。

A. 形声　B. 指事　C. 六书　D. 象形

2. 英语词汇中有很大一部分来自（　　）。

A. 日语　B. 汉语　C. 德语　D. 法语

3. 氽、汆、籴、粜四个字的读音分别是（　　）。

A. tǔn、cuān、dí、tiào　B. tiào、tǔn、cuān、dí

C. cuān、tiào、tǔn、dí　D. tǔn、cuān、tiào、dí

4. 下列不属于西方人思维模式的是（　　）。

A. 分析性　B. 逻辑性　C. 精确性　D. 模糊性

三、多选题

1. 下列属于文字的共性的是（　　）。

A. 有音　B. 有意　C. 有形　D. 有图

2. 下列属于英汉语言对比特点的是（　　）。

A. 综合语与分析语　B. 刚性与柔性　C. 形合与意合　D. 繁复与简短

E. 抽象与具体

3. 下列属于汉语思维方式的是（　　）。

A. 直觉性　B. 意向性　C. 模糊性　D. 逻辑性

E. 精确性

四、阅读题

语言文字作为文化符号，是社会存在的镜像。有什么样的社会现实，语言就会呈现出什么样的色彩与温度。类似“小鲜肉”这样的词汇，经由互联网传播，业已渗透进民众的日常生活中。网络语言的生命力为何如此顽强？道理亦不复杂：一方面，截至 2023 年 6 月，根据第 52 次《中国互联网络发展状况统计报告》，中国网民规模达 10.79 亿人。手机、平板电脑等语言传播设备已成为生活的必备。另一方面，网民接受新词且被新词浸染的速度异常迅速——因为传统媒体对新词有筛选和冷却的过程，而新媒体则原始而粗放得多，可谓山呼海啸、泥沙俱下。

互联网进入中国几十年了，语言在网络化进程中既在承续和扬弃，也在裂变和重生。就像王蒙所说：“老的语言也许沉淀了几千年，我们在使用语言的时候，语言本身也会发生变化。有人适应这种变化，有人讨厌这种变化。有些词流行过一阵就灭亡了，这样的自生自灭是很正常的。”

如同饮食上有人口味重、有人口味淡一样，对于网络流行语，基于审美与文化的差异，自然见仁见智、各有偏好。不过，专家学者对网络流行语的批判性思考，显然不算吹毛求疵：在文化炒作成为产业链的现实语境下，防止恶俗语言习惯对汉语言文字的侵蚀，恐怕也是相关部门的责任所在。这里包含相辅相成的两个层面：一方面，我们要相信汉语言文字的自净能力，没必要风声鹤唳，尊重语言文化的汰选规律；另一方面，在文化自信的前提下，能敏锐发觉网络流行语中的“病毒”，并在传播、使用的过程中多些规范意识、规则意识。

此前，中国人使用最广泛的语文工具书《新华字典》在第12次修订中，明确了结合时代特点加注常用网络用语的取向。可见，传统语言的严谨与网络语言的鲜活，并非鱼与熊掌般的矛盾。眼下而言，相信汉语言的自我净化“功力”，可以在欢迎美好网络流行语的同时，坚守好汉语言文字的“纯净花园”，这也是每个中国人应有的文化自觉。

1. 网络用语的兴起对维护汉语的纯洁性是否起到了反作用？
2. 某些网络新词是否也能像借用到英语中的法语词汇一样成为固定的汉语新词？
3. 对于网络用语的兴起，你怎么看？

五、思考题

学术界历来存在“语言决定论”的观点，认为语言对思维的方式有深刻影响。部分学者认为，汉语的模糊性和表意性特征可能制约了中国人的思维方式，特别是在逻辑思维方面，认为汉语在这方面远不如西方语言。伏尔泰在其《风俗论》中提到，中国的科技进步缓慢，部分原因在于“语言的性质”。他认为，语言是所有知识的根本要素，且中国的语言特性可能影响了中国人的创造力和科技发展。

汉语的语法结构与西方语言大相径庭。首先，汉语名词没有“性”“格”“数”的变化，动词不受“语态”“语气”“时态”“单复数”“人称”等限制，这些特点使得汉语在表达上具有一定的模糊性。其次，汉语的形象性词汇极为丰富，但抽象词汇相对较少，许多现代汉语中的常用抽象词汇其实是从西方语言翻译而来，而且这些翻译往往难以完全反映原词的精确意义，甚至会产生较大的偏差。汉语的这种特点对于艺术表现和诗意表达极为有利，但在理性思辨和逻辑推理方面，可能会表现出一定的局限性。

那么，语言与思维之间的关系究竟是怎样的？是否真的如语言决定论所言，语言的特性深刻影响了思维方式，导致了中国人在某些领域相对缺乏逻辑性？抑或，思维方式本身才是塑造语言的根本因素？语言的表达方式与思维的方式究竟是相辅相成，还是存在某种单向的决定性影响？我们是否可以从汉语独有的语言特点中发现其在某些文化领域的优势，例如在文学创作、艺术表现、文化传承等方面？

Section One

The Contrast of Chinese and Western Characters

I. Learning Objectives

1. To learn the developing process of Chinese and English

2. To compare the similarities and differences between Chinese and English, and summarize their effects on thinking

II. Key Points and Difficult Points

1. To get a grip of the special feature of Chinese character and its effect on Chinese thinking

2. To study the feature of English words and its effect on Western thinking

III. Lead-in Questions

1. Do you know the different originals of Chinese characters and English alphabets?

2. What is the ideographic feature of Chinese and phonographic feature of English?

3. What are the meanings of the graphemics of Chinese and morphology of English?

4. Do you know the development of Chinese characters and English words?

IV. Learning of English

1. History of English

English is a West Germanic language that originated from Anglo-Frisian dialects brought to Britain from the 5th to 7th centuries CE by Germanic invaders and settlers from what is now northwest Germany, west Denmark and the Netherlands.

The Old English of the Anglo-Saxon era developed into Middle English, the language as spoken between the Norman Conquest and the late 15th century. A significant influence on the shaping of Middle English came from contact with the North Germanic languages spoken by the Scandinavians who conquered and colonized parts of Britain during the 8th and 9th centuries; this contact led to much lexical borrowing and grammatical simplification. Another important influence came from the conquering Normans, who spoke a form of French called Old Norman, which in Britain developed into Anglo-Norman. Many Norman and French loanwords entered the language in this period, especially in vocabulary related to the church, the court system and the government. The system of orthography that became established during the Middle English period is by and large still in use today—later changes in pronunciation, however, combined with the adoption of various foreign spellings, mean that the spelling of modern English words appears highly irregular.

Early Modern English—the language used by Shakespeare—is dated from around 1500. It incorporated many Renaissance-era loans from Latin and Ancient Greek, as well as borrowings from other European languages, including French, German and Dutch. Significant pronunciation changes in this period included the ongoing Great Vowel Shift, which affected the qualities of most long vowels. Modern English proper, similar in most respects to that spoken today, was in place by the late 17th century. The English language came to be exported to other parts of the world through British colonisation, and is now the dominant language in Britain and Ireland, the United States and Canada, Australia, New Zealand and many smaller former colonies, as well as being widely spoken in India, parts of Africa, and elsewhere. Partially due to United States' influence, English has taken on the status of a global lingua franca.

Old English consisted of a diverse group of dialects, reflecting the varied origins of the Anglo-Saxon kingdoms established in different parts of Britain. The Late West Saxon dialect eventually became dominant; however, a greater input to Middle English came from the Anglian dialects. Geographical and social variation between English dialects and accents remains significant today. Scots, a form of English traditionally spoken in parts of Scotland and the north of Ireland, is often regarded as a separate language.

单词表

Scandinavian	*adj.*	斯堪的纳维亚（人）的；斯堪的纳维亚语的
	n.	斯堪的纳维亚人；斯堪的纳维亚语
Anglo-Norman	*n.*	诺曼系英国人，盎格鲁－诺曼语
	adj.	诺曼系英国人的，盎格鲁－诺曼语的
orthography	*n.*	正确拼字，正字法，正字学
incorporate	*v.*	包含；吸收
vowel	*n.*	元音
	adj.	元音的
colonisation	*n.*	殖民
lingua franca		混合语，交际语，通用语
Anglo-Saxon	*n.*	盎格鲁－撒克逊人；盎格鲁－撒克逊语
	adj.	盎格鲁－撒克逊人的；盎格鲁－撒克逊语的
geographical	*adj.*	地理学的，地理的
variation	*n.*	变化，变动；变异，演变；变奏曲；变量

2. 六书——汉字的六种构造条例

六书，即汉字的六种构造条例，是后人根据汉字的形成所做的整理，而非造字法则。象形、指事、形声、会意、转注、假借，其中象形、指事、会意、形声主要是“造字法”，转注、假借是“用字法”。

“六书”一词出于《周礼》：“保氏掌谏王恶，而养国子以道，乃教之六艺：一曰五礼，二曰六乐，三曰五射，四曰五驭，五曰六书，六曰九数。”然而，《周礼》只记述了“六书”这个名词，却没加以解释。

中国东汉学者许慎在《说文解字》中记载：“周礼八岁入小学，保氏教国子，先以六书。一曰指事。指事者，视而可识，察而见意，上下是也。二曰象形。象形者，画成其物，随体诘诎，日月是也。三曰形声。形声者，以事为名，取譬相成，江河是也。四曰会意。会意者，比类合谊，以见指撝，武信是也。五曰转注。转注者，建类一首，同意相受，考老是也。六曰假借。假借者，本无其字，依声托事，令长是也。”许慎的解说，是历史上首次对“六书”下定义的正式记载。后世对六书的解说，仍以许慎的见解为核心。

V. Story Links

1. 汉字的起源

大概在战国时期，中国人就开始关注文字的起源。有人认为结绳是汉字的起源。但不少人表示异议，结绳是上古用以记事的方法，差不多一切原始民族都曾用过。它即便是记事，也毕竟不能算是文字。也有人认为中国的文字源于八卦。此外，尚有河图洛书演进为文字说。中国古代最通行之说是仓颉（jié）造字，这至少在战国末年已经在广大学者中流传。

仓颉画像

仓颉到底是什么人呢？传说他是黄帝的史官，黄帝是古代中原部落联盟的领袖。由于社会进入较大规模的部落联盟阶段，联盟之间外交事务日益频繁，故迫切需要建立一套各联盟共用的交际符号，于是搜集及整理共用文字的工作便交在史官仓颉的手上了。宋代淳化年间，有一部著名的书法集叫《淳化阁帖》，其卷五载有古篆书二十八字，传说是仓颉所写。

其实，文字的形成是一个渐进的过程，绝非一时一人所能胜任。文字应当是古代劳动人民在长期的生产实践中不断创造、发明、发展、完善下来的符号。数量也是从少到多积累起来的。

2. 英文字母的起源及发展

大家都知道汉字是象形文字，但如果说英语也是象形文字，你一定会认为是无稽之谈。其实，追根溯源，英语的26个字母确实来自象形文字。这26个字母最初起源于埃及象形文字，后经腓尼基人改进为腓尼基字母，希腊人对腓尼基字母加以改进后创造了希腊字母，古罗马人对希腊字母加以改进后发明了拉丁字母，英文字母就属于拉丁字母。几千年的变迁，古代字母和现代字母的发音已经有很大的区别，但其基本的象形含义仍或多或少地被保存下来。每个字母的原始意义又渗透到各种词根之中，最终在现代词汇中留下了明显的痕迹。

26个字母的象形之处到底在哪呢？下面是部分字母所对应的含义：A—牛头，B—房子，C—骆驼，D—门，E—举着双手的人，F—沙粒，G—房角，H—荷花，I—手，K—皇帝，L—鞭子，M—水、波浪，N—鼻子，O—圆的东西，P—嘴，R—人头，S—太阳、沙丘，T—十字架，V—龙，X—十字架，Z—闪电。

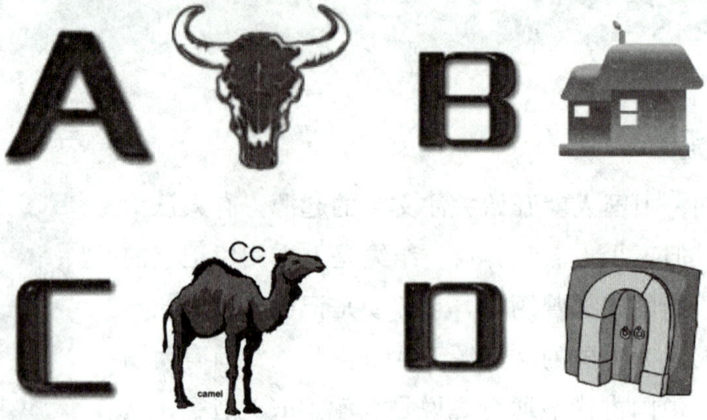

字母与象形图案

我们需要知道古人写字是不分上下左右的，因此一些象形文字可以横过来看，也可以倒过来看。比如 A 为什么来自牛头呢？如果你将 A 倒过来看就知道答案了。

VI. Did You Know?

1. 说文解字——“秋”

“秋”——火烧蟋蟀

中国古代有个民间游戏，叫斗蟋蟀。蟋蟀是一种典型的秋虫，入冬即死。我们来看一下甲骨文的“秋”字——上边是一只蟋蟀，代表秋虫，下边放了一个火盆。再来看“秋”字大篆体的写法——左边是秋天的禾苗，沉甸甸的麦穗已经压弯了腰；右边是个“火”字。火烧秋虫也好，火烧秸秆也好，都是秋天麦收后的一种行为，旨在秋收后通过烧秋虫、烧秸秆来重新滋养大地，也象征着一种成熟的状态。这就是“秋”的意思。《说文解字》里说：“秋，禾谷熟也。”秋天是收获的季节，谷子都熟了。“禾谷垂下头”经常被用来形容君子不忘本。底下是根，经常垂下头来注视自己的根基，是谦虚的表现，也是做人不要忘记根本的意思。

2. Root and Affix（词根与词缀）

A root, or a root word, is a word that does not have a prefix in front of the word or a suffix at the end of the word. The root word is the primary lexical unit of a word, and of a word family (root is then called base word), which carries the most significant aspects of semantic content and cannot be reduced into smaller constituents. The root of a word is unit of meaning (morpheme) and, as such, it is an abstraction, though it can usually be represented in writing as a word would be.

An affix (in modern sense) is a morpheme that is attached to a word stem to form a new word. Affixes may be derivational, like English -ness and pre-, or inflectional, like English plural -s and past tense -ed. They are bound morphemes by definition; prefixes and suffixes may be separable affixes. A prefix is an affix which is placed before the stem of a word. Adding it to the beginning of one word changes it into another word. For example, when the prefix un- is added to the word happy, it creates the word unhappy. Particularly in the study of languages, a prefix is also called a preformative, because it alters the form of the words to which it is affixed. A suffix is an affix which is placed after the stem of a word.

（资料来源：https://en.wikipedia.org/wiki/Suffix）

VII. Cultural Reflection

英语属印欧（Indo-Europe）语系中日耳曼语族（Germanic）的西日耳曼语支（West Germanic）。英语的起源和发展与英语民族历史发展密切相关。英语，最初指大不列颠（Great Britain）的盎格鲁－撒克逊人（Anglo-Saxon）的语言，是在各种因素的影响下得到发展、充实并逐渐规范化、标准化的。

汉语属于汉藏语系的汉语语族。我们现在所说的汉语是指以北京语音为标准音，以北方话为基础方言，以典范的现代白话文作品为语法规范的普通话。

虽然文字的起源与象形有关，但在长期的演变过程中，文字逐渐朝着两个不同的方向发展，一是以字母拼写词语为主的表音文字，一是用简单线条画下事物轮廓的表形文字。汉字与西方拼音文字所属的语系不同，表形、表音各有所长，在都具有文字的整体性质和功能的同时，表现出异中有同、同中见异的特点。汉语英语文字的相同点主要表现在：

一、具有文字的共性——有形、有音、有意

要揭示、界定一种文字的性质，首先当全面了解世界各种文字的特点，然后掌握一切文字的共性，这样才能揭示出有别于文字共性和他种文字个性的特性来。统观世界各国文字，世界文字的共性表现在以下三个方面：

所有文字都是作用于视觉的可见形体符号。也就是说文字都是有形的，比如英文的“Aa、Bb、Gg……”、中文的“目、石、下、休、捞……”，这些字符都是由可视的线条书写出的形体样子。不能被眼睛看见的，不是文字。

任何文字都有固定的读音。所有文字，或表语言中的音素（音位），或表一个音节。如英文的“A”读 [eɪ]，“B”读 [biː]，中文的“白”读“bái”，“苍”读“cāng”，“帆”读“fān”。某个字的读音长期固定于这些字上不变。

所有文字的功能都是为了表意。每一种文字都是以它的形体（字母和笔画结构）和读音为媒介而与语言的基本元素词相联系来传达思想从而实现交际目的的。言语和文字的功能职责就在于表意。在世界文字中，有的字符本身就有字义，如汉字；有的字符个体不表意，只有通过适当搭配构成词句才能表意。如“k.a.n.g.a.r.o.o”这些单列的字母并不表意，但按规则组合在一起构成单词，如“kangaroo（袋鼠）”就表意了。所以从总体上看，有形、表音、表意其实是所有文字的共性。所有文字，一是有形体，二是有读音，三是最终的功能、目的都是表意交际（虽然有些单字本身不表意）。可见形、音、意是文字固有的三要素。形、音、意也可被称为文字的三维性。

二、文字的源头都是象形文字

文字的源头——无论中西，其最早的文字都是象形文字直至图画文字，以至在其源头，要判断一幅图文是艺术描绘还是原始文字符号绝非易事。

汉字起源于象形，英语字母表中的每个字母一开始都是描摹某种动物或物体形状的图画，而这些图画最后演变为符号。但这些符号和原先被描摹之实物的形状几乎无相似之处。谁也不能肯定这些象形字母起初究竟代表什么。我们的解释只能是学者们基于史料做出的有根据的猜测。一般认为希腊字母乃西方所有字母，包括拉丁字母的始祖。其实希腊人的字母又是从腓尼基人那儿借过来的。

在腓尼基字母表中字母 A 读 aleph，写起来形似字母 V，中间再加一横，代表牛头或牛角。后来希腊人将它倒过来写。对于古代腓尼基人来说，牛意味着财富，吃、穿、耕作都少不了它。这也许就是 A 被列为第一个字母的缘故吧。

B 和 A 一样，也可以追溯到古代腓尼基。在腓尼基字母表中 B 叫 beth，代表房屋，在希伯来语中 B 也叫 beth，也含房屋之意。字母 B 原来形似原始社会的两室房屋，小写字母 b 是后来由大写字母 B 衍变出来的。犹太教、基督教圣地为 Bethlehem，在今约旦河西岸。该词中至今还包含着 beth 这一部分。B 在字母表中之所以排在第二位也许是因为对人类的生存来说“住”的重要性仅次于“衣食”。

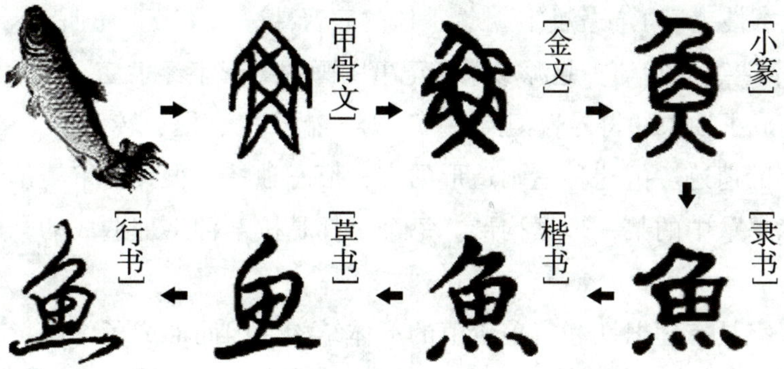

汉字的演化示例

方块汉字和英语拼音文字存在巨大差异，主要表现在以下四个方面：

一、汉语是表意文字，英语是表音文字

表意文字是一种用象征性书写符号记录词或词素的文字体系，不直接或不单纯表示语音。汉字作为世界上最早的文字之一，由于多方面的原因，它至今仍然停留在表意阶段，成为世界上现存唯一的表意文字——每个字都表示个别词或词素的形体。汉字的表意方式，一方面是在表形文字的基础上，使单纯的表形文字逐渐脱离因形及物、因物及义的轨道，变成纯然的表意符号；另一方面是创造纯粹的表意符号，或者利用已有的表形字，加上别的符号来表示新的意义，如“上、三、出、至、明、林”等。现代汉字虽然有 90% 以上的形声字带表音成分，如“洋、汪、湖、涨”等字的声旁“羊、王、胡、张”，但它们并没有摆脱表意性。一方面形旁“氵”保留着明显的表意作用，另一方面声旁本身往往还是一个能够单独使用的表意字，只是偶然被借来表示一些字的读音，这只能说汉字在应用上有了音化倾向，但与表音文字还是有本质区别的。表意文字具有较大的适应性，抛开古今语音的变化和方言的分歧，它的字形可以直接为不同时代、不同方言区的人们所共同使用。但是，表意文字也有缺点，一个词或一个词素都得用一个字来记录，而且文字本身不能直接表示声音，学习和使用都有困难。

表音文字是用书面符号即字母表示语词读音的文字系统。它的书面符号既不是实物的图像也不直接代表词或语素这些语言的意义单位，而只表示不含意义的较小的语音单位。因此，表音文字与语言的语音物质材料有直接的联系。根据表音文字的字母拼合起来的读音，人们就能辨认出它们所代表的词或语素这些意义单位。因而，通过语音单位的书写就能记录和表达相应的意义单位。由于语言中较小的语音单位为数不多，表音文字的书面符号也比较少，远没有表意文字那样复杂，所以掌握和使用起来都比较方便。现代许多民族大多使用表音文字。

二、汉字的表意性决定了汉字重视觉，英语的表音性决定了英语重听觉

“象形”是汉字造字的基础。起源于象形记事图画的象形字经隶变、楷化后虽完全摆脱了象形图画的特征，变成了抽象的符号，但点、横、竖、撇、捺、提、转、折、钩之类的笔画部件，仍保留着象形文字的遗迹。由这种笔画造形的字，形态独特，很具有审美价值。与此同时，每个字都是根据“六书”中的某一理据构形。每个字都是按某种字理造成的，这样就能给识字者带来一定的记忆线索。

方块字形的汉字具有理据性和审美价值的形体结构，因而形成了中国特有的书法艺术。书法是指按照文字特点及含义，以其书体、笔法、结构和章法写字，使之成为富有美感的艺术作品。汉字书法艺术的巨大魅力主要表现在两个方面：一是其神韵与意境，二是其极其丰富的思想内涵。正是由于汉字书法艺术具有这两大审美特点，并且二者高度融合，所以，汉字书法艺术被誉为无言的诗、无行的舞、无图的画和无声的乐。

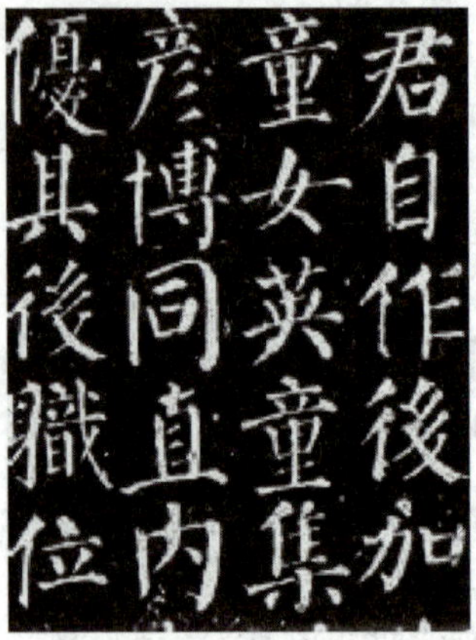

颜真卿的书法艺术

在英语当中，有 calligraphy 一词，英文字典里对此的解释是“漂亮的手写体”。但是表音文字的表现形象非常有限，因为是字母重复地使用，横向排列，所以它们在表现上显得比较单一。这是表音文字的局限。所以外国有些艺术史家说，中国的汉字本身都具有非常丰富的图形美，每一个汉字就像一个抽象的雕塑，它具有天然的艺术的素质。

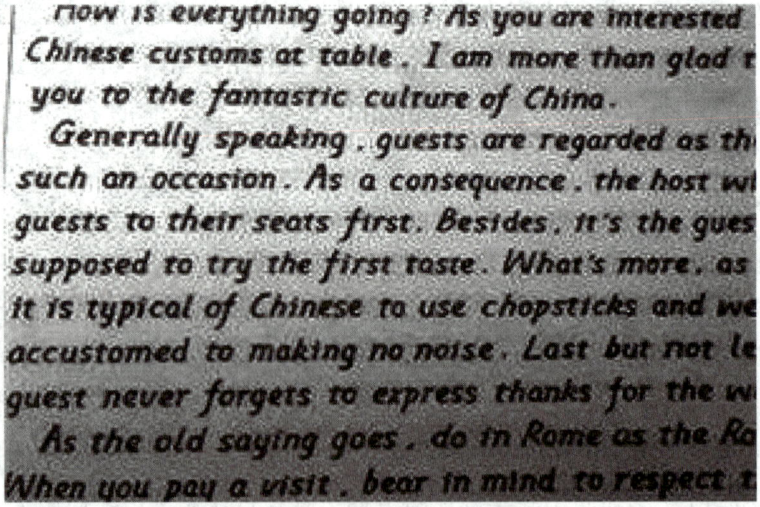

漂亮的英文手写体

三、汉字字词合体，英语有词无字

在表意上，汉字最大的特点是字词合体。也就是每个字同时就是一个意义完整的词。遍观汉语字典，我们可以发现，绝大部分的汉字（99% 以上）的单字本身就是一个有意义、可自由运用的词，所以在汉语书面语中，字不像西方拼音文字那样仅是一个只表语音音素的符号，更重要的是它又是一个可承载意思的词。这一特点在世界各国文字中，可以说是独一无二的。有人说汉字代表的只是语素而不是词。统观《新华字典》全书，绝大部分的字都是可作词用的，现代汉语中的许多双音节的所谓的“合成词”，实际上大多是由两个词义组成的复合词。例如：声音、选择、眉目、始终、方圆、车辆、笔直、提高、阐明、书本、枪支、举重、注意、理事、地震、自卫……这些合成词实际上是由两个词义合起来组成的复合词，这些词实际上是两个意思的复合体。这些双音节合成词拆开仍可以作词用。如“选择”一词，抽出“选”可作一个单音节词，如“任你选一个”，只取“择”也可作词用，如“择其要者”。这种复合词的每一个字表示的意义在以前称“词素”，后来受国外语言学的语素理论影响，称为“语素”。由于汉语的每个单字大都是一个有意义的单音词，所以凡汉语字典，实际上就是汇集汉语单音节词的词典。事实上汉语字典也是对汉字逐个标音释义的辞书。为什么汉字能够逐一释义呢？就因为汉字的每个字都是一个词。相反，为什么英、法等使用拼音文字的国家只有词典而没有字典呢？就是因为拼音字母没有意义，不需要解释。在汉语中，可取两个单音词组成合成词（或复合词），而单音词与合成词是同一级别的语言单位。在汉语中“选”是一个词，“择”是一个词，“选”与“择”结合成为“选择”后仍是一个词。由此可见,汉字绝大部分单字本身就是词。字词同体（或一体）是汉字与其他文字最根本的区别。

四、汉语和英语的变化发展不同

英语和汉语都经历了数千年的发展和变化。英语在历史上多次受到外来民族的入侵，在语言的发展上也经受了几次巨大的影响和冲击。古英语受到古希腊文明的影响。公元前 43 年恺撒大帝征服不列颠，罗马人统治英国，带来了他们使用的拉丁语；日耳曼民族于公元 449 年在英格兰登陆，将日耳曼语带到英国，而发展成现在的英语；公元 1066 年的诺曼征服更是使法语成为英国上流社会的语言，这些法语借词几乎涵盖了所有上流社会的生活用语和抽象概念，中古英语的词汇有一万多个借自法语；文艺复兴重新激起了人们对拉丁语和古希腊语的研究，后来随着英国的发展和世界范围的殖民扩张，英语不断受到外来语言的影响。在现代英语单词中，很多词根和词缀都带有外来语的深刻烙印。如 epilog 就保留了相应的希腊词 epilogos 中的前缀 epi 和词根 log，credible 保留了拉丁词 credi-，empire、crown、pedition 则是直接从法语中借来的词。这些各具特色的外来语使得英语的词汇非常丰富，而且带来了很多用途广泛的词缀。

汉字从最初的甲骨文到现在的楷书，也经过多次演变，字形、字义也不断发生变化，有些会意字已无法考证出是如何会意的。近代以来，随着中国与世界的交流越来越频繁，汉字也开始受到外来语言的影响，一些外来语也进入了中文的词汇。但是这些影响同外来语言对英语单词的影响是不同的，汉字不像英语那样出现了很多新的单词和词缀，汉字本身的结构并没有大的变化，只是出现了一些新的汉字，一些原有的汉字具有了新的意义，还有就是很多本来就存在的汉字结合起来表示新的意义。

VIII. Homework

1. 唇枪舌剑

你支持下面的观点吗？

中西语言一个重词汇，一个重语法，其根本原因在于中西语言属于不同类型的语言，即西方语言是典型的语法型语言，汉语是典型的语义型语言。这两者的差异主要表现在编码方式、结构框架和基本结构单位不同。

2. 汉语和英语句法结构的基本单位是什么？（小组协作讨论）

Section Two

The Contrast of Chinese and Western Grammars

I. Learning Objectives

1. To learn the Chinese grammar and English grammar

2. To contrast the differences between Chinese grammar and English grammar, and summarize their effects on the way of language expression

II. Key Points and Difficult Points

1. To contrast the basic grammar features of Chinese and English

2. To contrast the basic language unit of Chinese and English

III. Lead-in Questions

1. What are implicit feature and explicit feature of grammar?

2. What is the difference between synthetic language and analytic languages?

3. Do you know the Zi-centered theory of Chinese and word-centered theory of English?

4. What is the basic sentence structure of Chinese and English?

IV. Learning Contents

1. What is Grammar?

In linguistics, grammar is the set of structural rules governing the composition of clauses, phrases, and words in any given natural language. The term refers also to the study of such rules, and this field includes morphology, syntax, and phonology, often complemented by phonetics, semantics, and pragmatics.

For linguists, grammar refers to cognitive information underlying language use. Speakers of a language have a set of internalized rules for using that language. These rules constitute grammar, and the vast majority of the information in the grammar is—at least in the case of one's native language—acquired not by conscious study or instruction, but by observing other speakers. Much of this work is done during early childhood; learning a language later in life usually involves a greater degree of explicit instruction.

The term "grammar" can also be used to describe the rules that govern the linguistic behavior of a group of speakers. The term "English grammar", therefore, may have several meanings. It may refer to the whole of English grammar, that is, to the grammars of all the speakers of the language, in which case, the term encompasses a great deal of variation. Alternatively, it may refer only to what is common to the grammars of all, or of the vast majority of English speakers (such as subject-verb-object word order in simple declarative sentences). Or it may refer to the rules of a particular, relatively well-defined variety of English (such as standard English for a particular region).

单词表

linguistics	*n.*	语言学
morphology	*n.*	形态学
syntax	*n.*	句法；语法
phonology	*n.*	音韵学；音系学；语音体系
complement	*v.*	补充；补足
phonetics	*n.*	语音学；发音学

semantics	*n.*	语义学；词义学
pragmatics	*n.*	语用论；语用学
cognitive	*adj.*	认知的；认识的
underlying	*adj.*	潜在的，含蓄的
	v.	位于……的下面；构成……的基础（underlie 的现在分词形式）
explicit	*adj.*	明确的，清楚的
encompass	*vt.*	环绕，包围；包含或包括某事物；完成

2. Synthetic Languages and Analytic Languages

In linguistic typology, a synthetic language is a language with a high morpheme-per-word ratio, as opposed to a low morpheme-per-word ratio in what is described as an analytic language. This linguistic classification is largely independent of morpheme-usage classifications (such as fusional, agglutinative, etc.), although there is a common tendency for agglutinative languages to exhibit synthetic properties.

Synthetic languages are frequently contrasted with analytic languages. It is more accurate to conceive of languages as existing on a continuum, with the analytic pole (consistently one morpheme per word) at one end and highly polysynthetic languages (in which a single inflected verb may contain as much information as an entire English sentence with various words such as a noun, an adjective, and an adverb) at the other extreme. Synthetic languages tend to lie around the middle of this scale.

Synthetic languages are numerous and well-attested. Most Indo-European languages, all Kartvelian languages such as Georgian, some Semitic languages such as Arabic, and many languages of the Americas, including Navajo, Nahuatl, Mohawk and Quechua are synthetic.

单词表

typology	*n.*	类型学；象征主义，象征论
synthetic	*adj.*	合成的；人造的；综合的
	n.	合成物；合成纤维；合成剂
morpheme	*n.*	形态素，词素
analytic	*adj.*	解析的；分解的；分析型的

fusional	*adj.*	熔化的，熔合的
agglutinative	*adj.*	会胶合的，会黏着的
polysynthetic	*adj.*	多词合成的，多式综合的
Kartvelian	*n.*	卡尔特维里语
Georgian	*n.*	格鲁吉亚人；格鲁吉亚语；佐治亚州人
	adj.	佐治亚的；格鲁吉亚人的；格鲁吉亚的；乔治王朝时代艺术风格的
Semitic	*adj.*	闪米特人的；闪族语系的
	n.	闪语；闪语族
Navajo	*n.*	纳瓦霍人（美国最大的印第安部落）；纳瓦霍语
Nahuatl	*n.*	纳瓦特人（墨西哥南部和中美洲印第安各族）；纳瓦特尔语
Mohawk	*n.*	（北美印第安人中的）莫霍克族；莫霍克语
	adj.	（有关）莫霍克人的
Quechua	*n.*	盖丘亚族（南美印第安人的一大分支）；盖丘亚族人；盖丘亚族语

V. Story Links

1. 诗歌翻译赏析

英文诗歌：

You say that you love rain,
but you open your umbrella when it rains.
You say that you love the sun,
but you find a shadow spot when the sun shines.
You say that you love the wind,
but you close your windows when wind blows.
This is why I am afraid,
because you say that you love me too.

汉语译文：

普通版

你说你喜欢雨，但是下雨的时候你却撑开了伞；

你说你喜欢阳光，但当阳光播撒的时候，你却躲在阴凉之地；
你说你喜欢风，但清风扑面的时候，你却关上了窗户。
我害怕你对我也是如此之爱。

文艺版

你说烟雨微茫，兰亭远望；
后来轻揽婆娑，深遮霓裳。
你说春光烂漫，绿袖红香；
后来内掩西楼，静立卿旁。
你说软风轻拂，醉卧思量；
后来紧掩门窗，漫帐成殇。
你说情丝柔肠，如何相忘；
我却眼波微转，兀自成霜。

诗经版

子言慕雨，启伞避之。
子言好阳，寻荫拒之。
子言喜风，阖户离之。
子言偕老，吾所畏之。

离骚版

君乐雨兮启伞枝，
君乐昼兮林蔽日，
君乐风兮栏帐起，
君乐吾兮吾心噬。

五言诗版

恋雨偏打伞，爱阳却遮凉。
风来掩窗扉，叶公惊龙王。
片言只语短，相思缱绻长。
郎君说爱我，不敢细思量。

七言绝句版

恋雨却怕绣衣湿，喜日偏向树下倚。
欲风总把绮窗关，叫奴如何心付伊。

七律压轴版

江南三月雨微茫，罗伞叠烟湿幽香。
夏日微醺正可人，却傍佳木趁阴凉。
霜风清和更初霁，轻蹙蛾眉锁朱窗。
怜卿一片相思意，犹恐流年拆鸳鸯。

2. 标点小故事

有一个富翁生性吝啬，聘请教书先生时，讲明膳食供给很微薄。当时，这位教书先生一口应允了。二人恐怕口说无凭，写了一张没有加标点符号的合约：“无鸡鸭亦可无鱼肉亦可青菜一碟足矣。”富翁根据自己的主观愿望理解为“无鸡鸭亦可，无鱼肉亦可，青菜一碟足矣。”欣然签字。哪知道吃第一顿饭时，教书先生就大喊大叫：“怎么尽是素菜，没有荤菜？我们不是约定了‘无鸡，鸭亦可，无鱼，肉亦可；青菜一碟，足矣’的吗？”弄得这个富翁哭笑不得。

VI. Did You Know?

1. 汉语的“字本位”理论

字本位，人们将以字为汉语基本结构单位的语言研究思路称为“字本位”。“字本位”这个概念最早见于郭绍虞写于1938年的《中国语词的弹性作用》一文，以“字本位的书面语”与“词本位的口头语”相对。后来，由于人们越来越感到现行的语言理论难以有效地分析汉语的结构，于是探究原因，重新提出“字本位”的问题，不过它不限于书面语，而是指称以字为汉语基本结构单位的一种新的研究思路。以“字”为汉语基本结构单位的“字本位”理论与现在通行的以“词”为汉语基本结构单位的语言理论是两种不同的理论体系，因而必然会产生尖锐的冲突。徐通锵在《汉语结构的基本原理：字本位和语言研究》中就提到，“词”是印欧系语言的一种基本结构单位，汉语的“词”是西方语言学输入的一种语言结构单位，其内涵与“字”有重要的区别。我们为什么要弃“词”而选“字”，倡导“字本位”呢？就是由于“词”是一种舶来品，汉语中没有“根”，而形、音、义三位一体的字是汉语的载体，是汉文化的“根”，因而需要以“字”这个“纲”为基础探索汉语的结构规律、演变规律、习得机制、学习规律和运用规律，不然就难以有效地实现语言研究的预期目标，找到普遍有效的规律。

《汉字频率词典》统计，汉语一级字库常用字为3755个，二级字库为不常用字，共有3008个。根据国家出版局抽样统计，汉字中最常用字560个，常用字807个，次常用字1033个。

汉语还有一个特点，就是汉字构词能力非常强，就拿“树”这个字来说，可以组成柳树、松树、杨树等词汇，而且组成的这些词在概念上有类属联系（都是树），“树”这个语素在词汇中的意义变化也很小。但是在英语中，对应的则是 willow（柳树）、pine（松树）、poplar（杨树）。单看这些词，根本看不出它们之间的联系。而且，汉语不同于屈折语，字和词没有形态的变化，再加上汉字的表意性很强，记起来也会容易一些。一旦掌握了常用字，就可以攻克非常多的词汇。

2. 英语的“词本位”理论

据《圣经》记载，世界是上帝通过命名的方式创造的，而命名通常应用的是词语。因此，西方语言的研究以 word 为基本单位。而在中国，原始人类对世界的认知，是通过观察自然万物，慢慢体悟，然后再拟象造字，创造出刻在兽骨、龟甲上的甲骨文。仓颉造字的传说就体现了中国原始人类对世界慢慢感知的过程。因此，中国的语言有表意性的特点，强调语言的分析性。通过这两个传说的对比，我们就可以发现英语、法语等西方语言与汉语是有很大的区别的。英语中的 word 包含了语言研究的各个层面——语音、词汇和语法，潘文国把这叫作“一体三相”。他在他的论文《“字”与“Word”的对应性（上）》中，总结了 word 作为英语研究本位所具备的四个条件：（1）词是英语的天然单位；（2）词是英语民族认知世界的基本单位；（3）词是语言各个层面的交汇点；（4）词在语法上处于承上启下的枢纽位置，是词法与句法的交接点。

VII. Cultural Reflection

语言是一面镜子，它反映着一个民族的文化，揭示该民族文化的内容；语言既是社会的产物，又是人类历史和文化的结晶。同时语言与文化互相影响，互相作用；理解语言必须了解文化，理解文化必须了解语言。

汉语和英语则是在不同的历史背景和社会形态中形成的两个截然不同的语种，本质上都浸透着各自民族文化的特征，但是东西方不同的历史文化背景又使得汉英两种语言在交流中产生了碰撞。

下面将从综合语与分析语、刚性与柔性、形合与意合几个角度对英汉两种语言的语法进行对比与分析，进一步认识英语和汉语的特性与差异，从而使我们对英语的学习有更深刻的认识。

一、综合语与分析语

综合语的特征是运用形态变化来表达语法关系，分析语的特征是不用形态变化而用词序及虚词来表达语法关系。其中形态变化、词序和虚词是表达语法关系的三大手段。汉语为典型的分析语。

首先，英语有形态变化，而汉语则没有严格意义的形态变化。形态变化主要体现在构词形态和构形形态上。在构词方面，英语的词缀灵活多变，有大量的前缀、后缀，而汉语则不多见。在构形方面，英语常常是将动词、助动词和情态动词结合起来表示时态、语态和语气的变化，而汉语同一个词就可以表示主格、宾格，单数、复数，或者现在、过去等。其次，英语词序较灵活，汉语则较固定。英语词序倒置的现象比较多，汉语主要表现为功能性倒装。汉语的定语一般在名词前，英语的定语位置较灵活。再次，在虚词方面，英语经常使用定冠词、不定冠词、介词和连接词，汉语则没有冠词，表并列和从属关系的连接词的使用频率也较低，较常使用的是丰富多彩的助词，如动态助词、语气助词等。最后，英语是语调语言，汉语是声调语言。语调和重音的变化是英语语音的主要表意手段，两者的密切配合可以表达意义的差别，而汉语的语音手段主要是声调。汉语语音音节匀称，具有均衡美和节奏美。

二、刚性与柔性

（一）英语的刚性

英语句子有严谨的主谓结构，句子主次分明，层次清楚，多层递进，严密规范，句型重形合，句式为“聚集型”。英语的主谓结构有五种基本句型，即SV，SVC，SVO，SVoO，SVOC，而上述句型和变式可以通过增加修饰语扩展基本句型的成分，基本句型也可通过组合、省略、倒装等方式来实现扩展。英语注重句子结构完整，通过形态标志、连接词和填补词的使用来保持其完整性。此外，句子成分、词语之间必须在人称、数、性和意义等方面保持协调一致，即：语法一致、意义一致、就近原则等，这也是英语句子呈“聚集型”的重要因素。英语受形态变化的约束，有词性标记、关系词和连接词，语句关系结构比较清楚，因此语法歧义较少。

（二）汉语的柔性

汉语不受形态的约束，没有主谓协调一致的关系，其主谓结构具有多样性、复杂性和灵活性，句型重意合，句式呈“流散型”。汉语的主谓结构要比英语复杂得多。汉语的主语形式多样，可有可无，即：它可以表示施事、受事，也可以表示时间、地点，可用名词、动词，也可用形容词、数量词，句子可以没有主语，也可以省略主语，还可以变换主语予以隐含；谓语也复杂得多，即：它可以是动词、名词和形容词，可以是一个动词，也可以是多个动词，可以是一个单词，也可以是多个词组，可以是连动式、兼语式、把字式、紧缩式和主谓式。按表意功能和表达形式，汉语句型可以分为话题句、施事句、关系句、祈使句、描写句、说明句等。此外，汉语句式既有完全句也有大量的不完全句，两者混合交错，组成流水句。汉语缺乏形态变化和词性标记，较少使用连接词，重意会，因此语法歧义较多。

总之，英语重形合，词有形态变化，造句注重形式接应，要求结构完整，句子以形寓意，以法摄神，语法呈现显性、刚性，因而严密规范；采用的是焦点句法，具有严谨的客体意识。汉语重意合，字词缺乏形态变化，造句注重意念连贯，不求结构齐整，句子以意役形，以神统法，语法呈现隐性、柔性，因而流泻铺排，采用的是散点句法，具有灵活的主体意识。

三、形合与意合

形合指的是词语或分句之间用语言形式手段连接起来，表达语法意义和逻辑关系，意合指的是词语或分句之间不用语言形式手段连接，其中的语法意义和逻辑关系通过词语或分句的含义表达。英语造句主要采用形合法，汉语造句主要采用意合法。

（一）英语的形合法

英语造句常用各种形式手段连接词、语、分句或从句，注重显性接应和句子形式，结构完整，比较严谨；英语通常综合运用关系词、连接词、介词和其他连接手段、形式，把各种成分连接起来，构成长短句子来表达一定的语法关系和逻辑联系。意合法在英语里属于“变态”，主要是一些简练谚语、表达复合句内容的简单句，以及表达状语从句意义的定语从句。

（二）汉语的意合法

汉语造句少用甚至不用形式连接手段，注重隐性连贯、逻辑事理顺序，比较简洁。汉语的意合法的手段有语序、反复、排比、对偶、四字格等。汉语的许多主从复合句，虽然不用关联词，形式类似并列复句，但分句含义却有主次之分。紧缩句句式简明紧凑，分句之间的语法关系和逻辑关系往往是隐含的，四字格是汉语运用最广的语言形式。

四、繁复与简短

（一）英语的繁复

英语书面句子显得长而复杂，其原因是多方面的，而主要原因在于英语的从句和短语结构的复杂性。从属结构是现代英语最重要的特点之一。从句可以层层相扣，短句往往不短，而且能够充当英语句子成分的短句和从句其长短几乎是不加限制的，从句中还可以有从句，再加上各种并列成分、附加成分（例如同位语、插入语、独立成分），以及其他形形色色的修饰成分。这样一来，这些各式各样的长短成分，通过丰富而灵活的连接手段，可以接成枝叶横生的“参天大树”。英语以主谓核心协调控制全句结构，有词的形态变化约束，有连接手段连接词语和从句，有代词使词语前呼后应，这些因素都可以使冗长的句子平衡且协调，不致流散。因此，英语句子，尤其是书面语的句子，常常是环扣镶嵌，盘根错节，句中有句。换言之，英语句子一般有完整的结构，许多有关的成分通过各种表示关系和连接的手段组成关系联结，直接或间接地黏附在这个句子结构的里外、前后、左右或中间，整个句子成了庞大复杂的“高楼大厦”。

（二）汉语的简短

相比之下，现代汉语没有形态变化，少用甚至不用关联词，词语之间的语法关系主要是通过安排语序和使用助词来表达的，词语的先后次序一般是按照时间顺序和事理关系来排列的。换言之，汉语造句主要采取“流水记事法”，常用分句或流水句来逐层叙述。这些特点，大大限制了汉语单句的长度。此外，汉语定语修饰语一般前置，一个词语所能承受的修饰词语是有限的。一个名词前面不可“的”“的”（定语）不休，一个动词前后也不可“地”“地”（状语）或“得”“得”（补语）不已。一个词语若有两个以上稍长的修饰语，就显得“负荷过重”了。

VIII. Homework

1. 唇枪舌剑

英语句子呈现句首封闭、句尾开放的特征；而汉语句子则呈现出句首开放、句尾收缩的特征。你同意这个观点吗？请解释原因。

2. 根据下列提示，讨论汉英语言在句法方面的不同（小组协作讨论）

由于语言类型的不同，中西语言在句法结构、句法文化方面呈现出一些各异其趣的风貌。语法型的西方语言的句法结构具有层次线性、结构封闭的特点，其样貌就如同一条扣起的西式项链，结构紧锁，不容拆散。语义型的汉语的句法结构具有层次立体、结构开放的特点，样貌好像一套层层相套的俄罗斯套娃，结构松散，便于拆装。

立体与线性：________________

散点与焦点：________________

对偶与主从：________________

真实与虚拟：________________

Section Three

The Contrast of Chinese and Western Language Expression

I. Learning Objectives

1. To know the characteristics of both Chinese and English in expression

2. To contrast the expression difference of both Chinese and English and study their influence on Chinese and Western thinking modes

II. Key Points and Difficult Points

1. To contrast the hypotactic of English and paratactic of Chinese

2. To contrast *Wuxing* (悟性) and rationality

III. Lead-in Questions

1. Do you know the rigid feature of English and the supple feature of Chinese?

2. Do you know the comparative differences between the logical feature of English and the intuitive feature of Chinese?

IV. Learning Contents

1. 散文《匆匆》的不同译本（节选）

匆匆（节选）

朱自清

去的尽管去了，来的尽管来着；去来的中间，又怎样地匆匆呢？早上我起来的时候，小屋里射进两三方斜斜的太阳。太阳他有脚啊，轻轻悄悄地挪移了；我也茫茫然跟着旋转。于是——洗手的时候，日子从水盆里过去；吃饭的时候，日子从饭碗里过去；默默时，便从凝然的双眼前过去。我觉察他去得匆匆了，伸出手遮挽时，他又从遮挽着的手边过去，天黑时，我躺在床上，他便伶伶俐俐地从我身上跨过，从我脚边飞去了。等我睁开眼和太阳再见，这算又溜走了一日。我掩着面叹息。但是新来的日子的影儿又开始在叹息里闪过了。

在逃去如飞的日子里，在千门万户的世界里的我能做些什么呢？只有徘徊罢了，只有匆匆罢了；在八千多日的匆匆里，除徘徊外，又剩些什么呢？过去的日子如轻烟，被微风吹散了，如薄雾，被初阳蒸融了；我留着些什么痕迹呢？我何曾留着像游丝样的痕迹呢？我赤裸裸来到这世界，转眼间也将赤裸裸地回去吧？但不能平的，为什么偏要白白走这一遭啊？

Transient Days (excerpt)

By Zhu Ziqing

张培基译

What is gone is gone, what is to come keeps coming. How swift is the transition in between! When I get up in the morning, the slanting sun casts two or three squarish patches of light into my small room. The sun has feet too, edging away softly and stealthily. And, without knowing it, I am already caught in its revolution. Thus the day flows away through the sink when I wash my hands; vanishes in the rice bowl when I have my meal; passes away quietly before the fixed gaze of my eyes when I am lost in reverie. Aware of its fleeting presence, I reach out for it only to find it brushing past my outstretched hands. In the evening, when I lie on my bed, it nimbly strides over my body and flits past my feet. By the time when I open my eyes to meet the sun again, another day is already gone. I heave a sigh, my head buried in my hands. But, in the midst of my sighs, a new day is flashing past.

Living in this world with its fleeting days and teeming millions, what can I do but waver and wander and live a transient life? What have I been doing during the 8,000 fleeting days except wavering and wandering? The bygone days, like wisps of smoke, have been dispersed by gentle winds, and, like thin mists, have been evaporated by the rising sun. What traces have I left behind? No, nothing, not even gossamer-like traces. I have come to this world stark naked, and in the twinkling of an eye, I am to go back as stark naked as ever. However, I am taking it very much to heart: why should I be made to pass through this world for nothing at all?

(From Zhang P J, 1995, *Selected Modern Chinese Essays,* Shanghai Foreign Language Education Press.)

Rush (excerpt)

By Zhu Ziqing

朱纯深译

Those that have gone have gone for good, those to come keep coming; yet in between, how swift is the shift, in such a rush? When I get up in the morning, the slanting sun marks its presence in my small room in two or three oblongs. The sun has feet, look, he is treading on, lightly and furtively; and I am caught, blankly, in his revolution. Thus the day flows away through the sink when I wash my hands, wears off in the bowl when I eat my meal, and passes away before my day-dreaming gaze as reflect in silence. I can feel his haste now, so I reach out my hands to hold him back, but he keeps flowing past my withholding hands. In the evening, as I lie in bed, he strides over my body, glides past my feet, in his agile way. The moment I open my eyes and meet the sun again, one whole day has gone. I bury my face in my hands and heave a sigh. But the new day begins to flash past in the sigh.

What can I do, in this bustling world, with my days flying in their escape? Nothing but to hesitate, to rush. What have I been doing in that eight-thousand-day rush, apart from hesitating? Those bygone days have been dispersed as smoke by a light wind, or evaporated as mist by the morning sun. What traces have I left behind me? Have I ever left behind any gossamer traces at all? I have come to the world, stark naked; am I to go back, in a blink, in the same stark nakedness? It is not fair though: why should I have made such a trip for nothing!

(From Zhu C S, 1994, "Rush", *Chinese Translators,* [3]: 63–64.)

Haste (excerpt)

By Zhu Ziqing

Howard Goldblatt 译

What's gone is gone, and what is coming cannot be halted. From what is gone to what is yet to come, why must it pass so quickly? In the morning when I get up there are two or three rays of sunlight slanting into my small room. The sun, does it have feet? Stealthily it moves along, as I too, unknowingly, follow its progress. Then as I wash up, the day passes through my washbasin, and at breakfast through my rice bowl. When I am standing still and quiet, my eyes carefully follow its progress past me. I can sense that it is hurrying alone, and when I stretch out my hands to cover and hold it, it soon emerges from under my hands and moves along. At night, as I lie on my bed, agilely it strides across my body and flies past my feet. And when I open my eyes to greet the sun again, another day has slipped by. I bury my face in my hands and heave a sigh. But the shadow of the new day begins darting by, even in the midst of my sighing.

During these fleeting days what can I, only one among so many, accomplish? Nothing more than to pace irresolutely, nothing more than to hurry along. In these more than 8,000 days of hurrying, what have I to show but some irresolute wanderings? The days that are gone are like smoke that has been dissipated by a breeze, like thin mists that have been burned off under the onslaught of the morning sun. What mark will I leave behind? Will the trace I leave behind be so much as a gossamer thread? Naked I came into this world, and in a twinkling still naked I will leave it. But what I cannot accept is: why should I make this journey in vain?

单词表

slanting	*adj.*	倾斜的，歪斜的
squarish	*adj.*	近似方形的，呈方形的
reverie	*n.*	想入非非；白日梦，冥想
nimbly	*adv.*	敏捷地，机敏地
flit	*vi.*	轻快地掠过
fleeting	*adj.*	疾驰的，飞逝的；短暂的；稍纵即逝的

wisp	*n.*	小捆；小束；小缕
	vt.	把……卷成小把
gossamer	*n.*	蛛丝，游丝
	adj.	轻而薄的；虚无缥缈的；如蛛丝的
oblong	*n.*	长方形；椭圆形
furtive	*adj.*	鬼鬼祟祟的
bustling	*adj.*	繁忙的，熙熙攘攘的
evaporate	*v.*	（使某物）蒸发掉
stark	*adj.*	完全的；荒凉的；僵硬的
	adv.	赤裸；完全
stealthily	*adv.*	暗地里，偷偷摸摸地
irresolutely	*adv.*	优柔寡断地
dissipate	*v.*	驱散；使消散；挥霍；耗尽
onslaught	*n.*	猛攻，攻击；突击；大量的倾泻

2.Why Chinese Is So Damn Hard (excerpt)

by David Moser

University of Michigan Center for Chinese Studies

(1) *Because the writing system is ridiculous.*

Beautiful, complex, mysterious—but ridiculous. I, like many students of Chinese, was first attracted to Chinese because of the writing system, which is surely one of the most fascinating scripts in the world. The more you learn about Chinese characters the more intriguing and addicting they become. The study of Chinese characters can become a lifelong obsession, and you soon find yourself engaged in the daily task of accumulating them, drop by drop from the vast sea of characters, in a vain attempt to hoard them in the leaky bucket of long-term memory.

The beauty of the characters is indisputable, but as the Chinese people began to realize the importance of universal literacy, it became clear that these ideograms were sort of like bound feet—some fetishists may have liked the way they looked, but they weren't too practical for daily use.

For one thing, it is simply unreasonably hard to learn enough characters to become functionally literate. Again, someone may ask "Hard in comparison to what?" And the answer is easy: Hard in comparison to Spanish, Greek, Russian, Hindi, or any other sane, "normal" language that requires at most a few dozen symbols to write anything in the language.

(2) ***Because the writing system just ain't very phonetic.***

So much for the physical process of writing the characters themselves. What about the sheer task of memorizing so many characters? Again, a comparison of English and Chinese is instructive. Suppose a Chinese person has just the previous day learned the English word "president", and now wants to write it from memory. How to start? Anyone with a year or two of English experience is going to have a host of clues and spelling rules-of-thumb, albeit imperfect ones, to help them along. The word really couldn't start with anything but "pr", and after that a little guesswork aided by visual memory ("Could a 'z' be in there? That's an unusual letter, I would have noticed it, I think. Must be an 's'...") should produce something close to the target. Not every foreigner (or native speaker for that matter) has noted or internalized the various flawed spelling heuristics of English, of course, but they are at least there to be utilized.

Now imagine that you, a learner of Chinese, have just the previous day encountered the Chinese word for "president" (总统 zǒngtǒng) and want to write it. What processes do you go through in retrieving the word? Well, very often you just totally forget, with a forgetting that is both absolute and perfect in a way few things in this life are. You can repeat the word as often as you like; the sound won't give you a clue as to how the character is to be written. After you learn a few more characters and get hip to a few more phonetic components, you can do a bit better. ("Zǒng 总 is a phonetic component in some other character, right?...Sōng? Zēng? Oh yeah, cōng as in cōngmíng 聪明.") Of course, the phonetic aspect of some characters is more obvious than that of others, but many characters, including some of the most high-frequency ones, give no clue at all as to their pronunciation.

(3) ***Because you can't cheat by using cognates.***

I remember when I had been studying Chinese very hard for about three years, I had an interesting experience. One day I happened to find a Spanish-language newspaper sitting on a seat next to me. I picked it up out of curiosity. "Hmm," I thought to myself. "I've never studied Spanish in my life. I wonder how much of this I can understand." At random I picked a short article about an airplane crash and started to read. I found I could basically glean, with some guesswork, most of the information from the article. The crash took place near Los Angeles. 186 people were killed. There were no survivors.

The plane crashed just one minute after take-off. There was nothing on the flight recorder to indicate a critical situation, and the tower was unaware of any emergency. The plane had just been serviced three days before and no mechanical problems had been found. And so on. After finishing the article I had a sudden discouraging realization: Having never studied a day of Spanish, I could read a Spanish newspaper more easily than I could a Chinese newspaper after more than three years of studying Chinese.

(4) *Because even looking up a word in the dictionary is complicated.*

One of the most unreasonably difficult things about learning Chinese is that merely learning how to look up a word in the dictionary is about the equivalent of an entire semester of secretarial school. When I was in Taiwan, I heard that they sometimes held dictionary look-up contests in the junior high schools. Imagine a language where simply looking a word up in the dictionary is considered a skill like debate or volleyball! Chinese is not exactly what you would call a user-friendly language, but a Chinese dictionary is positively user-hostile.

(5) *Because tonal languages are weird.*

Okay, that's very Anglo-centric, I know it. But I have to mention this problem because it's one of the most common complaints about learning Chinese, and it's one of the aspects of the language that westerners are notoriously bad at. Every person who tackles Chinese at first has a little trouble believing this aspect of the language. How is it possible that shùxué means "mathematics" while shūxuě means "blood transfusion", or that guòjiǎng means "you flatter me" while guǒjiàng means "fruit paste"?

单词表

ridiculous	*adj.*	可笑的，荒谬的；荒唐的，愚蠢的
indisputable	*adj.*	无可争辩的；不容置疑的；无可否认的
fetishist	*n.*	盲目崇拜者
cognate	*adj.*	同宗的，同根的，同语系的
	n.	同家族的人，同源词

V. Story Links

1. 英语前重心与汉语后重心

英语句子呈现句首封闭、句尾开放的特征，使得英语句子变得繁复。具体表现在以下几个方面：

（1）修饰语、插入语后置，又有关系词与被修饰语连接，句子可以不断向句尾伸展、延伸。

（2）先行代词“it”及其他预指性代词，把真正的主语或宾语移到后面，并根据需要加以不断扩充，形成句子的末端重量（end-weight）。

（3）英语句子可以顺线性向后延展（natural linear expansion）的特点，导致句子长度大大超过汉语，也使句子变得繁复。

以一首著名英语儿歌为例：

基本句：This is the farmer that sowed the corn,

向后延伸：That kept the cock that crowed in the morn,

再延伸：That waked the priest all shaven and shorn,

再延伸：That married the man all tattered and torn,

再延伸：That kissed the maiden all forlorn,

再延伸：That milked the cow with the crumpled horn,

再延伸：That tossed the dog,

再延伸：That worried the cat,

再延伸：That killed the rat,

再延伸：That ate the malt,

再延伸：That lay in the house that Jack built.

从理论上说，英语 right-branching（右向分枝）的扩展是无限的，因而句子可以拉得很长，但汉语句子无法借助连接词不断地向后扩展，必须在适当的地方收缩，另行处理其余信息：杰克盖了那栋房子，房子里堆放着麦芽，麦芽让老鼠吃了，老鼠被猫宰了。

汉语句子则呈现句首开放、句尾收缩的特征：

（1）句首虽可开放，向左伸展，但扩展的长度和程度受到种种限制。

（2）汉语句子只能逆线性向前延伸，因而句子显得简短。

基本句：学术报告。

向前延伸：关于当代语言学研究动向的学术报告。

再延伸：李教授关于当代语言学研究动向的研究报告。

再延伸：你们到语言学院听了李教授关于当代语言学研究动向的学术报告。

再延伸：我听说你们到语言学院听了李教授关于当代语言学研究动向的学术报告。

再延伸：昨天我听说你们到语言学院听了李教授关于当代语言学研究动向的学术报告。

2. 段连城在《怎样对外介绍中国》一书中曾经举过一个例子，说的是某市举办国际龙舟会，彩色打印了宣传品，原文和译文如下：

中华大地，江河纵横；华夏文化，源远流长……（然后才讲到本地，再讲到龙舟节）轻快的龙舟如银河流星，瑰丽的彩船似海市蜃楼，两岸那金碧辉煌的彩楼连成一片水晶宫，是仙境？是梦境？仰视彩鸽翔飞，低眸漂灯流霓，焰火怒放火树银花，灯舞回旋千姿百态，气垫船腾起一片春潮，射击手点破满天彩球，跳伞健儿绽空中花蕾，抢鸭勇士谱水上凯歌，还有雀鸟争鸣，花卉盆景竞艳，书画、工艺展览铺出琳琅满目的画廊……啊，（某某）城是不夜城，龙舟会是群英会。

The divine land of China has its rivers flowing across; the brilliant culture of China has its roots tracing back long...

The light-some dragon-boats appear on the river as though the stars twinkle in the milkyway. The richly decorated pleasure boats look like a scene of mirage. The splendent awnings in green and gold chain into a palace of crystal. Is this a fairy-land or a mere dream? Looking above, you can see the beautiful doves flying about. Looking below, you can see the sailing lamps glittering. Cracking are the fireworks, which present you a picture of fiery trees and silver flowers. Circling are the lantern-dancers, who present you a variation of exquisite manner. Over there the motor-boats are plowing the water, thus a tide stirs up. Over there, the marksmen are shooting to their targets; thus colourful beads whirl around. Besides, the birds' chirping, the potted landscape's charm, the exhibition of arts and painting, all claim a strong appeal to you. Therefore, we should say: XXX is a city of no light; its Dragon-Boat Festival a gathering of heroes.

Come on, Dear Friends! Come on, Honorable guests!

翻译这类辞藻华丽的宣传品，译者可谓煞费苦心。一位外国友人读了之后，觉得不知所云，文中充满了极度夸张（full of hyperbole）的手法，于是坦率地写出了以下评语：

不幸的是，我的第一个反应是发笑，因为文字首先就充满了错误。文中没有提供关于龙舟会的必要材料，例如其历史起源和举行的时间，这些材料都是重要的。文中用种种离奇的、夸大的说法表明龙舟会多么了不起，但无意中却使用了滑稽的语言，而得不到什么信息。这份彩页文字还有一个常见的毛病，就是缺少必要的背景说明，作者是假定外国读者对中国历史和文化的许多方面都已熟知。这篇介绍也没告诉你：怎样去参加龙舟会，地点在哪里，何时开幕和闭幕，要花多少钱，等等。这些都是要到一个地方去参观的人需要知道的。

中国语言在描述时善于通过生动的形象和修辞手法传达画面感，给读者带来强烈视觉和感官冲击，虽然表述方式可能在外国人眼中显得不拘一格，而这正是语言的差异所在，也是汉语独特的韵味和魅力所在。

VI. Did You Know?

1. 英语是静态（Static）语言；汉语是动态（Dynamic）语言

英语有一种少用动词，或使用其他手段表示动作意义的自然倾向，而汉语往往大量采用兼语式或连动式的说法。

英语的静态特征表现是多维的，如使用非谓语动词或非限定动词（动词的-ed 形式、-ing 形式和不定式）、省略动词（如 be 或谓语成分）以及将动词名词化等——如使用动词的同源名词（如 realize—realization，free—freedom，master—mastery）、同源形容词（如 support—supportive，doubt—doubtful）、介词及副词等。相对而言，汉语的动词由于无英语动词那样的形态变化，若要表达动作意义，往往别无选择，只能采用动词本身。试比较下列各句：

I fell madly in love with her, and she with me. 译文：我疯狂地爱上了她，她也疯狂地爱上了我。（英语可省略动词，汉语却不可。）

A woman with fair opportunities, and without an absolute hump may marry whom she likes. 译文：一个女人只要不是十分驼背，就有平等机会，想嫁给谁就嫁给谁。（英语用介词，汉语得用动词。）

Back and forth his head swiveled, desire waxing, resolution waning. 译文：他来回晃着脑袋，欲望在膨胀，意志在萎缩。（英语用独立结构，汉语则用动词。）

I am afraid of you misunderstanding me. 译文：我担心你误解了我。（英语用动名词复合结构，汉语却用动词。）

But this very formulation is indicative of the underlying attitude. 译文：但这一说法已表明其内心态度。（英语用同根形容词 indicate—indicative，汉语只能用动词。）

This would be the confirmation that it was in general use. 译文：这将证实它的使用是十分普遍的。（英语用同根名词，confirm—confirmation，汉语不得不用动词。）

其实，英语除上述同源词外，还有众多的词可用来表示动作意义。例如：glance，glimpse，

look, mention, close, 等等。形容词如 able, afraid, aware, capable, good, 等等。例如: The very sight of it makes me nervous. 一看见他，我就感到紧张。I'm sure of it. 对此我深信不疑。

2. 英语重物称（Impersonal）；汉语重人称（Personal）

英语的重物称倾向在其造句中十分明显。最具代表性的是对主语的择定，英语常常出人意料地选择不能施行动作或无生命的词语作主语。相对而言，汉语一般更习惯人称化的表达，尤其是主语，能施行动作或有生命的物体为主语首选。这也是英汉表达的显著差异之一。试读以下内容：

（1）A wave of cigar smoke accompanied Ogilvie in. 奥格尔维进门时带进来一缕雪茄烟雾。（汉语不说：一缕雪茄烟雾伴随着奥格尔维进来了。）

（2）"Hi！ Hi!" said the cab driver, whose door popped open at the very sight of a traveler. "嗨！嗨！"出租车司机嚷道，他一瞅见乘客就"砰"的一声打开车门。（汉语不说："嗨！嗨！"出租车司机嚷道，车门在瞅见乘客时"砰"的一声打开了。）

（3）Bitterness fed on the man who had made the world laugh. 这个曾给全世界带来笑声的人自己却饱尝辛酸。（汉语不说：痛苦哺育了这个使全世界的人发出笑声的人。）

VII. Cultural Reflection

关于英汉语常用的表达方式，连淑能在《英汉对比研究》一书中进行了详细的阐述。可以简单地归结为一点：汉语是悟性表达，英语是理性表达。具体说来两种语言的表达差异在于以下几点：

一、汉语常用的表达方式

汉语的哲学背景是儒、道、佛的悟性，遣词造句的最大特点是采用意合法（parataxis），重意义组合而轻形式结构，让读者和听者领悟其中的意义和关系；词没有严格意义的形态变化，用词注重功能、意义；句子不受严谨的主谓结构的约束，少用或不用关联词词语，摆脱形式的束缚，直接表达现实和思维过程，体现悟性的象似性（iconicity），词语之间的关系常在不言之中，语法意义和逻辑关联常隐含在字里行间；造句富于弹性，灵活多变，着重意念，颇多隐含；讲究语意、文气和语感的通畅，言不尽意，富于领悟空间，对语境依赖较多；流水句很常见，话如行云流水，随意自然流动；完全句与不完全句混合交错，松句、散句、紧缩句、无主句、省略句、并列式复句交替并用；句子之间可断可连，流泻铺排；主谓难分，主从难辨，形散神聚，言简意赅，“意尽为界”。悟性和“约定俗成”的语用规则决定句义。要正确理解句义和语意，必须从词语的意义、功能以及语段、篇章和语境中去分析、领悟、体味。

汉语语篇注重话题，注重“意识流”，注重事理和先后顺序，常常采用非演绎式的，往往是领悟式的归纳型、经验式的临摹型或螺旋式、漫谈式的思维模式；注重隐性连贯，经常只把事情或意思排列起来，让读者自己去领悟其间的关系，呈现曲折起伏、断续离合、若即若离的风格；喜欢“摆事实，讲道理”，信息安排常常按照“自然”语序（natural order）：由远及近，“层层剥笋”，逐层深入，头长尾短，先叙述一些背景、历史、条件、环境、事实、情况、情节、理由、原因、分析、例证等，再给出主要的或重要的判断、结论、观点、态度、要旨、结果、行为等（specific-to-general sequence）；或按照“开篇说明—历史回顾—现状解释—观点态度—今后任务”这类模式。语篇开头注重的是“where the argument/talk is coming from”，通常反映了现实的时间和事理顺序，犹如对现实生活经历的临摹；也有类似英语的逻辑顺序。大多数语篇缺乏主题句，类似“点评式”议论或“体会式”言论。章句以意役形，以神统形，传神写意，画龙点睛，言简意赅，重意会而轻法则。

悟性有模糊性的特征，因而汉语模糊性较大，歧义现象较多：一个深层结构（语义结构）可表现为多个表层结构（句法结构），多个深层结构可表现为一个表层结构（如：这锅饭能吃十个人／十个人能吃这锅饭、神秘的少女的心、我差一点没跟他结婚）。许多表达方式在英美人看来是非逻辑的（例如：救火、晒太阳、在家养病、一匹马骑两个人、你想死我了、昨晚我盖了两条被子），但中国人通过“约定俗成”的悟性，并没有产生任何误解。

二、英语常用的表达方式

英语的哲学背景是亚里士多德开创的严密的形式逻辑，以及 16 至 18 世纪风行欧洲的理性主义。英语用词造句成章的最大特点是采用形合（hypotaxis），重形式结构协调，让读者和听者分析其中的意义和关系：词有严格意义的形态变化，用词强调“人称”“数”“格”等的一致；句子受严谨的主谓结构协调一致（S.V. concord）及“逻辑主语”与“逻辑谓语”协调一致的制约（这相当于亚里士多德判断结构的逻辑“主词”和逻辑“宾词”）；多用或常用关联词语，注重形式接应；“前呼后应”，显性衔接（explicit cohesion），以形显义、以形统意、以法摄神，以形态变化制约句子结构，注重语法关系和语义逻辑；大量句子虽枝叶横生、盘根错节、环扣镶嵌、句中有句、繁复多变，犹如“参天大树”，但结构完整、形态外露、主从分明、严谨规范、语法和意义协调一致，对语境依赖较少；语法和逻辑决定句义，要正确理解句义和语意，必须分析词的形式、句子的结构和前后的逻辑关系。

英语语篇常受亚里士多德的演绎法逻辑思维模式的影响，突出主语和主题句，注重分析推理，直线性、有秩序、有层次地围绕主题展开；信息安排往往采用“突显”语序（salient order）：

由近及远，开门见山，一语中的，头短尾长，先点出主要的或重要的判断、结论、观点、态度、要旨、结果、行为等，再追叙一些与此有关的背景、历史、条件、环境、事实、情况、情节、理由、原因、分析、例证等；语篇开头注重的是“where the argument/talk is going”；也有受培根的归纳法逻辑思维模式的影响，采用相反的语序，或按照时间先后的自然语序。

理性有确定性的特征，因而英语表达方式比较严谨、精确，模糊性较小，歧义现象较少；定义、概念明确，用词造句遵守严格的词法和句法；造句成章也服从某种逻辑规则，适合于科学思维和理性思维，也便于“以理服人”。

VIII. Homework

1. 唇枪舌剑

语言决定思维还是思维决定语言？

2. 思辨研讨

古希腊语是极为明晰、精确的语言，因而有人认为古希腊人极强的逻辑思辨能力是由古希腊语造就的。对此，你怎么看？

参考资料

一、书籍

连淑能 . 英汉对比研究 [M]. 北京：高等教育出版社，2010.

刘宓庆 . 汉英对比研究与翻译 [M]. 南昌：江西教育出版社，1991.

潘文国 . 汉英语言对比概论 [M]. 北京：商务印书馆，2010.

潘文国 . 字本位与汉语研究 [M]. 上海：华东师范大学出版社，2002.

Celce-Murcia, Marianne, and Diane Larsen-Freeman. The Grammar Book: An ESL/EFL Teacher's Course[M]. Boston: Heinle & Heinle, 1999.

Brown, H. Douglas. Principles of Language Learning and Teaching[M]. White Plains, NY: Pearson Education, 2007.

Swan, Michael. Practical English Usage[M]. Oxford: Oxford University Press, 2005.

Odlin, Terence. Language Transfer: Cross-Linguistic Influence in Language Learning[M]. Cambridge: Cambridge University Press, 1989.

二、网站

http://www.cssn.cn/yyx/（中国社会科学网）

Chapter Six

The Contrast of Chinese and Western Customs and Habits

课前成果检测

中西方习俗阅读测试题

一、单选题

1. 介绍两人相识的顺序一般是 ________。

A. 先把上级介绍给下级　　B. 先把晚辈介绍给长辈

C. 先把主人介绍给客人　　D. 先把早到的客人介绍给晚到的客人

2. 吃西餐时，若需中途离开，可将刀叉摆成 ________。

A. 八字形　　B. 二字形　　C. 十字形　　D. 随意形状

3. 参加宴会时，筷子不应该 ________。

A. 交叉摆放　　B. 插在碗里　　C. 搁在碗上　　D. 放在桌上

4. “庖丁解牛”出自我国古代著作 ________。

A.《论语》　　B.《孟子》　　C.《庄子》　　D.《春秋》

5. 我国最早阐述“药食同源”理论的书籍是 ________。

A.《黄帝内经》 B.《千金要方》 C.《饮膳正要》 D.《本草纲目》

6. 我国传统节日之一的重阳节又称 ________。

A. 敬老节 B. 女儿节 C. 天中节 D. 踏青节

7. 地理环境是中、西方社会形态和文化模式的横向决定因素之一。因此工业革命前西方社会中的 ________ 特别发达，而中国社会中的 ________ 特别发达。

A. 畜牧业和商业；农业 B. 农业；商业

C. 工业和农业；畜牧业 D. 商业；工业

8. 西方特殊的地理、气候条件促成的游牧业，尤其是商贸活动，强化了西方文化的动态性，导致西方人的家庭观念相对薄弱，促使他们的 ________ 等价值观念发展非常充分。

A. 集体主义 B. 利他主义

C. 博爱主义 D. 个人主义、自由主义

9. 新婚蜜月旅行起源于 ________。

A. 英国 B. 法国 C. 西班牙 D. 美国

10. ________ 是美国独创的，是最具美国特色的节日。

A. 情人节 B. 圣诞节 C. 五朔节 D. 感恩节

二、填空题

1. 人生中标志不同年龄阶段和身份变化的重要环节及相关的各种仪式，主要包括 ________、________、________ 和 ________。它是一种世俗仪式，一般又称为“通过仪式”。

2. 满汉全席原是 ________ 举办宴会时 ________ 和 ________ 合做的大型筵席。满汉全席上菜一般起码 ________ 种，分 ________ 吃完。其既有宫廷菜肴之特色，又有地方风味之精华；突出满族菜点的特殊风味，同时又展示了汉族烹调的特色。

3. 岁时节日，主要指与 ________、________ 的周期性转换相适应，在人们的社会生活中约定俗成的、具有某种 ________ 的特定时日。

4. 服役婚是指原始社会 ________ 向 ________ 转变时期的一种婚俗。男子在婚前或婚后住在妻方 ________ 一段时间，作为代价偿还妻方 ________ 的损失，换娶妻子到本氏族或本家族中来。

5. 中国的葬俗有 ________、________、________、________、________、________、________、________、________ 等。

三、问答题

1. 请写出下列白兰地酒龄标识的含义：

V.O　　　　V.S.O　　　　V.S.O.P　　　　X.O

2. 分享一下你们当地春节、元宵节、清明节、端午节、中秋节等节日的食俗。

3. 谈谈中国百姓神灵崇拜的主要特征。

4. 如今中国人对于西方节日的态度日渐开明，庆祝西方节日的隆重程度有赶超中国节日之嫌，对于这种现象，你怎么看？

5. 中国人一起吃饭总爱抢着付账单，而西方人通常都是 AA 制，你更倾向于哪一种？为什么？

四、思考题

诗仙李白在《月下独酌·其二》中写道："天若不爱酒，酒星不在天。地若不爱酒，地应无酒泉。天地既爱酒，爱酒不愧天。"诗句表达了中国人对于酒的热爱。西方的葡萄酒之父路易·巴斯德也曾经说过"没有葡萄酒的一餐，犹如没有阳光的一天"，由此可见西方人对于酒的喜爱。试从酒的原料、酒的制作方法、品酒的方式、饮酒礼仪以及饮酒的目的等方面思考并总结中、西方的白酒文化和红酒文化的差异。

Section One

The Contrast of Chinese and Western Cuisines

I. Learning Objectives

1. To study the characteristics of the Western and Chinese food culture
2. To summarize the reasons for the differences between Western and Chinese food

II. Key Points and Difficult Points

1. To compare Chinese and Western attitudes towards food
2. To understand and summarize the differences of table manner in China and the West
3. To compare the different ways of hospitality in China and the West

III. Lead-in Questions

1. Can you name some famous Chinese and Western cuisines and dishes?
2. What is the relationship between the geographical location and food culture?
3. How can different philosophies influence food culture?
4. What are different table manners and business etiquette in China and the West?

IV. Learning Contents

1. European Food History

European food has a distinct flavor and rich history. The food in Europe can be characterized by four categories: meats, sugar, cereals, and fats. Meats include tripe, fish, blood sausages, and wild game. Brought from India and the New World, cane sugar became a necessary ingredient in European recipes and foods. Europeans loved the sweet taste and the demand for sugar cane grew at the end of the 17th century. Cereals are the most important ingredients in European cuisine. Flour, bread, wheat, oats, and other grains provide people with the most nutritious and healthy meals. During the 18th century, though, new crops rose to popularity. Maize and potatoes were brought from the New World and became favorite foods in Northern Europe. Rice and pasta especially grew famous in Spain and Italy. Peas and beans are still a staple food in Europe. However, their popularity diminished over time as potatoes and cereals took their place as the main foods. The most used fats in Europe are olive oil, lard, and butter. Today, fats are indispensable as they are almost always used when cooking. Coffee, tea, alcoholic beverages, and chocolate are the most well-known drinks in Europe. Since water was not being purified until recently and was not safe to drink, it was not considered a beverage for a long time. Instead, wine, beer, ale, gin, and whiskey were the most popular drinks in Europe. Coffee, chocolate, and tea were brought from Africa, America, and Asia. Today, all of these drinks are popular, but pure water is consumed a lot more than it was a few centuries ago.

单词表

tripe	*n.*	内脏
ingredient	*n.*	成分，材料
maize	*n.*	玉米
staple food		主食
diminish	*v.*	减少，缩减
lard	*n.*	猪油

2. Chinese Food History

With origins dating back millennia, the history of Chinese food is certainly long and incredibly delicious. Chinese cuisine is said to have originated in the central part of China, and is one of just three cuisines (French and Turkish are the other two) that profoundly influenced countries throughout East Asia. Studies of Chinese food history point to literature that indicate China was cooking barbecued meat, grilled fish, and other "common" foods over 5,000 years ago.

Chinese cuisine as we now know it evolved gradually over the centuries as new food sources and techniques were introduced, discovered, or invented. Although many of the characteristics we think of as the most important appeared very early, others did not appear or did not become important until relatively late. The first chopsticks, for instance, were probably used for cooking, stirring the fire, and serving bits of food and were not initially used as eating utensils. They began to take on this role during the Han Dynasty, but it was not until the Ming that they became ubiquitous for both serving and eating. It was not until the Ming that they acquired their present name (kuaizi) and their present shape. The wok may also have been introduced during the Han, but again its initial use was limited (to drying grains) and its present use (to stir-fry, as well as boiling, steaming, roasting, and deep-frying) did not develop until the Ming. The Ming also saw the adoption of new plants from the New World, such as maize, peanuts, and tobacco.

Chinese cuisine was crafted around the five flavors—sweet, sour, bitter, pungent, and salty. Dishes tend to be prepared following one or a number of preparation methods. A Chinese cook—whether domestic or commercial—will know how to braise, steam, stir-fry, deep-fry, boil, or roast. Fermentation is also a feature of Chinese food, making its way into sauces, side dishes, and condiments. And of course, there is the ubiquitous presence of steamed rice at virtually every meal.

In addition to rice, Chinese cuisine is also famous for its diverse array of noodle and dumpling dishes. Noodles, made from wheat flour, are a staple in many regions, especially in the north, where the climate favors wheat over rice. They can be served in soups, stir-fried, or boiled, and are often paired with rich broths, meats, or vegetables. Dumplings, another quintessential part of Chinese cuisine, are typically made from flour dough filled with a variety of fillings such as pork, beef, or vegetables. These can be steamed, boiled, or pan-fried, offering a delightful array of textures and flavors. Both noodles and dumplings reflect the regional diversity and culinary ingenuity of Chinese cuisine.

单词表

millennia	*n.*	一千年
utensil	*n.*	厨具
ubiquitous	*adj.*	十分普遍的
pungent	*adj.*	辛辣的
fermentation	*n.*	发酵

V. Story Links

1. 5 Famous Chinese Dishes

(1) Jiaozi (Chinese dumplings)

Chinese dumplings are made with a wheat-based flour dough and filled with a stuffing of pork, beef, shrimp, or vegetables. They are commonly eaten during Chinese New Year and eaten all year round in the northern provinces. As legend tells it, during the Eastern Han Dynasty (25–220 CE), there lived a famous physician of Traditional Chinese Medicine, named Zhang Zhongjing, who was returning to his ancestral village one winter. It was a difficult winter and many living in impoverished conditions were experiencing ill effects from the cold. To help people, Zhongjing took mutton, herbs, and chilis and wrapped them in the dough, forming them in the shape of an ear. He then steamed them to bind everything together and keep them warm. These steaming, pillow-like treats helped people overcome the cold conditions, while the herbs that Zhongjing put inside worked to improve blood circulation and prevent frostbite.

(2) Dongpo Pork

Dongpo Pork is named after Su Dongpo, a famous poet, writer, artist, and statesman who lived during the Northern Song Dynasty (960–1127). He was also a famed gastronome, noted for inventing the braised pork belly dish, Dongpo Pork. As the story goes, one day Su had a pot of braised pork simmering on the stove when an old friend visited him and challenged him to a game of Chinese chess. As the challenging game consumed his focus, Su lost track of time and consequently overcooked his pork to the point where it gave off a fragrance as it began to burn, thus creating this culinary dish. The pork was rich in flavor, deep red color, tender and crispy, but not burnt. His friends named this fragrant dish after him. Su made this dish when he served as an official in Hangzhou which is the heartland of the country's gastronomy. This dish can be found in many restaurants across Hangzhou, where the signature preparation of Dongpo Pork features tender braised pork belly, served with a rich, flavorful sauce, often accompanied by steamed buns or rice. The pork is traditionally cooked slowly to achieve a melt-in-the-mouth texture, allowing the flavors to fully develop.

(3) Kung Pao Chicken

Kung Pao chicken, also known as Kung Po or Kung Po chicken, is a popular Chinese dish that is believed to have originated in the Sichuan Province of China. The dish is characterized by its spicy and savory flavors, as well as its combination of peanuts, vegetables, and meat (usually chicken). It is believed that Kung Pao Chicken was named after Ding Baozhen (1820–1886), a governor in the late Qing Dynasty (1616–1911) of Sichuan Province. Ding Baozhen was a "foodie" who loved eating diced chicken, peanuts and especially loved spicy flavors. During his time as governor, he frequently treated his guests with this dish. He was granted the title of Taizi Shaobao, also known as Kung Pao, which means the "Prince's Guardian". People named this dish to honor and remember him.

(4) Mapo Tofu

Mapo Tofu can be found in nearly any Chinese restaurant around the world with hundreds of variations adapting the piquant original to suit local tastes. Mapo Tofu is a popular dish from Sichuan Province, where spicy food is king and the signature spice of the region—the Sichuan peppercorn—gives dishes a unique "numbing" effect.

Mapo Tofu is consisted of tofu set in a spicy sauce, typically a thin, oily, and bright red suspension, based on doubanjiang (fermented broadbean and chili paste) and douchi (fermented black beans), along with minced meat, usually pork or beef. Variations exist with other ingredients such as water chestnuts, onions, other vegetables, or wood ear mushrooms.

"Ma" stands for "ma-zi" which means pockmarks. "Po" is the first syllable of "popo" which means an old woman or grandma. Hence, mapo is an old woman whose face is pockmarked. It is thus sometimes translated as "pockmarked grandma's beancurd". Mapo lived in Chengdu, the capital city of Sichuan, in the middle of the 19th century. She operated a makeshift roadside café on the outskirts of town; her customers were mainly small tradesmen and porters. They often brought beef and tofu to the café asking Mapo to cook for them. Over time, Mapo mastered the unique tofu cooking technique and local people named the dish Mapo Tofu. For an authentic Sichuan style Mapo Tofu, the floral tongue-numbing Sichuan peppercorn is a must. Along with the fiery heat from the chili pepper, it provides a circus of sensation in your mouth.

(5) Beggar's Chicken (Jiao Hua Ji)

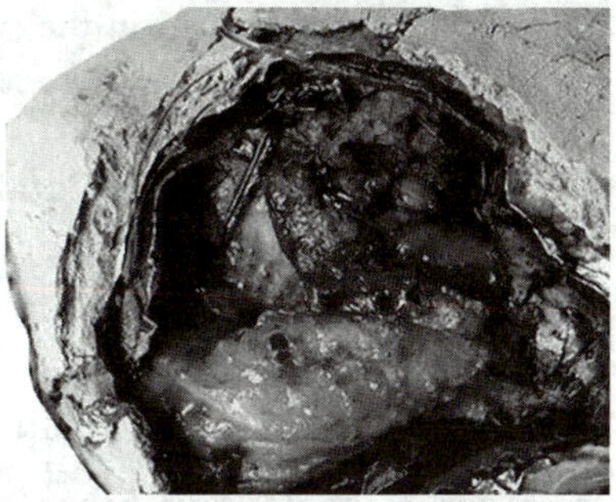

This dish is also known as yellow mud stewed chicken, a famous dish in Changshu, Jiangsu Province. The prepared chicken is covered with clay and lotus leaves and baked slowly using low heat. Preparation may take up to six hours. There are various legends surrounding the origins of beggar's chicken. One version of the story is: A beggar stole a chicken from a farm but had no pot or utensils, so he wrapped the bird in lotus leaves and packed clay or mud around it, set it in a hole where he had lit a fire, and buried it. When he dug up the chicken and cracked open the clay, he found the meat was tender and aromatic.

2. Five fabulous foods of Europe

(1) Germany—Eisbein

Essentially a boiled pork knuckle, Eisbein is best enjoyed with sauerkraut and mustard, and washed down with a tasty German beer.

(2) Italy—Pizza

The origins and styles of pizza-making are incredibly varied, making it hard to know what a "real" pizza should be like! The idea of adding toppings to hot bread probably dates back to the cavemen, and it was actually the Greeks who probably debuted what we think of as pizzas today. But the word "pizza", meaning "pie", was coined in around 1800 CE near Rome and Naples. By the end of the 18th Century, people had discovered that tomatoes (which were brought over from the New World) were edible, and had begun to top bread with tomatoes, essentially creating pizza as we know it. In around 1889, Italy's Queen Margherita and King Umberto I toured their kingdom, and the queen developed a taste for the flat bread. Her chef created a variety of pizzas for her, including one that featured basil, tomatoes and mozzarella cheese—the colors of the Italian flag. She loved it, and even today the ingredients for a Margherita pizza remain the same!

(3) Belgium—Moules-frites

A classic from Belgium and also enjoyed in Northern France, moules-frites is a pretty simple dish, consisting of a load of mussels (typically cooked in white wine and cream) and a load of fries. The mussels are often served in the pan, making for a rustic—and very tasty—traditional meal.

(4) Spain—Faves a la Catalana

This is a great example of Catalan cuisine. In fact, it's considered one of the three most important dishes in Catalonia! Traditionally it's made with butifarra negra, Spanish blood sausages, fresh garlic shoots, fava beans, pancetta and a range of herbs and spices.

(5) Switzerland—Fondue

Fondue is a Swiss melted cheese and wine dish served in a communal pot (caquelon or fondue pot) over a portable stove (réchaud) heated with a candle or spirit lamp, and eaten by dipping bread into the cheese using long-stemmed forks.

VI. Did You Know?

1. 西方的饮食文化

西方的饮食文化实际上就是面包文化，因为面包和黄油是西方人最常吃的食物，所以英文中以 bread and butter 表示“生计”。live on the breadline 的意思是“勉强维持生计”，其中 breadline 指领取救济食品的队伍。He knows which side his bread is buttered on. 其引申的意思是“他知道自己的利益所在”。Bread is the staff of life. 与我们的“民以食为天”意思相近。

2. 关于食物的习语

（1）Radish and ginger keep away from doctor. 冬吃萝卜夏吃姜，不劳医生开药方。

（2）Diet cures more than doctors. 自己饮食有节，胜过上门求医。

（3）Eat at pleasure, drink with measure. 随意吃饭，适度饮酒。

（4）Don't put all your eggs in one basket. 不要把一切希望寄托在一件事上。

（5）It's no use crying over spilt milk. 覆水难收，后悔无益。

（6）A corn was good till bread was found. 饥不择食。

（7）As you brew, so must you drink. 自作自受。

（8）It is difficult to cater for all tastes. 众口难调。

VII. Cultural Reflection

作家陆文夫说："饮食是一种文化，而且是一种大文化。所谓大文化是因为饮食与地理、历史、物产、习俗和社会科学、自然科学的各个方面都有关联。"不同民族和国家有着各具特色的食物和饮食方式，中西方饮食文化差异的表象主要体现在中西方对于饮食的态度、食材的内容、用餐方式以及餐桌礼仪的不同。

孔子曾说"饮食男女，人之大欲存焉"，告子也曾说"食色，性也"。自古至今，中国文化中一直崇尚"民以食为天"，这种"泛食主义"的文化倾向在汉语中得到了充分体现。中国人常通过与食物相关的词语来表达情感，例如，职业被称为"饭碗"，思考被比作"咀嚼"，体验被称作"品味"，嫉妒说成"吃醋"，用"小菜一碟"形容做某事轻而易举。除此之外，还有像"家常便饭"、"一口吃个胖子"、"吃得开"、"吃不了兜着走"、"喝西北风"和"吃一堑长一智"等这样将食物与情感、心理活动、生活态度等紧密相连的形象表达。这种文化现象体现出食物在中国社会和语言中的特殊地位和丰富的象征意义。在中国文化中，食物不仅仅是维持生命的必需品，更是与情感、社会关系紧密相连的重要符号。中国的饮食观念注重感性体验，重视食物的味道及其带给人的心理感受。食物还是一种保持健康的手段，人们通过食疗来调节身体与情绪。此外，饮食在中国文化中有着重要的社会功能，它是人与人之间增进感情、解决矛盾、维系关系的重要方式。在现代社会，食物依旧是商务交往中的关键工具，承载着深层次的文化意义。与此不同的是，西方国家的饮食观念则更多着眼于理性，食物主要被视为生存必需品和交际工具，侧重于营养和实用性，人们较少关注其带来的情感体验或文化象征。在西方，饮食的功能更多是用来庆祝、感谢或进行社交活动，其文化意义相对简单，而不会像在中国那样产生深远的影响。因此，食物在中国文化中的地位与功能远远超出了日常生活的需求，成为情感表达、社交互动与文化传承的重要载体。

在食材的选择上，中国人大多"求精、求美"，而西方人可能更讲究营养均衡。中国地大物博，饮食文化内容丰富，迄今为止已经孕育出了诸多菜系和流派。中国人重"吃味"，在菜看的选材用料上选择范围比较广泛。中国饮食文化起源于农耕文化，决定了中国人的饮食结构以农作物为主，肉类为辅，强调荤素搭配，喜食果蔬，讲究杂食。而西餐文化中食物只是用作充饥而已，因此大块肉、大块鸡被作为食材。西方饮食文化起源于畜牧业文化，决定了西方饮食结构偏重肉类与肉制品。

中国人请客吃饭采取“共享”的形式，共享一个圆桌，共享一桌美食，餐后还要争相地结账，突出了一个“和”字。而西方深受个人主义思想的影响，多采用长桌，餐饮一人一份，餐后AA制付钱，体现了对个性、自我的尊重。

饮食受到文化的制约，又跟民族文化密不可分。中西方在自然地理环境、社会发展、传统文化思想、生活习俗等方面的差异，造就了中西饮食文化的差异。

早期中国文化受地理环境的制约很大。中国位于亚洲大陆的东南部，西北部是茫茫的沙漠、草原和戈壁，东南则是无垠的大海，地理环境差异很大，因此中国人一般“靠山吃山、靠海吃海”。中国人的主食以米、面为主，这主要是因为我国的很多地区适宜农作物生长。

西方文明的发源地所提供的天然生活材料不是那么充裕。因此为了生存，探索自然界的奥秘、开发和利用自然资源服务于人类就成了欧洲精神的主流。西方许多国家属于温带海洋性气候区，这种气候很适合畜牧业和渔业的发展，广阔的牧场和海洋给人们提供了乳制品、牛羊肉及各种海产品，这就决定了西方人以肉食为主的饮食习惯。

饮食观念是人们在食物的制作和食用过程中所形成的观念，深受自然科学、人文科学，尤其是哲学的影响。不同的哲学思想及由此形成的文化精神和思维方式将产生不同的饮食观念。中国的饮食观念是五味调和，西方的饮食观念是突出个性。这主要是由中国和西方国家不同的哲学思想及因此形成的文化精神和思维方式而产生的。首先，从哲学思想看，中国哲学思想的一个重要核心是讲究“气”与“有无相生”；西方哲学思想则讲究实体与虚空的分离与对立。其次，从文化精神来看，中国人讲究天人合一，强调整体功能；西方人讲究物我二分，强调形式结构。再次，在认识事物的思维方式上，基于哲学思想的不同，西方的思维注重思辨和条分缕析，而中国人的思维倾向于综合和整体，强调对整体与部分的关系。

中西方饮食在观念、礼仪、内容等方面存在的差异，都可以在文化上找到根源。饮食文化也是跨文化交际中非语言文化的一部分，了解中西方饮食文化的具体差异和造成差异的原因，可以避免在交际过程中由于不当的饮食行为而造成误解。中国是饮食之邦，也是礼仪之邦，地域辽阔，民族众多，经过几千年的发展形成了丰富多彩的饮食文化，我们应努力弘扬中华民族的优秀饮食文化传统，使之不断得到更新与发展。

VIII. Homework

1. 美食对对碰

从 BBC 美食网站（http://www.bbc.co.uk/food/recipes/）上选择一个让你垂涎欲滴的美食菜谱分享给大家，感受一下西餐与中餐带给味蕾的不同体验吧！

2. 五分钟演讲

"一方水土养一方人"，谈谈你对这句话的理解。

3. 美食视频制作

挑选一道家乡美食，以"舌尖上的中国"为例，制作一个长度为 5～10 分钟的美食视频，把你的家乡推广到全世界吧！

4. 调查报告

茶庄 vs. 星巴克

一壶茶，一本书；一杯咖啡，一个闲适的午后。茶与咖啡展现的是怎样的人生态度和文化差异呢？

Section Two

The Contrast of Chinese and Western Holidays

I. Learning Objectives

1. To understand the different origins of traditional festivals in China and the West
2. To compare and contrast different traditions and customs of festivals
3. To understand different social functions of traditional festivals

II. Key Points and Difficult Points

1. To compare different cultural connotations conveyed by Halloween and Chinese Ghost Festival, Western Valentine's Day and Chinese Double Seventh Day
2. To learn the legends concerning the festivals
3. To learn how to write business holiday cards
4. To study cultural differences of Chinese and Western festivals

III. Lead-in Questions

1. What are the origins of Western festivals?
2. Can you name some Chinese farming festivals?
3. What is the relationship between the economy and the holidays?

IV. Learning Contents

1. Top 5 Most Famous Carnivals in Europe

(1) Santa Cruz de Tenerife Carnival, Spain

The Carnival of Santa Cruz de Tenerife, in the Canary Islands, is the second most popular and internationally known celebration after Brazil's. Rhythm, color, luxury and a lot of spectacles during fifteen days overflow the streets of this Canarian city. For the entire week the people of Tenerife party to the rhythm of a lively Latin soundtrack, with performances by renowned artists adding to the festive atmosphere.

(2) Cologne Carnival, Germany

The Cologne Carnival is a carnival that takes place every year in Cologne, Germany. Traditionally, the "fifth season" (carnival season) is declared open at 11 minutes past 11 on the 11th of November. The time of merrymaking in the streets is officially declared open at downtown square "Alter Markt" on the Thursday before the beginning of Lent. Street carnival, a week-long street festival, also called "the crazy days", takes place between Fat Thursday (Weiberfastnacht) and Ash Wednesday (Aschermittwoch). The highlight of carnival is Rose Monday (Rosenmontag), two days before Ash Wednesday. All through these days, Cologne folks go out masqueraded. The typical greeting during the festival is Kölle Alaaf!, a Kölsch phrase.

(3) Nice Carnival, France

The famous Carnival of Nice is one of the greatest cultural events of the French Riviera and one of the most important carnivals in the world and France. Musicians and dancers will walk down the streets. A creative procession composed of 2 different events: the Carnival Parade and the Parade of Flowers will take place.

(4) Cadiz Carnival, Spain

The Cadiz carnival is known throughout the world as a huge street party. Eleven days of non-stop fun, originality and, more than anything else, mass participation. The whole city is transformed, the streets are filled with people intent on having a good time and making sure everyone else has a good time, singing, and enjoying themselves. This is one of the most long-awaited events on the calendar and attracts thousands of people every year.

(5) Basil Carnival, Switzerland

The Basel Carnival is the largest popular festival in Switzerland. It begins with the "Morgestraich" (the Monday after Ash Wednesday) when the clock of the tower of St. Martin touches the 4 of the dawn and the lights of the city are extinguished completely. It is then when the lights of the flashlights and the resounding crowd of basilican drummers and flute players fill the void of the night.

单词表

Canarian	*adj.*	加纳利群岛的
extinguished	*adj.*	熄灭的；灭绝的
basilican	*adj.*	巴西利卡式的

2. Chinese Traditional Festivals Introduction: History, Rituals, and Customs

Traditional Chinese festivals compose an important and brilliant part of Chinese culture. The formation of traditional festivals is a long process of historical and cultural accumulation in a nation or a state. Festival activities always reflect primitive sacrifice, superstitious taboo and earthly life, people's spirit and religious influence. Sometimes historical figures become the focus of a festival, showing people's commemoration for them and endowing some historical sense to it.

Moreover, traditional Chinese festivals were often connected with ancient astronomy, calendars and mathematics. Jieqi, or the 24 solar terms, is a key factor in forming traditional festivals.

The origin of the Spring Festival now is too old to be traced. It is widely believed that the word "Nian", was first the name of a monster beast that started to prey on human being at the night before the beginning of a new year. It would swallow many people with one bite. People were very scared. One day, an old man came to their rescue, offering to subdue "Nian". He said to "Nian" that "I hear that you are quite capable, but can you swallow other beasts on earth instead of people who are by no means of your worthy opponents?" Hence, "Nian" did swallow many of the beasts of prey on earth that also harassed people and their domestic animals from time to time. After that, the old man who turned out to be an immortal fairy disappeared riding the beast "Nian". Before the old man left, he had told people to put up red paper decorations on their windows and doors at each year's end to scare away "Nian" in case it sneaked back again, because red is the color that the beast feared most.

过大年

Customs include: pasting couplets, family reunion dinner, staying up late on New Year's Eve, handing out red packets.

（资料来源：http://www.topchinatravel.com/china-guide/spring-festival.htm)

单词表

accumulation	*n.*	积累，积聚
astronomy	*n.*	天文学
prey	*v.*	捕食，以……为食
subdue	*v.*	制服，克服
harass	*v.*	骚扰，折磨，反复袭击
sneak	*v.*	鬼鬼祟祟，偷偷溜走

3. Business Holiday Writing

When you are ready to send greetings to your customers, clients, employees, mentors, and others who make you successful, apply these suggestions, and no matter where you and your customers live, it is good business sense to take every opportunity to thank the people who create your success.

Holiday Messages

If you are stumped about what to write in a holiday greeting, use the short messages below as examples. Adapt them to suit your reader, your relationship, and your culture.

At this joyous time of year, we are grateful for our work with you. We wish you abundance, happiness, and peace in a new year filled with hope. Happy holidays!

Thank you for giving me the opportunity to work with you this year. It has been an honor and a valuable experience for me. I wish you a happy Hanukkah and a new year filled with all good things.

As the year ends, we think about all we are grateful for. Our relationship with you is one thing we treasure. Thank you for the opportunity to serve you. We wish you a merry Christmas and much success in the new year.

Happy New Year Messages

For customers who do not celebrate Christmas, use a new year's message like one of this:

I wish you a wonderful new year filled with abundant joy and treasured moments. May 2025 be your best year yet!

Email vs. Handwritten

If email is the only way you communicate with your customers and employees or if mailed greetings are too expensive—then email is your choice. But even with email, use each person's name. A bland message that says "Dear Employee" or "Dear Customer" might as well say "Dear Stranger".

If you have people's addresses and a budget to send greetings by mail, choose a tasteful card to send. For most business associates, cards with religious messages are inappropriate. What's more, addressing envelopes by hand shows your personal involvement.

Printed vs. Handwritten Signature

Whenever possible, sign your cards rather than using a typed signature. Although a signature typed in gold or silver looks impressive, writing a message and signing your name show a relationship with your reader. Pass around cards at your workplace and have people who know the recipients sign them.

Holiday Letters for Business

Holiday letters are usually reserved for personal friends and family. However, if you want to bring your business network up to date on the progress you have made this year, or if you want to share your personal side with your business associates, write and send one.

Responding to Holiday Greetings

Although responding to holiday cards and greetings is not required, it is thoughtful to do so. Whenever you can spread peace, joys, and friendship in the world, do it!

单词表

stump	*v.*	把（某人）难住
abundance	*n.*	大量，丰富；繁荣，富裕
bland	*adj.*	平淡的，枯燥乏味的，（评论或话语）温和的，无关痛痒的
recipient	*n.*	接受者，领受者

V. Story Links

1. Saint Valentine's Day

The first official Saint Valentine's Day was declared on 14th of February by Pope Galasius in 496, in memory of a 3rd century martyred priest in Rome.

It is believed that a young priest named Valentine rose to distinction after betraying Emperor Claudius in 270 CE by conducting illegitimate wedding ceremonies in the capital. Emperor Claudius claimed that married men made poor soldiers and consequently decreed that all marriages of younger citizens would be outlawed. Bishop Valentine, however, maintained that marriage was part of God's plan and purpose for the world. He continued to conduct marriages in secret between young people, sometimes as young as twelve, in the name of love.

His success gained him unwelcome notoriety, which became Bishop Valentine's downfall. He was jailed and ultimately beheaded, but not before he fell in love with the jailer's daughter. It is thought that on the evening of his execution the bishop passed her a note which read "from your Valentine". This story has blossomed into the defining tradition of Valentine's Day.

主持婚礼的瓦伦丁

2. 中国的七夕故事

"纤云弄巧，飞星传恨，银汉迢迢暗度。
金风玉露一相逢，便胜却人间无数。"

这是中国宋代词人秦观所作咏叹七夕的词作。七夕节，传说中是牛郎织女相会的日子，是中国传统节日中最具浪漫色彩的一个，也正被越来越多的年轻人看作"中国情人节"。

七夕节的起源与牛郎织女的爱情故事有关。相传牛郎父母早逝，与一头老牛相依为命。老牛感其善待，教他如何娶织女为妻。有一天，众仙女们到河里沐浴，藏在暗中的牛郎突然拿走了织女的五彩衣。惊惶失措的众仙女穿衣飞走，唯独剩下织女。在牛郎的恳求下，织女答应做他的妻子。婚后，牛郎和织女过着男耕女织、相亲相爱的幸福生活，一年后织女生了一对龙凤胎。老牛临死之前叮嘱牛郎要把它的皮留下来，遇难时披上它的皮以求帮助。老牛死后，夫妻俩忍痛剥下牛皮，把老牛埋在山坡上。

玉皇大帝和王母娘娘得知织女和牛郎成亲之事，勃然大怒，立即命令天神下界抓回织女。牛郎回家后不见织女，急忙披上牛皮，担着一双儿女追去。眼看就要追上织女，王母娘娘拔下头上的金簪向空中一挥，一条银河霎时间出现，将牛郎与织女隔在两边。后来，王母娘娘准许牛郎和织女每逢七月初七相会，于是人间的喜鹊飞上天空为他们搭桥，这就是人们说的“鹊桥会”。

（资料来源：https://www.douban.com/group/topic/57654448/）

鹊桥相会

VI. Did You Know?

1. 有关中国节日的古诗词

清明

（唐）杜牧

清明时节雨纷纷，路上行人欲断魂。
借问酒家何处有？牧童遥指杏花村。

端午

（唐）文秀

节分端午自谁言，万古传闻为屈原。
堪笑楚江空渺渺，不能洗得直臣冤。

阳关曲·中秋月

（北宋）苏轼

暮云收尽溢清寒，银汉无声转玉盘。
此生此夜不长好，明月明年何处看。

九月九日忆山东兄弟

（唐）王维

独在异乡为异客，每逢佳节倍思亲。
遥知兄弟登高处，遍插茱萸少一人。

生查子·元夕

（宋）欧阳修

去年元夜时，花市灯如昼。
月上柳梢头，人约黄昏后。
今年元夜时，月与灯依旧。

不见去年人，泪湿春衫袖。

2. 圣诞节习俗——槲寄生下的亲吻

在西方国家有一个浪漫的习俗，在圣诞节当天，如果一对男女正好一起站在槲寄生下，他们就必须接吻。人们为什么要在槲寄生下接吻呢？

槲寄生在西方被称为“生命中的金枝”。在北欧神话中，主神奥丁（Odin）和爱神弗丽佳（Frigg）的儿子——光明之神巴尔德（Balder），被邪恶之神洛基（Loki）用槲寄生制成的飞镖射死。弗丽佳悲痛的眼泪化解了槲寄生的邪恶，救活了儿子。于是她承诺，无论谁站在槲寄生下，都会赐给他（她）一吻。爱战胜了死亡，这个神话流传至今，槲寄生也被赋予爱、和平和宽恕的寓意，成为圣诞节不可或缺的装饰植物。

VII. Cultural Reflection

传统节日的形成，是一个民族或国家的历史文化长期积淀凝聚的过程，也是最能真实反映民族文化的一个重要方面。经过人们世代的传承，节日的传统和内涵也根植于人们的心灵深处，帮助人们追根求源、发现自我、弘扬民族精神及寻求心理慰藉。节日体现了人们对生活的热爱，同时随着时代的变迁，节日也被赋予了更多的社会内涵。

一、节日是文化传承的生动体现

中国的传统节日集中体现了中华民族的传统信仰、伦理道德、价值观念等，与中华民族源远流长的悠久历史一脉相承。它以一种潜移默化的形式，展示了我国古代先民信神敬天、感恩知报的思想境界。我国曾长期处于自给自足的农业社会，传统节日具有浓厚的农业色彩，体现出农耕文明的社会特征。由于古代生产力和农业技术不发达，劳动人民十分重视气候对农作物的影响，从春生、夏长、秋收和冬藏的过程中认识到自然发展的规律，总结出包含四时、二十四节气等在内的历法体系。中国自古以来就是一个以农业为主的国家，农业的发展离不开天气的关照，因此逐渐形成了以节气为主的农事节日，春节、清明节、中秋节等都是重要的农事节日。人们通过丰收或农闲时举办的一些活动祭祀日月星辰，庆祝五谷丰登，祈求来年风调雨顺。

而西方传统节日的起源则大都具有浓厚的宗教色彩。虽然西方人类社会早期的节日活动也旨在企盼丰收，但是后来，由于基督教的兴起和普及，以及工业社会的商品经济取代了农业经济，所以敬奉土地、祈求丰收的传统节日习俗逐渐被各种宗教意识衍生出来的节日所取代。西方国家最初多以畜牧业为主，尽管后来农业、工业、商业都有较大发展，但农业大多没有成为立国之本，因此人们对季节、气候的重视程度不及中国，在漫长的岁月中，基督教的节日逐渐成为西方国家主要的传统节日。比如西方的复活节、万圣节和圣诞节都是典型的宗教节日。

二、中西节日的庆祝方式与寓意不同

每个节日都有自己独特的庆祝方式和节日习俗，中西方传统节日的庆祝方式和节日习俗也有很大的差异，中国传统节日主要以饮食为主题，而西方国家的传统节日主要以玩乐为主题。

饮食文化是中国节日文化的重要组成部分，春节、清明、端午、中秋、重阳等都有其独特的节日食物以及蕴含的文化寓意。中国的哲学观点讲究顺应自然，中国的节日也充分体现了以自然为取向、尊重自然的、强调人与自然和谐共生、万物平等的哲学思想。

中国的传统节日强调集体主义价值取向，几千年来儒家思想对中国社会的影响深远而广泛，儒家极力推崇社会的有序与和谐，倡导个人对于群体的忠诚与责任。因此中国注重血缘性、群体性，强调集体主义的价值观在中国传统节日习俗中得到了很好的体现，中国的传统节日也注重和平，关切人文、人道，注重伦理道德的传承。比如中国的春节一定要合家团圆，家人一起吃年夜饭，感恩祈福；大年初一到初五亲朋好友之间开始互相拜年，互赠美好祝愿；中秋节也是家人团圆的日子，月饼象征着团团圆圆，这也便有了“海上生明月，天涯共此时”“千里共婵娟”等明月寄相思的古诗词。

西方尽管也有一系列的节日食品，如圣诞节的烤火鸡和烤鹅、复活节的彩蛋和感恩节的火鸡、南瓜饼等，但西方的节日更多以玩乐为主题。复活节期间有寻找彩蛋的活动；万圣节有化妆派对，孩子们挨家挨户要糖果；一年一度的梅西感恩节大游行以及各种各样的圣诞节颂歌会、教堂集会等都体现出西方人重玩乐的节日习俗。可以说西方传统节日注重的是一种快乐的氛围和情感的释放，因此人们的庆祝方式以娱乐为主，往往表现为个性的张扬和人与人之间的情感诉求。节日为人们提供了放松身心的机会。

三、信仰的差异也是导致中西方节日习俗差异的一个重要原因

中国传统节日具有泛神性与世俗性。中华民族一直以来处于泛神的信仰状态，即多种宗教并存，但都不超过世俗的范围，中国的宗教信仰不在于神的有无，而在于要请诸神来净化人 的思想情感，帮助人们实现愿望。比如说中国人过小年，会用美食供奉灶王爷，希望他能在玉帝面前多多美言；过年时祭奠祖先、供奉神龛等也是希望祖先诸神可以保佑子孙后代，祈求多福多寿；放鞭炮，是为了驱邪避灾，以及辞旧迎新等。而西方的传统信仰主要是基督教，一些节日便具有鲜明的相关元素，比如在圣诞节的时候，家家户户都要装点圣诞树，上面挂着代表圣饼的小甜饼，象征赎罪；还点上蜡烛，象征基督的光和爱等。复活节的习俗之一是制作彩蛋，人们认为鸡蛋是生命力和新生命的象征，复活节时人们把鸡蛋染成红色，代表耶稣受难时流出的鲜血，同时也象征复活后的快乐。

总体来看，中国的传统节日多与农业生产、自然节气有关。例如春节（农历新年）是中国

最重要的节日，象征着农历的开始，家人团聚、辞旧迎新;中秋节则庆祝农作物丰收和家庭团圆。中国传统节日在强调家庭团聚、尊重传统和表达敬意的同时，还蕴含着丰收、团圆、祥和、幸福和希望的象征意义。而西方的节日往往与信仰、历史事件或文化习俗有关。同时，西方也有一些世俗的节日，如情人节、万圣节和感恩节。

中国的传统节日强调家庭团聚、尊重长辈和传统价值观。庆祝节日是人们重视传统文化和家族纽带的表现，家人聚在一起分享快乐和美食，尊重祖先和长辈。而西方节日更加注重个体表达，节日成为人们展示情感、交换礼物和庆祝的好机会。

需要注意的是，具体的节日和习俗可能因国家、地区和个人的差异而有所不同。同时，随着社会的发展，中国的传统节日也逐渐与时俱进。例如在春节期间，春节联欢晚会和春节旅游已成为一种时尚，网购和微信红包也成为庆祝方式的一部分。中国的传统节日逐渐融入现代生活，在保持传统的同时，也展现出创新和活力。

VIII. Homework

1. 节日配对

将功能相似的中西方节日连线，并分析一下不同节日的文化内涵。

春节	万圣节
七夕节	情人节
中元节	圣诞节

2. 调查报告

中西传统节日都有什么禁忌？这些禁忌的背后包含了怎样的文化差异？以小组为单位，搜集资料，对以上两个问题进行调查研究。

3. 商务贺卡写作

假设你在公司企划部工作，感恩节临近，请你代表公司给客户写一张感恩节贺卡。

Section Three

The Contrast of Chinese and Western Weddings and Funerals

I. Learning Objectives

1. To understand different influences about philosophies and religions on Chinese and Western weddings and funerals

2. To research on different funeral customs, death-related rituals and wedding customs

II. Key Points and Difficult Points

1. To understand different attitudes towards loss and different practices of funerals

2. To get to know different cultures on colors and numbers, and try to avoid these taboos in business intercourse

3. To compare and contrast the different customs concerning Chinese and Western weddings

III. Lead-in Questions

1. How do people practice funeral rituals in China and the West?

2. How do people conduct a wedding ceremony in China and the West?

3. What are cultural differences in dealing with death?

4. What is the significance of colors in China and the West?

IV. Learning Contents

1. History of Western Weddings

Western marriage traditions date back to Ancient Greece and Rome, where marriage was much more of a legal contract than a romantic endeavor. Instead of taking place between a man and woman, the marriage was actually a contract between two men: the groom and the bride's father. Women had no choice about whether they would marry or who would become their husband, and they may not even have laid eyes on the groom before the wedding day.

Marriage became a legal contract in Medieval Times around 1076 when laws began to affect how a marriage was performed. These laws meant that women were no longer allowed to be bartered, sold, or exchanged for goods of any kind. If a couple wanted to get married, a priestly blessing was required first.

During the Elizabethan era, which occurred between 1558 and 1603, most marriages were still arranged. Prior to the wedding, the groom accepted the bride's dowry. In many cases, this was the reason behind the wedding. A dowry wasn't necessarily money; it was also land or goods.

In Victorian times, which constituted most of the 1800s, a woman would "come out" into society as soon as she finished school (around the age of 17 or 18). New clothes and accessories would be purchased so she would look her best and impress any potential suitors. Men, of course, viewed courtship as more business than pleasure. Land, money, and the family business were all carefully researched, since what belonged to the woman would be turned over to the man upon marrying. After Queen Victoria wore a white dress to her wedding, brides in England and America began to take up this trend.

Although today's couples can choose whom they will marry and have unlimited options when it comes to their ceremony, attire, and customs, modern weddings still have their roots in Western weddings of the past.

单词表

barter	*v.*	以……进行交换，进行易货贸易
dowry	*n.*	嫁妆
accessory	*n.*	配饰，饰品
suitor	*n.*	求婚者
courtship	*n.*	求爱，求婚
attire	*n.*	服装

2. Traditional Han Chinese Marriage Customs

Han Chinese weddings involve six stages, called the Six Etiquettes. They start off with a marriage proposal (纳采), followed by an inquiry into the bride's birthplace and other personal information (问名) and divination (纳吉). Acceptance of the bridal gifts is next (纳征), then choosing the wedding day (请期), and finally the wedding ceremony (亲迎).

Na Cai denotes the man's family's sending of a matchmaker to the woman's family to initiate a marriage proposal. After her family accepts the overture, his family prepares gifts for a formal proposal—a tradition that has been preserved till present times. Nowadays, once a man and woman fall in love, he normally goes to her family to ask for her hand in marriage.

If the two families don't object to the proposal, the man's family will instruct the matchmaker to ask for the woman's name and birthdate.

The couple's birthdates are needed for fortunetelling, to see if they are compatible and to predict their shared future. This step is called Na Ji.

If the fortunetelling results are good, the man's family presents the woman's family with gifts in honor of the betrothal. There are no specific rules on what the gifts should be or their quantity. They vary according to the customs of different regions, as well as the economic conditions of the families involved.

Qing Qi is when the man's family picks a wedding date and asks for the approval of the woman's family. Qin Ying is when the groom fetches and welcomes the bride to his home on their wedding day. According to folk custom, the woman becomes formally married to the man after he fetches her and welcomes her to his family. Without the completion of this step, their marriage would not be accepted by the public.

In modern society, the marriage law stipulates that a man and woman legally become a couple once they register and get a marriage license from the Department of Civil Affairs. But in some places, the tradition has been kept that the two only become married once their wedding has been officiated.

单词表

initiate	*v.*	发起，接纳
matchmaker	*n.*	媒人，红娘
betrothal	*n.*	婚约，订婚

V. Story Links

1. Honeymoon

The concept of a honeymoon traditionally refers to a holiday taken by newlyweds shortly after their wedding to celebrate their marriage. In contemporary times, honeymoons are often associated with destinations considered exotic or romantic. However, the term can also refer to a phase in a couple's relationship—whether married or not—when they enjoy a period of intense affection and joy before transitioning into the routine of daily life together.

Historically, the honeymoon was first described in 1546 as a time "characterized by love and happiness" following marriage. The term may allude to the idea that the first month of marriage is the sweetest. Another interpretation, according to the *Oxford English Dictionary*, is that the word originally had no specific reference to time but compared the fleeting nature of mutual affection to the changing phases of the moon, where the fullness quickly gives way to the waning phase. Today, a honeymoon typically refers to the holiday spent by a newly married couple before settling into married life at home.

The purpose of a honeymoon varies across cultures. In arranged marriages, it may serve as a time for the couple to get to know each other better. In some cultures, it marks the couple's initiation into sexual intimacy. In others, it is mainly a time for relaxation, creating shared memories, and adjusting to married life. Regardless of cultural differences, the honeymoon remains a significant ritual for couples to bond and begin their life together.

（资料来源：https://en.wikipedia.org/wiki/Honeymoon）

2. 月老的传说

唐朝初年，杜陵有个书生叫韦固。他尚未娶妻时，一位朋友为他介绍原任司马潘昉的女儿，并约定次日一早在龙兴寺相见。韦固娶妻心切，连夜便来到龙兴寺。只见门口台阶上坐着一位老人，在月光下翻看一卷书。韦固很是好奇，便凑过去观看，但却一个字也不认识。韦固恭敬地问道："请教老人家，怎么您这本书我竟然一字不识？"老人笑道："这是幽冥之书，并非人间之物，你如何认识？"老人接着说："我是幽冥之人，专管天下的婚姻档案。"韦固闻言非常高兴，连忙把自己的烦恼向老人诉说一番，并请老人预测此次婚姻的成败。老人说："潘氏与你没有姻缘。你未来的妻子现在才三岁，要等到她十七岁时，才能和你成婚。"韦固将信将疑，又探问老人身上布囊中的物件。老人说："这是红绳子，一旦男女有姻缘，就会系住他们的脚。哪怕是冤家对头，贵贱悬殊，远在天边相隔千里，只要系上，终究会成为夫妻。"后来，果如老人所言，韦固和潘家女儿没有姻缘。十四年后，韦固到相州任参军。刺使王泰见他很有才干，就把自己的女儿香娘许配给他。婚后，妻子向他诉说自己的身世。韦固听后才相信月下老人所言不虚。这个故事的流传，使得大家相信男女婚姻是由月下老人系红绳加以撮合的，所以民间常把做媒之人叫作"月老"。

（资料来源：个人图书馆 http://www.360doc.com/content/16/0928/22/36931788_594507193.shtml）

月下老人与韦固

VI. Did You Know?

1. 西方葬礼中的祷告词

In sure and certain hope of resurrection to eternal life
through Our Lord Jesus Christ, we commend to Almighty God (Name),
and we now commit his/her body to the ground:
earth to earth, ashes to ashes, dust to dust.

2. 西方婚礼习俗

Something old, something new, something borrowed, something blue, and a silver sixpence in her shoe.

Something old represents the link with the bride's family and the past. Something new represents good fortune and success in the bride's new life. Something borrowed is to remind the bride that friends and family will be there for her when help is needed. Something blue is the symbol of faithfulness and loyalty. A silver sixpence in her shoe is to wish the bride wealth.

3. Flower Gifting Etiquette Around the World

Flower gifting is a universal tradition, but the meanings of flowers and the customs surrounding their presentation can vary greatly from one culture to another. To convey the intended sentiment, it's important to understand the local practices and taboos associated with flowers in different countries. Below is an overview of flower gifting traditions in various parts of the world.

Germany

In Germany, white flowers, particularly white lilies and roses, are commonly associated with funerals and are given as condolences. In contrast, red roses are the traditional choice to express romantic feelings.

France

France shares a similar approach regarding white flowers—specifically chrysanthemums, which are closely tied to funerals and are considered inappropriate for other occasions. Additionally, yellow flowers (such as yellow roses) symbolize infidelity, so they should be avoided. For expressing romance, tulips, orchids, and red roses are highly recommended.

Bulgaria

In Bulgaria, the tradition of giving an odd number of flowers is followed, and like France, yellow flowers—particularly yellow tulips—are associated with separation. Red roses and springtime tulips are popular choices for expressing love or admiration.

China

In China, flowers like lilies, orchids, and peonies are commonly gifted. However, you should avoid giving a bouquet of four roses, as the number 4 is associated with death in Chinese culture, and is considered an unlucky number.

Japan

In Japan, bright red flowers, such as roses and gerberas, represent passionate love and positivity. White lilies convey purity, and tulips are associated with thoughtfulness.

India

In India, colorful flowers are highly appreciated, with yellow and red roses being popular choices for many occasions. Frangipani, however, should be avoided, as it is primarily used in funeral ceremonies.

Ghana

In Ghana, there are no strict rules regarding flower gifting, and flowers are not typically given at family gatherings. However, offering a bouquet can be seen as a pleasant and thoughtful surprise.

Egypt

In Egypt, flowers are primarily given for specific occasions, such as weddings or as get well soon gifts. They are also appropriate at funerals. In other circumstances, giving flowers is not a common practice.

United States

In the United States, roses are the most popular flowers, particularly for occasions such as Valentine's Day, Mother's Day, and weddings. The color of the rose carries significant meaning—yellow roses symbolize friendship or cordial relations, while red roses are traditionally used to express love and romance.

Canada

Similar to the United States, red roses and daisies are common choices for expressing love, especially on Valentine's Day. However, white flowers, such as lilies and chrysanthemums, are typically associated with funerals and should be avoided for any occasion other than that.

Mexico

In Mexico, arriving at a business or social gathering without a gift is considered impolite. Flowers, particularly bouquets, are a versatile gift and can be a great way to make a positive impression.

Brazil

In Brazil, black and purple flowers are associated with death and should be avoided for celebratory occasions like dates or Mother's Day. Red roses are a popular flower to express love, and the Corsage Orchid, the national flower, is highly regarded in the country.

（资料来源：https://myglobalflowers.com/blog/lifestyle/traditions-of-flower-gifting-in-different-cultures）

VII. Cultural Reflection

英国人类学家爱德华·泰勒在《原始文化》一书中说："文化是一个复杂的整体，其中包括知识、信仰、艺术、道德、法律、习俗以及人们作为社会成员而获得的一切能力和习惯。"婚葬文化是文化中最具代表性的领域。婚姻不仅是两个人的结合，更是两个家族、两种价值观的融合；死亡则是生命的另一面，承载着各民族对生命意义、死后世界以及对逝者的尊重。中西方的婚姻文化与死亡文化差异，反映了两种文化在家庭、个体、社会责任以及生命终极意义等方面的理解。

一、中西婚姻文化的特点与差异

中国婚姻文化深受儒家思想影响，儒家提倡的是"家庭为本，社会为先"的理念，强调家族、传统和社会责任。因此，在中国传统婚姻中，婚姻并不只是两个人的结合，更是两个家庭之间的联结，涉及社会层面的认同和责任。中国古代的婚姻制度明确规定了婚姻是家族和社会的事务，婚姻的选择必须符合社会的规范和家庭的期待。

中国传统婚礼讲究"六礼"，即纳采、问名、纳吉、纳征、请期、亲迎，每一个步骤都代表着对长辈、祖先以及天地神灵的尊重与敬仰。这一系列仪式体现了"天人合一"的思想，即天地和人类之间的关系是和谐统一的，婚姻是家庭与社会的重要事务，因此必须得到社会、父母和祖先的认可。在中国古代社会，婚姻不仅是两个人的私人事务，更是整个家族乃至社会的集体事务。这种强调家族和社会责任的婚姻文化，塑造了中国人对于婚姻深厚的责任感和忠诚感。中国传统婚礼的另一大特点是注重仪式的庄重。婚礼上，新郎新娘不仅要拜天地、拜祖先、拜父母，表达对长辈的敬意，还要通过"婚车""闺房""新郎新娘拜堂"等一系列复杂的礼节，彰显家族的尊荣与婚姻的神圣性。这些仪式是中国传统文化中宗法观念的体现，传递着家族延续、责任担当的思想。

与中国婚姻文化的家族导向不同，西方婚姻文化更加强调个人的自由选择和爱情至上的理念。西方社会的婚姻常常注重个人意愿与情感的表达，婚姻更多被视为个人选择的一部分，是个人自由的体现。

西方婚礼的形式较为简单而浪漫，婚礼仪式通常在教堂、户外或宴会厅举行，新郎新娘穿着婚纱和礼服，交换戒指并宣读誓言，表达彼此的忠诚与承诺。西方的婚礼仪式更加注重个人的情感体验和对爱情的真诚承诺，而不再是两个家庭之间的联姻。在西方，婚姻的决定权更多掌握在男女双方手中，家长和社会的影响较小。

二、中西方"死亡文化"的特点及差异

中国的死亡文化受到儒家、道家和佛教的深刻影响，体现出一种尊重死者、传承文化和

延续家族的思想。儒家认为，死者的灵魂应该得到尊重，并继续守护家族的运势。儒家提倡孝道，认为子女应该对父母尽忠尽孝，因此，在中国的丧葬文化中，祭祀和丧礼占据重要地位。儒家文化中的“孝”思想也让中国的死亡文化充满了家族责任感，死亡不仅是个体的结束，更是家族责任的延续。道教的阴司神灵观念以及佛教的六道轮回思想，使中国的死亡文化充满了神秘感。中国传统的葬礼仪式繁复，通常包括守灵、哭丧、做七、百日等程序。葬礼后，家人还会定期祭拜逝者，表达对死者的尊敬和怀念。此外，中国还非常注重墓地风水，认为合适的墓地能够影响家族的运势。因此，选墓、安葬和风水的讲究也是中国死亡文化中的重要组成部分。

中国的死亡文化强调“天人合一”的思想，认为生死是一个自然的循环过程，死者的灵魂与家族紧密相连。在中国，葬礼不仅是对死者的尊重，更是对家族、社会和传统的尊重。葬礼是家族成员表达敬意的方式，也是文化传承的重要途径。

西方的死亡文化注重对死后灵魂的关怀与救赎。葬礼仪式通常包括追悼会、宗教仪式、致辞和葬礼等，旨在纪念逝者的生命和成就，强调个体的灵魂归宿。西方的丧葬文化注重对逝者的个体性纪念，葬礼通常由家人和朋友共同参与，形式较为简洁，但常通过追思会、颂歌等形式纪念逝者的生活与成就。在西方，葬礼仪式更多地表现出对逝者人生的尊重，强调个人的自由和信仰。西方社会中的死亡仪式更倾向于通过宗教仪式来缅怀死者，死者的家人和亲朋好友通过悼念活动来纪念逝去的生命。

中国的死亡文化强调家族责任与家族传承，认为死亡是生命自然延续的过程，死者的灵魂仍然与家族和祖先保持联系，因此葬礼是家族社会认同和责任的体现。而西方的死亡文化则更注重个人灵魂的独立性，死亡是个体与上帝之间的关系，更强调纪念逝者的个人成就与生前的行为。两种文化各具特色，共同反映了人类对生死的深刻关注和探索。

VIII. Homework

五分钟演讲

基督教的救赎观与中国传统文化中的“福报”是相似还是相悖？大胆说出你的想法吧。

参考资料

一、书籍

Geertz, Clifford. The Interpretation of Cultures [M]. New York: Basic Books, 1973.

Hofstede, Geert. Cultures and Organizations: Software of the Mind [M]. New York: McGraw-Hill, 1991.

Benedict, Ruth. The Chrysanthemum and the Sword: Patterns of Japanese Culture [M]. Boston: Houghton Mifflin, 1946.

易中天 . 闲话中国人 [M]. 上海 : 上海文艺出版社 , 1996.

林语堂 . 生活的艺术 [M]. 北京 : 外语教学与研究出版社 , 2009.

费孝通 . 乡土中国 [M]. 北京 : 人民出版社 , 2008.

二、网站

http://www.about.com/food/（各地美食）

http://weddings.lovetoknow.com（婚礼习俗知识）

三、影视作品

电影 :《傲慢与偏见》《理智与情感》《审判日》

纪录片: CCTV《舌尖上的中国》、BBC《发现中国美食之旅》、BBC《中国新年：全球最大庆典 Chinese New Year 2016》

Chapter Seven

The Contrast of Chinese and Western Social Lives

课前成果检测

中西方社会生活阅读测试题

一、填空题

1. 目前存在的娱乐节日可以划分成四种类型：首先是 ________，比如多年前的《综艺大观》。其次是 ________，它是娱乐节目盛行以来经久不衰的一个类别，以一种独特的方式一直吸引着观众的眼球。第三种是 ________，比如《开心辞典》，它是以益智问答构成节目的主要环节。最后一种是 ________，这也是目前发展最为迅速的一类娱乐节目。

2. 京剧，它形成于 ________，时间是在 ________ 年前后，盛行于 20 世纪三四十年代，时有 ________ 之称。现在它仍是具有全国影响的大剧种，是近代中国戏曲的代表。

3. 中国京剧是中国的 ________，已有 ________ 年历史。京剧之名始见于 1876 年的《申报》，是中国最大的戏曲剧种。其剧目之丰富、表演艺术家之多、剧团之多、观众之多、影响之深均为全国之冠。京剧是综合性表演艺术，有 ________、________、________、________ 四项基本功，通过程式的表演手段叙演故事、刻画人物，表达“喜、怒、哀、乐、惊、恐、悲”的思想感情。角色可分为 ________、________、________、________ 四大行当。人物有忠奸之分、美丑之分、善恶之分，各个形象鲜明，栩栩如生。我国非常重视非物质文化遗产的保护，2006 年 5 月 20 日，京剧被国务院批准列入第一批国家级非物质文化遗产名录。

4. 纵观中西方教育历史，可以发现中国教育注重的是 ________，而西方教育注重的是 ________。

二、知识荟萃

1. 中国古代娱乐的知识
2. 中国古代对教育思想有影响的人物
3. 西方教育思想发展脉络
4. 中国排球、乒乓球、体操、跳水等体育项目的发展历程
5. 体育与商业的关系
6. 娱乐与商业的关系

三、动脑想一想

1. 通过某些亲身经历或者书本知识，你所了解的中西方教育差异主要体现在哪些方面？其中你认为最主要的差异是哪些？形成这些差异的根源是什么？你能分析出中西方教育各自的优势和弊端吗？

2. 如今，娱乐明星和体育明星的个人广告代言费在常人看来已近天价，你能分析出其中的原因吗？体育、娱乐界与国家经济、商业之间是怎样的关系？其中的经济运作流程你知道吗？

3. 中西方的体育精神有何差异？

Section One

The Contrast of Chinese and Western Entertainments

I. Learning Objectives

1. To study the differences and similarities between Chinese and Western entertainments
2. To know the reasons of the differences, including the world views, ways of thinking, values, etc.

II. Key Points and Difficult Points

1. To contrast Chinese and Western attitudes toward entertainments
2. To understand the differences between Chinese and Western entertainments
3. To understand the reasons of the differences

III. Lead-in Questions

1. Can you make a list of differences between Chinese and Western entertainments?
2. What are the world outlooks and values that influence the forms and spirits of entertainments?
3. How to deal with the differences in intercultural communication?

IV. Learning Contents

1. Ballet in Western World

Dance is a form of cultural representation that involves not just dancers, but choreographers, audience members, patrons and impresarios coming from all over the globe and from vastly varied time periods. Even though dance traditions may be limited to one cultural group, they all develop. For example, ballet is an example of a highly developed western form of dance.

Ballet is a type of performance dance that originated in the Italian Renaissance courts of the 15th century and later developed into a concert dance form in France and Russia. It has since become a widespread, highly technical form of dance with its own vocabulary based on French terminology. It has been globally influential and has defined the foundational techniques used in many other dance genres. Becoming a ballet dancer requires years of training. Ballet has been taught in various schools around the world, which have historically incorporated their own cultures to evolve the art.

芭蕾舞

Ballet may also refer to a ballet dance work, which consists of the choreography and music for a ballet production. Traditional classical ballets usually are performed with classical music accompaniment and use elaborate costumes and staging.

单词表

choreographer	*n.*	编舞者
patron	*n.*	赞助人；顾客
impresario	*n.*	（歌剧、乐团、剧院等的）经理，主办人
originate	*v.*	起源，产生；始创
Renaissance	*n.*	文艺复兴（欧洲 14 至 16 世纪）
terminology	*n.*	（某学科的）术语；专门用语
choreography	*n.*	编舞；舞蹈艺术；舞艺
accompaniment	*n.*	伴唱（奏）；伴随物

elaborate	*adj.*	复杂的，详尽的；精心制作的
staging	*n.*	上演；演出风格

2. Chinese Dance

Dance in China is a highly varied art form, consisting of many modern and traditional dance genres. The dances cover a wide range, from folk dances to performances in opera, and may be used in public celebrations, rituals and ceremonies. There are also 56 officially recognized ethnic groups in China, and each ethnic minority group in China also has its own folk dances. Some Chinese dances today such as dancing with long sleeves have been recorded since the very early periods, dating from at least as early as the Zhou Dynasty. The most important dances of the early period were the ritual and ceremonial music and dances called Yayue, and these dances were performed at the imperial court until the Qing Dynasty, but only survive today as performances in Confucian ceremonies.

The imperial court from the Qin Dynasty onward established various departments responsible for the collection of music and dances. The art of dance reached a peak in the Tang Dynasty, and the dances of the period were highly diverse and cosmopolitan.

In some of the earliest dances recorded in China, dancers may have been dressed as animal and mythical beasts, and during the Han Dynasty, some forms of the Dragon Dance were mentioned. The Dragon Dance at that time included a dance performed during a ritual to appeal for rain at time of drought, as Chinese dragon was associated with rain. Modern Dragon Dance uses light-weight structure manipulated by a dozen of men using poles at regular intervals along the length of the dragon, and some forms of the dragon can be very long and involve hundreds of performers. There are more than 700 different dragon dances in China.

舞龙图

单词表

genre	*n.*	流派；体裁；种类
ritual	*n.*	（宗教等的）仪式，典礼；习惯，例行公事

Confucian	*adj.*	孔子的；儒家的；儒家学说的
cosmopolitan	*adj.*	世界主义的；国际性的，国际化的
mythical	*adj.*	神话的，神话中的
manipulate	*v.*	操纵

V. Story Links

1. Peking Opera

Peking Opera, China's national opera, originated in the late 18th century when the "Four Great Anhui Troupes" began performing in Beijing in 1790. Between 1840 and 1860, artists from Anhui, Han, and Beijing operas collaborated, incorporating elements from Kunqu, Qinqiang, and local folk tunes, ultimately forming the distinctive Peking Opera style. It is the most influential and representative of all operas in China. The operatic dialogues and monologues are recited in Beijing dialect, and some of the words are pronounced in a special fashion. The actors and actresses, in addition to singing, use well-established movements to express certain emotions and meaning. Peking Opera represents an important part of Chinese culture and has become a refined art form as a result of the hard work of hundreds of artists over the past two centuries.

2. The Entertainment Industry

The entertainment industry is one of the largest sectors of the USA economy and is in fact becoming one of the most prominent globally as well. It occupies an important position in movies, music, television programming, advertising, broadcasting, cable, casino gambling, wagering and sports. It attracts economics, financing, production and marketing of entertainment in the United States and overseas, which will interest investors, business executives, and accountants, lawyers and arts administrators.

VI. Did You Know?

1. The Origin of Rock and Roll

Rock and roll emerged as a defined musical style in the United States in the early to mid-1950s. It derived most directly from the rhythm and blues music of the 1940s, which itself developed from earlier blues, boogie woogie, jazz and swing music, and was also influenced by gospel, country and western, and traditional folk music. Rock and roll in turn provided the main basis for the music that, since the mid-1960s, has been generally known simply as rock music.

2. 中国古代的娱乐方式

一是文学艺术：

诗词文学是中国古代娱乐的重要形式之一。雅俗共赏的诗词被广泛流传，人们时常聚集在一起朗诵、吟咏或进行诗词对答的比赛。曲艺表演也是重要的娱乐形式，如评话、相声、杂剧等，以幽默、机智和艺术性的表演形式吸引观众。

二是戏剧表演：

京剧、豫剧、昆曲等各个剧种，以精彩的演唱、舞蹈、表演和化妆来展现故事情节，受到古代社会各阶层的欢迎。

三是赛事竞技：

在古代，人们会举行各类体育竞技活动，如射箭、马术、棋类比赛等。这些比赛不仅是娱乐，也体现了个人的技艺和体能。

四是游艺活动：

人们通过捉鸟、放风筝、放花灯、放纸船等户外游戏来放松身心，尤其是在一些传统节日和庆典时。

五是音乐舞蹈：

音乐演奏和舞蹈是古代娱乐的重要组成部分。演奏的乐器有琴、瑟、筝等，舞蹈形式有宫廷舞蹈、民间舞蹈等。

六是观赏游乐：

皇家园林和私人庭院提供了休闲和娱乐的场所，如宫殿花园、园林、游乐园等，人们可以欣赏自然风光、品味美食、观赏花灯等。

七是书法绘画：

中国古代文人喜欢从事书法和绘画活动，他们通过练习和欣赏书法绘画来陶冶情操，表达个人的审美追求。

VII. Cultural Reflection

在全球化的背景下，中西方文化的碰撞与交流日益频繁，娱乐方式作为文化的重要组成部分，展现出人们各自鲜明的价值观与哲学思考。中西方文明有着各自独特的发展路径，因此在娱乐方式和内涵上呈现出明显的差异。这些差异不仅体现在形式和内容上，更深层次地反映了人们对人生、社会以及人类价值的不同理解与追求。中西方娱乐方式反映文化的深层次差异，还能呈现中国娱乐方式中蕴藏的深厚文化底蕴与独特价值观。

一、中西方娱乐方式的文化背景与核心差异

中国的娱乐方式深深扎根于中华文化的传统理念之中，体现了中国人对个人与社会的关系、人与自然的关系的独特理解。总体来说，中国的娱乐更加注重个体感受和体验，强调通过内心的修养和智慧的锤炼来实现精神的升华。与此不同，西方的娱乐往往强调群体体验与象征意义，更注重集体活动和互动。中国的传统娱乐项目如围棋、象棋、歌舞、斗蟋蟀等，通常是单人或两人参与，技巧性强，对智力要求极高，但同时不失其社会功能和外部象征意义。而西方的娱乐形式，如奥林匹克运动、多人球类运动等，则更多强调群体的协作与互动，具有娱乐与社会交往功能。

从中西方娱乐方式的差异可以看出，娱乐的形式和内容与文化的内涵息息相关。中国传统娱乐更加强调和注重“自我修养”和“独立思考”，追求的是内心的平和与个人的独立思考，更多关注个体在有限空间内的沉浸式体验。而西方的娱乐更侧重于集体参与和社会互动，更多以寻求外部刺激的方式来增加娱乐性。

二、娱乐与文化价值观

（一）西方的个人主义价值观

西方文化以个人主义为核心，强调个体的权利、自由与独立，追求个人存在的意义，集体意识则比较淡漠。电影《克莱默夫妇》便是西方个人主义价值观的典型体现。剧中的泰德是一位广告策划师，虽然他尽力工作养家，却未能满足妻子乔安娜对个人自由和存在感的需求。乔安娜的离婚声明直白地表达了她对个人身份和自由的追求，体现了西方文化中对“自我”认知的高度重视。在这种价值观指导下，西方娱乐不仅仅是为了娱乐本身，更是个人表达、自由选择和自我实现的载体，而在表达自我、实现自我的过程中，较少关注家庭与社会的责任感。

（二）中国的集体主义价值观

与西方的个人主义不同，中国文化自古以来注重集体主义，强调个人利益要服从于集体利益，个人的价值在于服务于集体、为社会作贡献。中国的集体主义不仅体现在家庭、社会和国家的关系中，也深深渗透到中国传统的娱乐活动中。中国的许多传统娱乐项目，如围棋、象棋，虽注重个人智力的锤炼，但也讲究个人在集体和社会背景中的相互影响与合作。中国电影作品常常突出集体主义精神，强调个人在集体中的价值与责任。这些电影往往展现人们通过团结协作共同战胜困难，最终实现社会的进步和国家的强盛。中国电影中的主要人物往往表现为普通人在平凡的生活中做出不平凡的事迹，符合中国文化强调谦逊、谨慎与内敛的传统美德。

三、英雄主义的深层差异

西方文化中的英雄通常是突出个体的勇气与能力，许多电影通过夸张的个人英雄形象来呈现国家、民族的伟大力量。这种个人英雄主义反映了西方文化中对个体独立性、自由选择和自我实现的崇尚。以美国电影为例，众多以英雄为题材的影片，如《超级战舰》《复仇者联盟》等，往往集中展示英雄个体的伟大事迹和超凡能力，英雄不仅是拯救世界的“救世主”，也是文化身份的象征。

然而，中国文化中的英雄形象则更多体现了集体主义的精神。中国电影中的英雄常常是平凡人，他们或许没有超人的能力，但他们在面对困境时展现出的坚韧与智慧，最终定能带领集体走向胜利。中国电影如《红高粱》《地道战》等，彰显了集体合作和无名英雄的精神，他们代表了中国人民在艰难困苦中的坚持与团结，这种英雄主义体现了中国文化中的集体价值观和民族精神。

四、中西方娱乐方式背后的文化力量

通过中西方娱乐方式的对比，我们不仅能看到不同娱乐形式的外在差异，更能深刻理解这些差异背后的文化价值观。西方的娱乐方式强调个人的自由和选择，注重群体参与和社会互动，体现了个人主义的价值观；而中国的娱乐方式则更加注重个体的内在修养与智慧，强调在集体中找到个人的价值，体现了集体主义精神。

中国文化的优越之处，在于其强调集体和谐、社会责任和长远发展的智慧。集体主义文化从不排斥个体主义，只是个体主义能够与集体主义完美而高效地融合。这种智慧不仅塑造了中国传统的娱乐形式，也深深影响了中国社会的发展方向。通过更深入地理解中国传统娱乐的精神内核，我们不仅可以认识到其中的艺术价值和文化魅力，还能从中汲取实现社会和谐与个人发展的智慧。这种独特的文化价值观，正是当代中国文化崛起的重要基础，也为我们提供了无穷的民族自信和文化自豪感。

在全球化的今天，我们应当以更加自信的姿态，推广和弘扬中国优秀的文化遗产，尤其是其中蕴含的文化价值观，让世界更好地理解和认同中国文化的独特魅力。

VIII. Homework

1. 列举你所熟悉的娱乐活动，并讨论其对于你生活的意义。

2. 寻找中西方某一娱乐活动的起源，熟悉其历史发展过程，了解其社会意义及所体现的民族文化价值观。

3. 中西方主要娱乐活动所体现的娱乐精神是什么？

Section Two

The Contrast of Chinese and Western Education

I. Learning Objectives

1. To understand the different system and process of Chinese and Western education
2. To contrast the conceptions related to Chinese and Western education
3. To know the cultural reasons for the differences

II. Key Points and Difficult Points

1. To study the guiding ideas of Chinese and Western education
2. To contrast different process of Chinese and Western education
3. To learn the advantages and disadvantages of Chinese and Western education

III. Lead-in Questions

1. What are the different processes of Chinese and Western education?
2. What are the guiding ideas of Chinese and Western education?
3. What are the historical and cultural reasons for the different guiding ideas in education?
4. Which education methods or ideas do you agree with more?

IV. Learning Contents

1. Education in the United States of America

Education in the United States of America is provided by public schools and private schools. Public education is universally required from kindergarten through 12th grade (often abbreviated K-12), and its curricula, budgets, and policies are set through locally elected school boards. State governments set overall educational standards, often mandate standardized tests for K-12 public school systems, and supervise, usually through a board of regents, state colleges and universities.

Private schools are generally free to determine their own curriculum and staffing policies, with voluntary accreditation available through independent regional accreditation authorities. In the United States of America, about 87% of school-age children attend public schools, about 10% attend private schools, and roughly 3% are home-schooled.

Education is compulsory over an age range starting between five and eight and ending somewhere between ages sixteen and eighteen, depending on the state. This requirement can be satisfied in public schools, state-certified private schools, or an approved home school program. There are also a large number and wide variety of publicly and privately administered institutions of higher education throughout the country.

The United States of America spends more per student on education than any other country. According to a report published by the *US News & World Report*, of the top ten colleges and universities in the world, eight are American (The other two are Oxford and Cambridge, in the United Kingdom).

西方课堂

单词表

kindergarten	*n.*	幼儿园
curricula	*n.*	课程（名词 curriculum 的复数形式）
budget	*n.*	预算
mandate	*v.*	授权；强制执行
accreditation	*n.*	认证；委派
approve	*v.*	批准；赞成；同意
administer	*v.*	管理；执行；给予

2. Education in China

The ancient Chinese emphasis on education is on virtue, the ancients said: the pursuit of one's life is to be the ideal personality, which is able to uphold and fulfill the "benevolence" as the core of the ethical ideal of the gentleman. An important characteristic of traditional Chinese culture is to cultivate virtue for the existence and prosperity. The foundation for the traditional Chinese concept is the individual virtues of self-cultivation.

In the education content, the focus is on moral education and cultivation, and the ancient thinkers are constantly considering how to inspire people's moral consciousness and enhance the moral realm. Many famous articles of education, such as "Learning in mind", "The Great Learning", and "Mean", are all talking about moral education.

北京大学

Nowadays, education in China is a state-run system. All citizens must attend school for at least nine years, known as the nine-year compulsory education, which the government funds. It includes six years of primary education, starting at age six or seven, and three years of junior secondary education (middle school) for ages 12 to 15. Some provinces may have five years of primary school but four years for middle school. After middle school, there are three years of high school, which completes the secondary education. The Ministry of Education reported a 99.9 percent attendance rate for primary school.

单词表

uphold	*v.*	支持，维护（法规、制度或原则）
benevolence	*n.*	慈善，仁慈
prosperity	*n.*	繁荣，成功
self-cultivation	*n.*	修养，修身；自我修养；道德修养
inspire	*v.*	激励，鼓舞
compulsory	*adj.*	必须做的，义务的，强制的

V. Story Links

1. 孔丘学琴

孔丘幼时向鲁国乐官师襄子学琴，同一首曲子一连弹奏了十日，师襄子建议他换个曲子，孔丘说："我已经熟悉这支曲子了，但还没有领悟它的技术。"过了些时候，师襄子说："你已经掌握了弹奏这支乐曲的技术，可以弹别的了。"孔丘说："我还没领悟它的用意。"又过了一段日子，孔丘仍在弹那支曲子，师襄子不耐烦地说："你已经了解它的用意，可以换换曲子了。"孔丘说："我还没领悟它描写的人物形象呢。"过了些时候，孔丘终于停下不弹了，他若有所思，向远处眺望，说："领悟到了，这人又高又大，皮肤很黑，眼睛向上看，好像要统一四方，这不就是周文王吗？"师襄子听了非常惊讶，说："这支曲子就叫作《文王操》啊！"

2. A Real Lesson in Humility

Book T. Washington, the renowned black educator, was an outstanding example of the truth that true humanity is often demonstrated through action rather than words. Shortly after he took over the presidency of Tuskegee Institute in Alabama, he was walking in an exclusive section of town when he was stopped by a wealthy white woman. Not knowing the famous Mr. Washington by sight, she asked if he would like to earn a few dollars by chopping wood for her. Because he had no pressing business at the moment, Professor Washington smiled, rolled up his sleeves, and proceeded to do the humble chore she had requested. When he was finished, he carried the logs into the house and stacked them by the fireplace.

A little girl recognized him and later revealed his identity to the lady. The next morning the embarrassed woman went to see Mr. Washington in his office at the Institute and apologized profusely. "It's perfectly all right, Madam," he replied. "Occasionally I enjoy a little manual labor. Besides, it's always a delight to do something for a friend." She shook his hand warmly and assured him that his meek attitude had endeared him and his work to her heart. Not long afterward she showed her admiration by persuading some wealthy acquaintances to join her in donating thousands of dollars to the Tuskegee Institute.

VI. Did You Know?

1. The important thing in life is to have a great aim, and determined to attain it. — Goethe

人生最重要的是要有一个伟大的目标以及实现这个伟大目标的决心。—— 歌德

2. Success covers a multitude of blunders. — George Bernard Shaw

成功由大量的失望铸就。—— 萧伯纳

3. Education is a progressive discovery of our ignorance. — Durant

教育是一个逐步发现自己无知的过程。—— 杜兰特

4. Education is an admirable thing, but it is well to remember from time to time that nothing worth knowing can be taught. — Oscar Wilde

教育是一件令人钦佩的事情，但是要时刻牢记：没有什么值得知道的事是能够教会的。—— 奥斯卡·王尔德

5. Education has for its object the formation of character. — Herbert Spencer

教育的目的在于培养品德。—— 赫伯特·斯宾塞

6. A teacher affects eternity; he can never tell where his influence stops. — H. B. Adams

教师的影响是永恒的；无法估计他的影响会有多深远。—— 亚当斯

7. Education has produced a vast population able to read but unable to distinguish what is worth reading. —George Macaulay Trevelyan

教育造就了一大批人，他们会读书，但是不会区别什么书值得读。—— 特里维廉

8. Education is not the filling of a pail but the lighting of a fire. —William Butler Yeats

教育不是注满一桶水，而是点燃一把火。—— 威廉·巴特勒·叶芝

9. Education is the chief defence of nations. — Edmund Burke

教育是国家的主要防御力量。—— 埃德蒙·伯克

10. Education makes a people easy to lead, but difficult to drive; easy to govern, but impossible to slave. — Henry Peter Brougham

教育使一个民族易于领导，但是难以驱使；易于管理，却不可能奴役。—— 亨利·彼得·布隆厄姆

VII. Cultural Reflection

教育是一种文化现象，是构成文化系统的重要组成部分，然而不同的地域和文化造就了不同的教育理念和形式，中西方教育差异尤其明显，我们就以下几个方面对两者进行反思：

一、中西方教育思想发源的比较

古希腊的三大哲学家苏格拉底（Socrates）、柏拉图 (Plato)、亚里士多德（Aristotle）是毕生从事教育工作的教育家。他们的教育思想对以后两千多年西方教育思想的发展有深远的影响。中国教育源远流长，在几千年的华夏文明发展史中，中国传统教育发展演进的历程，已深深融入中华传统文化。中国古代也出现了三位著名的教育家——孔子、墨子、孟子，其中孔孟的儒家教育思想对以后的两千多年的中华民族产生了根深蒂固的影响。

中西方在各自出现三位形成学派的教育家之前，也都有过较长的演变历史。古希腊文化和教育自公元前 1100 多年开始，经历了荷马时代、古风时代、古典时代。而在中国，从夏商周的记载来看，公元前 11 世纪开始进入奴隶制高度发展时期，也是教育的开端。除此之外，中西方的历史也很相似，古希腊有荷马史诗，古代中国有《诗经》。可以说，中西方三哲时代是中西方教育思想的发源时期。

二、孔子与苏格拉底在教育目的上的比较

孔子从两个方面论述了教育的目的，一方面，教育工作本身就是一种政治教育，孔子强调通过教育取得民众的信任，主张“道之以德，齐之以礼”，把教育和政治、经济、军事、法律的关系进行了结合。另一方面，教育能够发展并完善人与人之间的关系，孔子曾说过“性相近也，习相远也”。而在西方，苏格拉底认为人天生是有区别的，但不管这种区别有多大，教育能使人得到改进，对于想学习建筑、金工、农艺、人事管理的人，想胜任将军职责的人，有治国本领的人，是可以通过教育，以及发展人的智力而实现的。但是，从孔子和苏格拉底各自的论述中我们可以看出，前者比后者更加夸大了教育的目的和作用。

孔子从为政的政治主张出发，主张把官职与学习紧密联系起来，有官职的人应该是受过教育并继续学习的人，受过教育的人应该得到一定的官职，就是“仕而优则学，学而优则仕”的基本含义。苏格拉底认为教育的目的是培养治国人才，在判断是非、荣辱、善恶时，应由具备专门知识的人支配，认为教育是实施人才培养的途径。两者在教育目的上的不同认识，对中西方教育的影响更加深远。

三、孔子与苏格拉底在道德教育上的比较

道德教育是孔子教育思想的重要组成部分，甚至可以说他的全部教学活动都是对学生进行道德教育。其道德教育的内容以“仁”和“礼”为核心，认为一个人能够树立远大的理想，确定宏伟目标，有为实现政治抱负和理想信念的献身精神，又能善于自省自克，严以律己，宽以待人，其道德修养就会不断进步，从而达到一个较高的道德境界。

苏格拉底也是将伦理、道德问题作为整个教育思想体系的中心，认为教育应从研究自然转向研究人类自身，聚焦于伦理和政治是他的立场。苏格拉底认为道德不是天生的，正确的行为基于正确的判断，做坏事的人按照错误的判断行事，没有人会明知故犯，所以教人道德就是教人智慧，智慧就是道德，并认为正义的行为和其他一切道德都是智慧。

四、孔子与苏格拉底在教育内容上的比较

从教育范围看，孔子的教育内容覆盖面更广。他以“六艺”（礼、乐、射、御、书、数）为教育核心，涵盖礼仪、艺术、军事和实用技能。而苏格拉底的教育内容则相对单一，集中于伦理学和哲学领域，鲜少涉及实用技艺。从教育的内容侧重点看，孔子强调“德”的培养，以“仁”“义”“礼”为核心，注重个人在家庭和社会中的伦理行为；教育内容多围绕人际关系展开，强调通过学习礼仪和修养德行达到个人与社会的和谐。而苏格拉底的教育内容则聚焦于培养理性，通过辩证法探讨抽象的哲学命题，如“正义”“善”等，追求思想的深度与逻辑的清晰。从传授知识的方式看，孔子的教育内容具有很强的规范性和实际可操作性，比如礼的具体实施、音乐的演奏与欣赏等，强调学生通过实践内化知识。与之相比，苏格拉底的教育内容更倾向于

抽象思辨，通过连续的对话和质疑促使他们自发探求问题的本质，其内容本身强调思想的内在逻辑与自我觉悟。总体而言，孔子的教育内容以道德伦理和实用技能为主，体现了中华文化对群体秩序与社会责任的重视；苏格拉底的教育内容则专注哲学探讨与理性批判，展现了希腊文化对个体智慧与思想自由的追求。

由此可见，中西方在教育思想渊源、教育目的和教育内容方面存在诸多异同。其相同之处延续了中西两种文明，其差异构成中西文明的明显区别。我们学习西方先进的教育理论时，必须考虑中国这个大的文化环境，不能盲目引进西方教育思想，这正是我们以史为鉴的目的，也正是本课程进行中西方文化比较的目的。

VIII. Homework

1. 比较中西方教育的主要差异，并且分析各自的优点和缺点。
2. 中西方不同的教育方法和理念，你更加赞同哪一方？为什么？
3. 如果你是教育部门的工作人员，你会对我国目前的教育进行哪些改革？为什么？
4. 列举对你有影响的著名教育家的格言。

Section Three
The Contrast of Chinese and Western Sports

I. Learning Objectives

1. To know the major sports in Chinese and Western countries
2. To know the origins and rules of some dominant sports
3. To understand the sportsmanship in Chinese and Western culture

II. Key Points and Difficult Points

1. To know the rules and origins of the major sports in China and Western countries
2. To describe the history and sportsmanship reflected in some major sports

III. Lead-in Questions

1. What are the major sports in Chinese and Western countries?
2. Do you know the origins and rules of the Chinese and Western sports?
3. What are the sportmanships in Western world and China?
4. What are the relationships between the sportsmanship and the cultural values?

IV. Learning Contents

1. General Introduction of Sports in the US

Sports in the United States are an important part of the country's culture. The four major professional sports leagues in the United States are Major League Baseball (MLB), the National Basketball Association (NBA), the National Football League (NFL), and the National Hockey League (NHL). All four enjoy wide-ranging domestic media coverage and are considered the preeminent leagues in their respective sports in the world, although only basketball, baseball, and ice hockey have substantial followings in other nations. Three of those leagues have teams that represent Canadian cities, and all four are among the most financially lucrative sports leagues in the world.

橄榄球

棒球

Professional teams in all major US sports operate as franchises within a league, meaning that team owners can relocate a franchise to another city if they believe it will bring financial benefits. However, such moves typically require approval from the league. All major sports leagues use a similar type of regular season schedule with a playoff tournament after the regular season ends. In addition to the major league-level organizations, several sports also have professional minor leagues, active in smaller cities across the country. Sports leagues in the United States are also unique in that they do not practice promotion and relegation, unlike sports leagues in Europe and almost all other parts of the world.

Sports are particularly associated with education in the United States, with most high schools and universities having organized sports. College sports competitions play an important role in the American sporting culture, and college football and college basketball are as popular as professional sports in some parts of the country. The major sanctioning body for college sports is the National Collegiate Athletic Association (NCAA).

单词表

league	*n.*	联盟；同盟
ice hockey		冰球，冰上曲棍球
lucrative	*adj.*	获利多的，赚大钱的
franchise	*n.*	特许经营权；获特许经营权的企业
playoff	*n.*	双方得分相等时的最后决赛；复赛；季后赛
relegation	*n.*	贬谪；驱逐；移交；归属

(1) Golf

Golf is played in the United States by about 25 million people. The sport's national governing body, the United States Golf Association (USGA), is jointly responsible with The R&A for setting and administering the rules of golf. The USGA conducts three national championships, open to professionals: the US Open, the US Women's Open, and the US Senior Open. In 2018, it added a fourth, the US Senior Women's Open. The PGA of America organizes the PGA Championship, Senior PGA Championship and Women's PGA Championship.

The PGA Tour is the main professional golf tour in the United States, and the LPGA Tour is the main women's professional tour. Golf is aired on several television networks, such as Golf Channel, NBC, ESPN, CBS and Fox.

高尔夫

Notable golfers include Walter Hagen, Ben Hogan, Jack Nicklaus, Arnold Palmer, Tiger Woods, Patty Berg, Mickey Wright, Louise Suggs and Babe Zaharias.

单词表

championship	*n.*	锦标赛；冠军称号
air	*v.*	使公开；播送，播放
golfer	*n.*	高尔夫球手

(2) Basketball

Basketball was invented in 1891 by Canadian physical education teacher James Naismith in Springfield, Massachusetts. Of those Americans citing their favorite sport, basketball is ranked second (counting amateur levels) behind American football. However, in regards to money, the NBA is ranked third in popularity. More Americans play basketball than any other team sport, according to the National Sporting Goods Association, with over 26 million Americans playing basketball.

篮球

The National Basketball Association (NBA) is the world's premier men's professional basketball league and one of the major professional sports leagues of North America. It contains 30 teams (29 teams in the US and 1 in Canada) that play an 82-game season from October to June. After the regular season, eight teams from each conference compete in the playoffs for the Larry O'Brien Championship Trophy.

Since the 1992 Summer Olympics, NBA players have represented the United States in international competition and won several important tournaments. The Dream Team was the unofficial nickname of the United States men's basketball team that won the gold medal at the 1992 Olympics.

Basketball at both the college and high school levels is popular throughout the country. Every March, a 68-team, six-round, single-elimination tournament (commonly called March Madness) determines the national champions of NCAA Division I men's college basketball.

单词表

amateur	*adj.*	业余（爱好者）的

premier	*adj.*	首位的；第一的；最初的
tournament	*n.*	锦标赛；比赛；联赛
elimination	*n.*	除去；消除；淘汰

2. General Introduction of Sports in China

Sports in China have long been associated with martial arts, reflecting the country's rich cultural heritage. Today, China boasts a wide variety of competitive sports, with physical fitness continuing to be a core value in traditional Chinese culture. China also holds its own national quadrennial multi-sport event, the National Games, akin to the Olympics, which showcases the country's growing athletic prowess.

羽毛球

Before the 1990s, sports like badminton and table tennis were largely funded by the government, with athletes often facing uncertainty about their careers after retirement. However, this began to change in the mid-1990s when sports such as football, basketball, volleyball, and ping pong were professionalized, providing athletes with better financial security and career prospects.

The professionalization of sports has led to commercialization, with sports associations evolving into profit-driven entities. This has resulted in the formation of professional leagues and sports clubs that handle ticket sales, advertising, transfers, and broadcasting. Chinese athletes, such as Yao Ming, who entered the NBA in 2002, have also joined international professional leagues, further increasing China's global sports presence.

With continued investment and development, China is poised to strengthen its position as a leading sports nation, both domestically and internationally.

单词表

martial arts		武术
quadrennial	*adj.*	每四年一次的；连续四年的
professionalize	*v.*	（使）专业化，职业化
commercialization	*n.*	商品化，商业化

(1)Table Tennis

In China, "ping pong" is the official term for the sport of table tennis. Beyond the national team, China has a deep pool of talent that consistently produces world-class players, enabling the country to maintain its overwhelming dominance in the sport for decades. This sustained excellence has led foreign media outlets to refer to China as the "unbeatable powerhouse" of table tennis, with many commentators praising its unmatched depth and skill. Such dominance has triggered a series of rule changes by the International Table Tennis Federation to keep the competition more balanced. Ma Long is currently one of the highest-ranked Chinese players and remains the top-ranked player globally. Deng Yaping is widely regarded as one of the greatest table tennis players of all time, having achieved legendary status in the sport.

Table tennis has also played a significant role in shaping China's international relations. A pivotal moment occurred in April 1972, when the US table tennis team was invited to visit China, an event later referred to as "Ping Pong Diplomacy." Today, table tennis remains the most popular amateur recreational sport in China, with an estimated 300 million players, reflecting its widespread appeal and cultural importance.

单词表

overwhelming	*adj.*	势不可挡的；压倒性的；无法抗拒的
trigger	*v.*	使发生；触发；使运行
recreational	*adj.*	娱乐的；消遣的

(2)Volleyball

Volleyball was introduced to Asia in 1908 and officially reached China in 1910. The Chinese Volleyball Association represents China in the Fédération Internationale de Volleyball (FIVB), the Asian Volleyball Confederation (AVC), and also in the All-China Sports Federation.

The China women's national volleyball team is one of the leading squads in international women's volleyball. In the 1980s, China won five consecutive world titles, capturing the FIVB Women's World Cup in 1981 and 1985, and the FIVB Women's World Championship in 1982 and 1986. Although the team experienced some instability in the 1990s, it won the FIVB World Grand Prix title in 2003 and went on to claim the gold medal at the 2016 Rio Olympics. The spirit of the Chinese women's volleyball team, known for its resilience, teamwork, and perseverance, has become globally recognized. Foreign media have hailed the team as the "Iron Army" of volleyball. Lang Ping, as the head coach of the team, has been widely respected for her leadership, guiding the team to numerous international successes and contributing significantly to the legacy of Chinese women's volleyball.

The China men's national volleyball team represents China in international volleyball competitions and friendly matches. The team participated in the Summer Olympics twice, finishing eighth at the 1984 Summer Olympics in Los Angeles, and fifth at the 2008 Summer Olympics in Beijing.

单词表

squad	*n.*	班；小队
consecutive	*adj.*	连续的；连贯的

V. Story Links

1. 刘长春单刀赴会洛杉矶

在太平洋上颠簸了21天后，中国第一位参加奥运会的选手刘长春于1932年7月29日下午4时到达美国洛杉矶码头。他是参加第十届洛杉矶奥运会的唯一中国选手。因长途旅行体力不支，刘长春在100米和200米短跑预赛中即遭淘汰，但他向世界宣告了中国奥林匹克运动的存在。

2. The Rise of the Olympic Games

The Olympic Games originated long ago in ancient Greece. We don't know exactly when the Games were first held and what circumstances led to their creation. However, Games were a direct outgrowth of the values and beliefs of Greek society. The Greeks idealized physical fitness and mental discipline, and they believed that excellence in those areas honored Zeus, the greatest of all their gods. One legend about the origin of the Olympic Games revolves around Zeus. It was said Zeus once fought his father, Kronos, for control of the world. They battled atop a mountain that overlooked a valley in southwestern Greece. After Zeus defeated his father, a temple and immense statue were built in the valley below to honor him. This valley was called Olympia, and soon religious festivals developed there as people came to worship Zeus and to approach as nearly as possible his great strength. It is believed that these religious festivals eventually led to the famed Games of the Olympics.

VI. Did You Know?

1. 体育经济

体育经济是指从生产和经营的角度出发，把大众的体育生活和与此相关的经济行为有机地融合在一起并作为一项特殊的产业来发展。而相对的体育产业，指的就是以活动的形式向全社会提供各类体育服务的行业，是体育服务业的总称。随着经济的发展，体育本身所蕴含的巨大经济功能与价值越来越被人们认同，在发达国家，体育产业的发展已经比较成熟。如在美国，体育产业总值超过千亿；在其他欧美发达国家，体育产业的产值达到上百亿美元；我国自 20 世纪 80 年代改革开放以来，伴随着经济的发展，体育产业也逐渐迅猛发展，被誉为我国的“朝阳产业”。

2. The Origin of *Ping Pong*

In about the year 1800 an American manufacturer of sports goods produced a game which was called Indoor Tennis. The Americans did not find it interesting at the time, so he exported to his London agents and it became very popular in Britain. The game was then played across dining-room tables, or on the floor with the net strung between chairs. The players used a ball made of cork or rubber, which was covered with a net of soft string to prevent it from damaging the furniture. A few years later, a hollow ball like the one we use today was invented. The game then quickly spread all over the world.

VII. Cultural Reflection

体育文化和社会发展是密切相关的，社会发展决定了体育文化的发展，一定的体育文化总是与一定的社会发展和生产方式相适应。社会发展本身就是一个长期、艰苦的过程，所以体育文化也必然循着这一历史过程。在发展过程中，不同民族、不同地域的体育文化就形成了不同的文化模式。我们从以下两个方面对中西方体育文化进行比较：

一、中国传统体育文化与西方竞技体育文化的差异与根源

中西方体育文化是世界文化中两个不同的体系。在 1840 年鸦片战争以前，两者是各自独立发展的，并没有明显的冲突和融合。随着社会生产力的发展，科学技术的进步以及国际间交流的频繁，才使两种文化开始正面接触，接触后人们才发现其差异所在，并且有机会来分析这些

差异的根源。

中国传统体育文化植根于“天人合一”、阴阳、八卦、五行等理论之中，而西方竞技体育文化是在重外在分析，以及重与自然的斗争等西方哲学观念的指导下发展起来的；中国传统体育文化注重人体自身的统一性以及与自然界的和谐，带有某种经验、直觉、模糊的性质，而西方竞技体育文化是科学实验、生理学、现代医学等的综合运用；中国传统体育文化重节奏、韵律、神韵、内涵、和谐美，重朦胧、抽象、含蓄美，而西方竞技体育文化则重力量、速度之美，重外在、形体美。除此之外，中国传统体育文化一贯向着娱乐性、表演性、礼仪性方向发展，注重个人修养，而西方竞技体育文化始终向着竞争性、惊险性、公开性、健美性、趣味性方向发展，并使体育形成体系，注重人的全面发展，而忽视了人在竞争中的道德教育，容易产生残忍与暴力。因此我们可以得出结论，西方竞技体育文化追求“强与险”，而中国传统体育文化追求“健与寿”。

二、中国传统体育文化与西方竞技体育文化的互补

由于现在各国之间的交流日益频繁，并且交流的覆盖面较广，所以体育文化也必然会受到这种交流局势的影响，即互相吸收文化中的精粹部分，最终实现体育文化相互融合。在中国，由于市场经济的发展和对外开放的政治经济条件，传统体育文化势必要注入新的血液，因此，西方的竞争观念、自我价值的彰显也成为中国传统体育文化的追求。在西方，一些知识分子也开始致力于东方体育文化精神的研究，试图从东方的处世之道和养生方法中获得身心自由。中国的某些体育项目，如气功、武术、龙舟竞渡等，开始向西方移植，冲破了西方竞技一统天下的局面。与此同时，篮球、足球、排球、乒乓球、田径等项目已深入中国人的内心，获得了大家的喜爱。

虽然中国传统体育文化与西方竞技体育文化的交流只有几百年的时间，但是它们不仅各自获得了新的文化血液，而且获得了新的文化生存空间。中国传统体育文化与西方竞技体育文化有着对立统一的一面，才有其交互影响的可能，这一东方与西方的体育文化对话，可以丰富世界体育运动的手段与形式，完善世界体育科学思想体系，拓展人类体育功能结构的外延。

总之，由于不同的文化价值观，中西方体育文化的交流会是一个缓慢的过程。但正是在这个过程中，中西方的体育文化才能够不断地充实、丰富自己，为各自的文化画卷上增添靓丽的一笔。

VIII. Homework

1. 列举中西方主要的体育强项，并分析出现这些强项的原因及所反映的文化价值观。
2. 中西方文化中的体育精神是什么?
3. 分享你所擅长的体育运动，并且列举这项体育运动的规则。
4. 试分析当今世界体育运动与经济之间的关系。

参考资料

一、书籍

崔怀猛 . 古代中西方体育文化 [M]. 北京：北京体育大学出版社，2010.

谷世权 . 中国体育史 [M]. 北京：北京体育大学出版社，1997.

霍建瀛 . 中国京剧艺术 [M]. 北京：今日中国出版社，1997.

王炳照 . 简明中国教育史 [M]. 北京：北京师范大学出版社，1994.

魏贤超，王小飞 . 在历史与伦理之间：中西方德育比较研究 [M]. 杭州：浙江大学出版社，2009.

张斌贤，王晨 . 外国教育史 [M]. 北京：教育科学出版社，2008.

朱立人 . 西方芭蕾史纲 [M]. 上海：上海音乐出版社，2001.

二、网站

https://www.chinadaily.com.cn/sports/

http://wenku.baidu.com/view/a7a6b0c75fbfc77da269b14c.html

Chapter Eight

The Contrast of Chinese and Western Etiquette

课前成果检测

中西方礼仪阅读测试题

一、单选题

1. 在中西社交场合中，哪种行为被认为是不礼貌的？

A. 直接注视对方的眼睛　　B. 保持适度的目光接触

C. 低头微笑　　D. 握手问候

2. 在中西餐桌礼仪中，哪个是西方通常使用的餐具？

A. 筷子　　B. 叉子　　C. 筷子和叉子同时使用　　D. 勺子

3. 在中西文化中，哪种社交场合中的问候通常包括握手？

A. 商务会议　　B. 家庭聚会　　C. 婚礼　　D. 礼拜堂

4. 在中西文化中，哪种社交场合中通常会给小孩子送礼物？

A. 生日派对　　B. 家庭聚会　　C. 结婚仪式　　D. 商务会议

5. 在中西文化中，哪个动作是在中国文化中表示尊重的方式？

A. 轻轻握住对方的手臂　　B. 握手作为问候

C. 握手表示感谢　　D. 鞠躬表达尊重

二、填空题

1. 在中西社交场合中，________ 是中国文化中常见的问候方式，而 ________ 是西方社交中常用的问候方式。

2. 在中西餐桌礼仪中，使用刀和叉的方式不同，西方人通常用 ________ 手拿刀，________ 手拿叉。

3. 在中西社交场合中，西方人更加注重个人的 ________ 和 ________，而中国文化中更加注重集体的 ________ 和 ________。

4. 在中西社交交往中，________ 是中国文化中被视为尊敬和尊重的行为，而在西方文化中，________ 是一种常见的表示尊敬的方式。

5. 在中西礼仪中，西方人通常习惯于在交谈中保持适度的 ___________ 接触，而中国文化中，人们更注重 ________ 和 ________。

三、问答题

1. 请举出一个中西社交礼仪中的差异，并解释其背后的文化价值观。

2. 你认为中西礼仪的差异对跨文化交流有何影响？请举例说明。

四、思考题

1. 以你的观察和经验，中西礼仪差异对你个人的跨文化交际经历产生了什么影响？你如何应对这些差异？请分享一个具体的经历。

2. 在当今全球化的背景下，为什么了解中西礼仪的差异和相似之处对于个人和商务交往都很重要？请阐述你的观点。

Section One

The Contrast of Chinese and Western Greetings and Introductions

I. Learning Objectives

1. To understand the key differences in greetings and introductions between Chinese and Western cultures

2. To develop cultural sensitivity and adaptability when engaging in cross-cultural greetings and introductions

II. Key Points and Difficult Points

1. To highlight the significance of titles and hierarchy in Chinese culture and how they influence greetings and introductions

2. To explore the role of non-verbal cues, such as body language, eye contact, and facial expressions, in greetings and introductions in both cultures

3. To explore the cultural nuances and subtleties involved in greetings and introductions, such as the concept of "saving face" in Chinese culture and the level of formality in Western contexts

III. Lead-in Questions

1.Have you ever experienced or observed differences in greetings and introductions when interacting with people from Chinese or Western backgrounds? What stood out to you?

2. What role do non-verbal cues play in greetings and introductions? Can you think of any specific examples where non-verbal cues might be interpreted differently in Chinese and Western cultures?

3. How might cultural differences in greetings and introductions impact business or professional interactions between individuals from Chinese and Western backgrounds?

4. How do you think titles and hierarchy influence greetings and introductions in Chinese culture? How does this compare to Western cultures?

IV. Learning Contents

1. Chinese Body Gestures

(1) How to Point to Yourself

In Chinese culture, when you're relating something to yourself, you may point to your own nose with your index finger. The meaning of this is completely different from its meaning in Western culture, where it may be considered rude to do so. However, remember to avoid pointing your finger to other people's nose. It's perfectly fine for yourself, but when referring to others, you may want to use your whole palm instead to show full respect.

(2) Hug People Carefully

When it comes to hugging, Chinese people might be a bit reserved. In Western culture, it's perfectly normal to hug someone when greeting, even someone you barely know. As for Chinese greetings, Chinese people cannot accept such closeness. If it's not someone you're extremely close with or it's not a very special occasion on which to show affection, remember to avoid hugging! This Chinese gesture may be considered rude. You may just want to offer a handshake instead.

(3) Fist and Palm Gesture

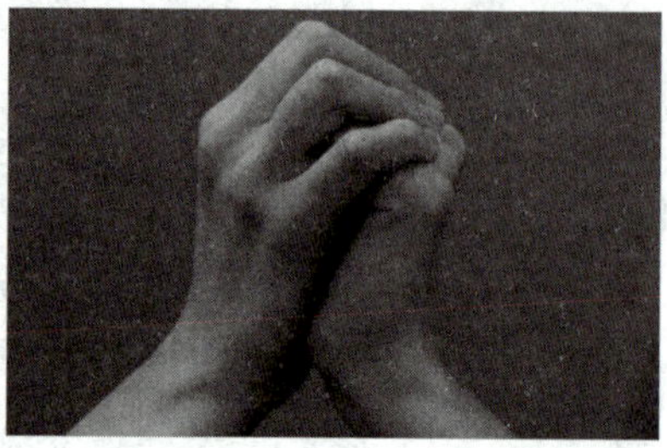

This is a Chinese tradition meaning "wish you good fortune." It may feel strange at first, but as you practice more and get used to it, it will become very fun and natural to do! Chinese people usually do it during New Years, especially young people; they do it to elders to show their respect and good wishes. If you show this gesture to elders during a Chinese New Year celebration, you might want to add "给您拜年了！" which is a way to say "wish you a happy new year!"

单词表

reserved	*adj.*	内向的；矜持的
affection	*n.*	感情；钟爱

2. Western Greetings

Greetings are usually informal, with first names often used in initial introductions.

A handshake is the most common greeting when meeting someone for the first time or in professional settings.

Handshakes should be firm and accompanied with direct eye contact throughout the greeting, especially in business contexts. Being the first person to offer your hand can reflect confidence. However, be aware handshaking can seem overly-formal and awkward in casual settings.

Many people hug in informal situations or to greet close friends and family.

It is important to smile during greetings. Americans generally smile a lot and are likely to appreciate when similar warmth is reciprocated.

A formal introduction is not always necessary in social settings. It is sometimes assumed that people will get to know each other as they mingle.

If you are a newcomer, take the initiative to introduce yourself to those around you. Your American counterpart may not always give individual introductions, expect you to do it yourself.

Many Americans greet by saying "How are you?". This is usually a form of greeting rather than an actual enquiry about your wellbeing. The common response is "I'm good, thanks. How are you?". Giving an answer that is deeply personal or less positive can make the situation uncomfortable if you are not very familiar with the person.

In opening deeper conversation, Americans often ask people about their occupation (e.g. "So, what do you do?").

单词表

initial	*adj.*	最初的；开始的
awkward	*adj.*	令人尴尬的；使人难堪的
reciprocate	*v.*	回应；回报
mingle	*v.*	混在一起；使联结；（尤指在社交场所）相交往

V. Story Links

1. How Do You Define "Face" Exactly?

As a sociological construct, the Chinese concept of face is difficult to define.

The famous Chinese writer and translator Lin Yutang (1895–1976) even went so far as to say that "face cannot be translated or defined." He did, however, characterize it as "...abstract and intangible, it is yet the most delicate standard by which Chinese social intercourse is regulated." The closest translations are along the lines of "pride", "dignity" or "prestige".

But these don't tell the whole story.

Face-management is much more than just impression management (or "protecting and enhancing your ego") in the Western sense. Of course, no one—regardless of culture—wants to look bad or have their ego bruised. But the Chinese concept goes beyond the narrow Western concept of face (and is perhaps closer to the Arab concept of "honor").

It's also worth noting that the concept of face in China is vastly different than the concept of "guanxi" in China. Although both are equally important to understand.

Unlike "Western face"—which is more self-oriented and individualistic—Chinese face is more other-directed and relational. In other words, it's less about your own personal pride or ego, and more about how one is viewed by others. Unlike Western face, Chinese face can be given or earned. It can also be taken away or lost.

2. The Origin of "Hello"

It may be true that OK is the most spoken word on the planet, but hello is a good candidate for the English word that most people learn first. The word is so ubiquitous that it's surprising how new it is: hello has only been in use for about the last 150 years of the 1000-year history of English.

An older term used for greeting or salutation is hail, which dates back to the Middle Ages but was still in use in Shakespeare's time; he used it both as a greeting ("Hail to your grace") and as an acclamation ("Hail, Caesar!"). Interestingly, this word is related to others that originally meant "health," such as hale, health, and whole. Since hail was presumably sometimes shouted (from a horse, across a river, from a tower), it isn't surprising that several variants are recorded, including hollo, hallo, and halloa. Another variant of this interjection has subsequently had a long life as a noun and verb: holler.

Hello is first recorded in the early 1800s, but was originally used to attract attention or express surprise ("Well, hello! What do we have here?"). But the true breakthrough for this now-common word was when it was employed in the service of brand-new technology: the telephone. Thomas Edison himself claimed to have initiated the use of hello upon receiving a phone call—which required people to address an unseen and unknown person. It was simpler and more efficient than some other greetings used in the early days of the telephone, such as "Do I get you?" and "Are you there?"

Hello obviously caught on, and spread along with the telephone. But had the actual inventor of the telephone, Alexander Graham Bell, had his way, our greetings might be very different today. For his entire life, he preferred to answer the phone with "Ahoy."

VI. Did You Know?

1. Some Western gestures are considered taboo in China:

Pointing the index finger—use the open hand instead

Using the index finger to call someone—use the hand with fingers motioning downward as in waving

Finger snapping

Showing the soles of shoes

Whistling is considered rude

2.Chinese customs that are annoying to Westerners:

Belching or spitting on the street

Lack of consideration when smoking and failure to ask permission to smoke

Slurping food

Talking while eating

VII. Cultural Reflection

在中国文化中，问候语和介绍语通常涉及家庭和健康，如“你吃了吗？”“身体好吗？”等，反映了中国文化中对亲近和关怀之人身体的重视。与之相比，西方问候语更注重个人和工作，如“你好吗？”“工作顺利吗？”等，反映了西方文化中对个人成就和事业发展的关注。

由此可见，中国文化中的问候语强调人与人之间的情感联系，更加关注个体的身体和家庭状况。这反映了中国文化中的家庭价值观和人际关系的重要性。在跨文化交流中，我们可以通过关心他人的家庭和身体来表达友好和关怀。而西方问候语更注重个人的状况和职业发展，体现了个人主义和成就导向的文化价值观。在跨文化交流中，我们可以更多地关注对方的职业和兴趣以及工作上的成就和目标，以表达尊重和关注。

对中西方问候和介绍的对比教学也因此具有非常重要的意义。首先，这种对比教学可以使学生了解中西方问候和介绍的差异，可以帮助人们在跨文化交流中更加得体地表达自己的问候和介绍他人的方式，有助于建立良好的沟通和互动，减少误解和冲突，增进文化间的理解和尊重。再者，由于中西方的问候和介绍方式反映了各自文化对人际关系的重视和处理方式，通过教授中西方问候和介绍方式的比较，可以帮助人们更好地适应和理解不同文化中人际交往的规则和习惯，从而在社交场合中建立更加融洽的关系。第三，教授中西方问候和介绍方式的对比，可以培养学习者的跨文化意识和尊重。学习者能够认识到不同文化中的多样性和差异，避免将自己的文化标准强加于他人。这有助于培养开放包容的心态，拓宽视野，增进文化交流和全球化意识。最后，通过对比中西方问候和介绍的方式，学习者可以拓展自己的语言技能。学习者可以学习不同语境下适用的表达方式和用语，提升自己的口语和书面表达能力。这对于学习者的语言学习和应用能力有着积极的影响。

除此之外，中西方问候与介绍方式的差异也有着更加深刻的文化意义。如上所述，中西问候和介绍方式的差异反映了不同文化对人际关系的重视和处理方式。中国文化注重家庭和亲密关系，问候常涉及家人和身体状况，介绍时强调社会关系。而西方文化注重个人和独立性，问候和介绍更侧重于个人状况和工作领域。这反映了中西方文化中不同的人际关系观念和价值取向。另外，中西问候和介绍的方式也反映了不同文化中的社交规范和礼仪。中国文化强调亲近和关怀，问候时常使用亲切的称呼，介绍时注重人际关系的介绍。而西方文化更注重礼貌和尊重，问候和介绍更直接简洁。了解中西方问候和介绍的文化差异，可以帮助人们在不同文化背景下更好地适应社交规范和礼仪。更重要的是，问候和介绍是展示个体文化身份和归属感的方式之一。使用适当的问候和介绍方式可以表达对自己文化传统的认同和尊重，同时也有助于与其他文化背景的人建立联系和理解。通过了解和尊重中西方问候和介绍的差异，我们能够更好地维护自己的文化身份，同时拓宽自己的跨文化视野。

由此可见，通过比较中西方问候和介绍的方式，可以促进跨文化交流和理解。了解对方的问候和介绍方式，尊重并适应对方的习惯，有助于建立良好的沟通和互动。这种跨文化交流和理解有助于打破文化隔阂，增进不同文化间的互相学习和尊重，促进文化多样性的发展。

VIII. Homework

1. 情景对话：编写一份对话脚本，展示中西方问候和介绍的差异。可以选择常见的社交场合，如聚会、约会、商务会议等，并根据情境设计对应的问候和介绍对话。

2. 观看 TED 演讲 “The Difference between Chinese and Western Communication” (Wu You)，并展开讨论。

3. 观看电影《迷失东京》(*Lost in Translation*)。

Section Two

The Contrast of Chinese and Western Dining Etiquette

I. Learning Objectives

1. To understand the key differences in dining etiquette between Chinese and Western cultures

2. To develop cultural competence and adaptability when participating in cross-cultural dining experiences

II. Key Points and Difficult Points

1. To highlight the specific table manners and etiquette expected during meals, such as chewing with closed mouths, using napkins, and not reaching across the table

2. To understand the intricacies of Chinese and Western dining etiquette, such as when to start eating, how to handle communal dishes, and the appropriate pace of eating

3. To develop sensitivity to cultural nuances related to dining, such as accepting or declining certain foods or beverages, observing dietary restrictions, or understanding the symbolism of certain dishes

III. Lead-in Questions

1. Have you ever experienced or observed differences in dining etiquette when dining with individuals from Chinese or Western backgrounds? What aspects stood out to you?

2. Can you think of any specific examples where the use of utensils differs between Chinese and Western dining cultures? How do these differences impact the dining experience?

3. In your opinion, why is it important to understand and respect the cultural norms and dining etiquette when interacting with people from different backgrounds?

4. How does seating arrangement and hierarchy influence dining experiences in Chinese culture? How does this compare to Western dining settings?

IV. Learning Contents

1. Chinese Dining Etiquette

Since China is known for its state of ceremonies, China has always attached great importance to etiquette. Chinese dining etiquette is an important portion of Chinese food culture. Good dining etiquette and table manners can show one's good self-cultivation and leave a good impression on your Chinese host. We have sorted some basic dining etiquette for you at the following.

(1) Table

In China, people share dishes communally. In order to permit easy sharing, square and rectangular tables are normally used for small groups of people, while round tables for large groups.

(2) Place Settings

In restaurants, a basic place-setting includes a set of chopsticks, a spoon, a small teacup, a large plate and a rice bowl. In a more formal occasion, a chopstick holder, a large water or wine glass and a small glass for baijiu are provided. Tissues are provided on the table in low-end restaurants, while high-end restaurants provide cloth napkins as part of the place-settings.

(3) Seating Order

In a formal dinner, the seating order is very strict. Chinese seating order is based on seniority and organizational hierarchy. In general, the seat of honor is usually the one in the center facing east or facing the entrance. This seat is usually reserved for the guest with highest status or a foreign guest of honor. Others with higher status sit in close proximity to the seat of honor, and those with positions sit further away. While as a host, he may take the least prominent seat, usually the one nearest the kitchen entrance or service door. Only after the senior or the guest of honor sit down, can other people be seated.

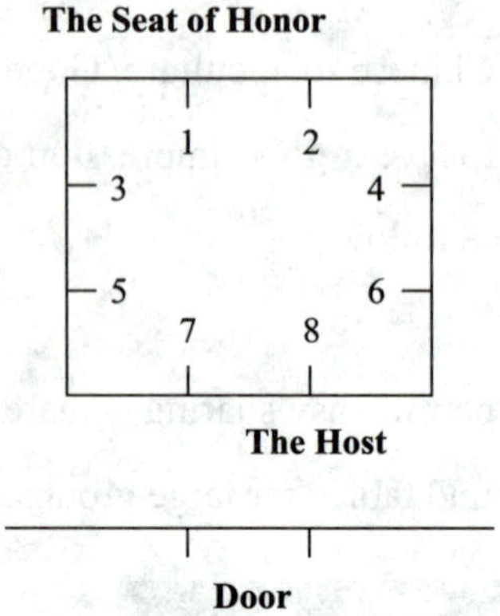

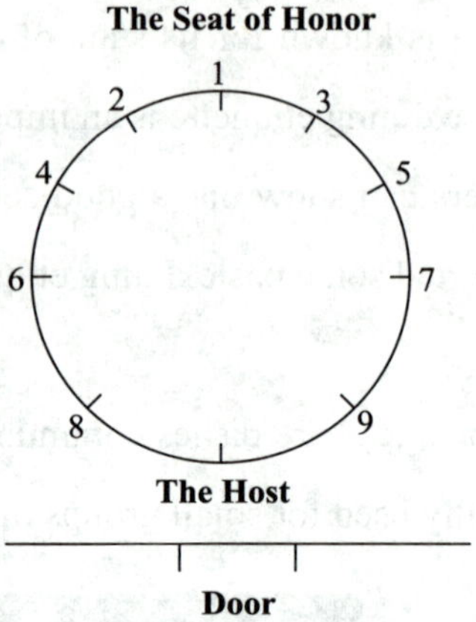

(4) Table Manners in Dining

Guests should start eating after the host gives a signal to begin.

Don't pick up too much food in your bowl at once; instead, eat up the food in the bowl first and then take more. Quiet and slow chewing will suggest good manners. When you pick up food, don't touch people next to you and remember, it's not polite to push the food out of the plate and spill the soup.

Talking to other people with a full mouth is also impolite.

Don't eat the food which is dropped on the table.

When you pick your teeth, use your hand or napkin to cover in front of your mouth.

单词表

rectangular	*adj.*	矩形的；长方形的
seniority	*n.*	年长；级别高
hierarchy	*n.*	等级制度（尤指社会或组织）
proximity	*n.*	（时间或空间）邻近；靠近

2. Western Dining Etiquette

(1) Making Restaurant Reservations:

Restaurant reservations are like any other appointment. If you make a reservation, stick to it. Call ahead if you are going to be more than 15 minutes late, and cancel as far in advance as possible if your plans change so that someone else can get a table.

(2) How to use napkins:

As soon as you are seated, remove the napkin from your place setting, unfold it, and put it in your lap. Do not shake it open. At some very formal restaurants, the waiter may do this for the diners, but it is not inappropriate to place your own napkin in your lap, even when this is the case. The napkin rests on the lap till the end of the meal.

Do not clean the cutlery or wipe your face with the napkin. NEVER use it to wipe your nose!

If you excuse yourself from the table, loosely fold the napkin and place it to the left or right of your plate. Do not refold your napkin or wad it up on the table either. Never place your napkin on your chair.

At the end of the meal, leave the napkin semi-folded at the left side of the place setting. It should not be crumpled or twisted; nor should it be folded. The napkin must also not be left on the chair.

(3) How to use your silverware and dinnerware:

Use the silverware farthest from your plate first. Here is the silverware and dinnerware rule: Eat to your left, drink to your right. Any food dish to the left is yours, and any glass to the right is yours.

Starting with the knife, fork, or spoon that is farthest from your plate, work your way in, using one utensil for each course. The salad fork is on your outermost left, followed by your dinner fork. Your soup spoon is on your outermost right, followed by your beverage spoon, salad knife, and dinner knife. Your dessert spoon and fork are above your plate or brought out with dessert. If you remember the rule to work from the outside in, you will be fine.

Use one of two methods when using the fork and knife:

American Style: Knife in right hand, fork in left hand holding food. After a few bite-sized pieces of food are cut, place the knife on the edge of the plate with blades facing in. Eat food by switching the fork to your right hand (unless you are left-handed). A left hand, arm or elbow on the table is bad manners.

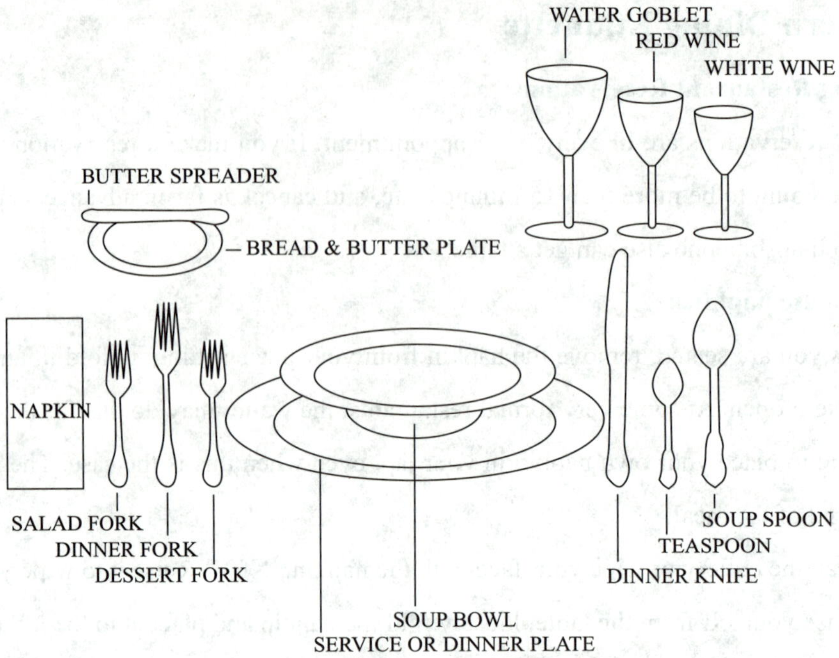

Continental/European Style: Knife in right hand, fork in left hand. Eat food with a fork still in your left hand. The difference is that you do not switch hands—you eat with your fork in your left hand, with the prongs curving downward. Both utensils are kept in your hands with the tines pointed down throughout the entire eating process. If you take a drink, you do not just put your knife down, you put both utensils down into the resting position: cross the fork over the knife.

Once used, your utensils (including the handles) must not touch the table again. Always rest forks, knives, and spoons on the side of your plate in the 4:20 position.

单词表

crumple	*v.*	弄皱；起皱
utensil	*n.*	器具；用具
beverage	*n.*	（除水以外的）饮料

V. Story Links

1. Chopsticks Etiquette

Do not place your chopsticks vertically into your rice. This is likely to remind your Chinese dining companions of rice bowls and incense sticks offered to ancestors at Chinese funerals.

Do not pass food from chopstick to chopstick. This is another taboo related to funeral rites. Indeed, when someone passes and is cremated, some bones are usually left among the ashes. The family of the deceased is then asked to sift through the ashes and pass the bones from chopstick to chopstick. Mimicking this gesture at the dining table is a sure way to make everyone feel uncomfortable.

Do not separate chopsticks to spear, skewer or stab food. Chopsticks are always to be used in pairs, and only to pick up food.

Do not rinse off your chopsticks in your soup or drink.

Do not point at other people with chopsticks or wave chopsticks around.

Do not play with chopsticks or use them to strike and move tableware.

Do not lick, chew or use the tip of your chopstick to pick teeth.

2. Western Dining Etiquette History

Manners in Europe date back to the eleventh century, to the days of chivalry and knights-errant.

In the thirteenth century, Frederick II inaugurated courtly manners, which emphasized intellect, wit, and beauty. Our word courtesy is a diminutive of "courtier's customs," while manners comes from thc Lutin manuaruu, meaning "of the hand".

The fifteenth and sixteenth centuries gave birth to modern table manners. With the invention of movable type around 1440, books on social deportment based on consideration of others began to circulate. William Caxton, the first printer in England, published *The Book of Curtesye*, around 1477, a tome that set forth the duties of knighthood and chivalrous conduct.

Renaissance women of the aristocracy played a more passive and decorative role than today, and it was gentlemen with leisure time who contemplated social deportment and wrote etiquette books. In 1528 Baldassare Castiglione, an Italian diplomat, penned *IL Cortegiano*, which was translated into English as *The Courtier* in 1561.

Court etiquette was so elaborate in the seventeenth century that it bordered on the ridiculous.

Aristocrats were given tickets of admission to court ceremonies with a code of conduct printed on the reverse side. Gradually, etiquette came to mean a mode of behavior, not only for the French court but in social situations everywhere.

VI. Did You Know?

1. Chinese Dining Taboo

Do not lick the food attached to the chopsticks and don't use them to move the bowl or plate.

Do not use your chopsticks to strike the bowl or tea cup.

Do not stick your chopsticks vertically into your food owing to a Chinese practice of leaving such dishes for the dead.

Do not "dig" or "search through one's food for something" in particular. This is sometimes known as "digging one's grave" and is extremely poor manners.

Do not turn the Lazy Susan when others are serving themselves.

Do not tap your foot. Tapping your foot or shaking your leg is seen as disrespectful in various Asian cultures, including Chinese culture. This is because the tapping gesture is believed to shake off good luck and wealth, and a woman should be gentle and elegant rather than fidgeting.

Do not use your individual chopsticks to serve food. Since dishes are generally served in shared portions in China, they are usually accompanied by their respective communal serving chopsticks (公筷), or other cutleries.

2. Western Eating Taboo

Do not talk with food in your mouth! This is very rude and distasteful to watch! Wait until you have swallowed the food in your mouth.

Do not blow on your food to cool it off. If it is too hot to eat, take the hint and wait until it cools.

Do eat a little of everything on your plate. If you do not like the food and feel unable to give a compliment, just keep silent. It is acceptable to leave some food on your plate if you are full and have eaten enough. If the food served is not to your liking, it is polite to at least attempt to eat a small amount of it. It is never acceptable to ask a person why they have not eaten all the food. Don't make an issue if you do not like something or can't eat it—keep silence.

Do not "play with" your food or utensils. Never wave or point silverware. Do not hold food on the fork or spoon while talking, nor wave your silverware in the air or point with it.

VII. Cultural Reflection

中西餐桌礼仪的对比包括就座礼仪、餐具使用、用餐方式等，这些知识表面上看起来琐碎微小，但是，正是这些细小的差异，承载着巨大的文化差异。

教授中西餐桌礼仪，能够促进中西文化交流。中西餐桌礼仪是不同文化背景下的一种社交规范，了解和学习这些礼仪可以促进不同文化之间的理解和交流。通过了解餐桌礼仪，人们可以更好地适应并尊重其他文化中的饮食习惯和行为规范。

同时，餐桌礼仪是一种表达对他人的尊重和关注的方式。懂得适当的礼仪可以让人们在就餐时更加文雅得体，不会给他人带来困扰或冒犯他人。再者，教授中西餐桌礼仪对于培养儿童的良好习惯和礼貌也非常重要。适当的餐桌礼仪可以培养孩子的自律性、分享精神和团队意识。更重要的是，在商务场合，餐桌礼仪是一种重要的社交技巧。正确的餐桌礼仪可以给他人留下良好的印象，增强个人形象和职业信任度。

中西餐桌礼仪的差异也蕴含着深刻的文化意义，通过对比，可以更加清晰且深刻地了解中西文化的本质区别。

首先，中西餐桌礼仪中的座位安排和就餐顺序常常反映了社会等级观念。座位的安排往往以地位、权力或年龄为依据，强调了社会上的等级差异。这反映了西方社会中关于地位和权力的重视。对此进行文化反思时，我们可以思考社会等级观念对人际关系的影响。

其次，中西餐桌礼仪反映了不同文化中个人主义和集体主义价值观的差异。西方餐桌礼仪注重个人卫生和个人空间，每个人有自己的餐具和盘子。而中餐则注重共享和团体意识，大家共同享用同一桌的食物。这反映了西方文化中个人自主和独立的价值观，以及中西方文化对个人与集体关系的不同理解。文化反思可以帮助我们思考个人主义和集体主义对社会关系和社会凝聚力的影响。第三，中西餐桌礼仪都有一定的社交规范和礼仪要求，但其具体内容和强调的方面可能不同。中餐注重家庭团聚和亲密感，强调尊重和关怀。而西餐礼仪注重正式场合的社交礼仪，强调礼貌和行为规范。文化反思可以使我们审视社交规范和礼仪意识在不同文化中的起源和作用，并思考如何在跨文化交流中尊重他人的习俗和价值观。

由此可见，通过中西餐桌礼仪的对比学习，有助于我们更好地理解中西餐桌礼仪背后的文化观念，从而拓展视野，促进跨文化交流和相互尊重。

VIII. Homework

1. 梳理一下中西餐桌礼仪的异同。哪些礼仪是两种文化共同的要求？为什么？

2. 追根探源：中国的筷子文化有什么特点？与西方刀叉文化有什么本质差异？

3. 请在网络上搜索一些关于中西餐桌礼仪的博客和视频，并在课上进行分享。

4. 企划书设计：以小组为单位组织一场西式商务宴会，注意考虑菜单、餐具、酒水饮料、餐桌座位安排、餐桌布置、宴会流程、餐桌礼仪要求等，做一份企划报告书，享受一场高端宴会吧。

Section Three

The Contrast of Chinese and Western Social Interactions

I. Learning Objectives

1. To understand the key differences in social interactions between Chinese and Western cultures
2. To develop cultural awareness and adaptability when engaging in cross-cultural social interactions

II. Key Points and Difficult Points

1. To highlight the expectations and norms surrounding dress codes and appearance in social settings, including formal and casual attire, grooming standards, and the influence of fashion trends
2. To navigate the balance between formality and informality in social interactions
3. To overcome stereotypes and biases that may exist regarding social interactions in Chinese and Western cultures

III. Lead-in Questions

1. Have you ever noticed or experienced differences in social interactions when engaging with individuals from Chinese or Western backgrounds? Can you provide any specific examples?
2. How do you think cultural values and norms influence social interactions in different cultures? Can you think of any examples where these differences may be particularly noticeable?
3. Can you think of any examples where attitudes towards public displays of affection vary between Chinese and Western cultures? How might this impact social interactions and relationships?
4. How might language barriers or differences in communication styles, such as direct versus indirect communication, impact social interactions between individuals from Chinese and Western backgrounds?

IV. Learning Contents

1. Chinese Gift-Giving Etiquette

(1) General Tips for Gifts-Giving in China:

Bringing gifts to the host when you are invited is quite common in China. It is a suitable way to say thank you to give gifts to the people who invite you.

Recipient often declines the gift while the giver has to insist a bit. The recipient should not appear greedy when others give gifts to him/her in China. So the recipient often declines the gift you give twice or three times before accepting. You should offer the gift again after the recipient declines the gift, and he or she may finally accept your gift.

(2) General Tips for Receiving Gifts:

Recipient should receive the gift with both hands.

A little different than the west, Chinese recipients usually won't open gifts in front of the giver immediately. They believe opening gifts immediately will show visitors that you care about the value of gifts more than their visiting and this is slightly impolite.

(3) Note for Other Taboos:

In China, it is not a good idea giving clocks (送钟 sòng zhōng), umbrellas (伞 sǎn), pears (梨 lí) or shoes (鞋 xié) as they all have "bad" homophones: (送终 sòng zhōng) "attending a funeral ritual", (散 sàn) "to separate" , (离 lí) "leaving or parting" and (邪 xié) "evil".

It's also a bad idea to give mirrors that are believed to attract ghosts and sharp objects as it might seem that you want to cut off your relationship with the recipient.

Do not give gifts in sets or multiples of four as the number four (四 sì) sounds similar to 死 (sǐ) which means death. 6 and 8 are good and lucky numbers in China as the first sounds like "smooth" (溜 liū) and the second one (八 bā) sounds like "发" (fā) "to prosper". Furthermore, there is also a visual resemblance between 88 and 囍 (shuāng xǐ) literally: "double joy".

Necklaces, ties, and belts are considered personal gifts, so they should only be exchanged between boyfriends and girlfriends.

单词表

recipient	*n.*	收件人；接受者
homophone	*n.*	同音异形异义词

2. Western Gift-Giving Etiquette

(1) What to give: Americans are pretty generous when it comes to gift-giving and may give gifts when invited to someone's home for the first time, or as a token of friendship. While this isn't always expected, it's much appreciated. If you're unsure what to give, you can't go wrong with a gift that represents your home country, food such as chocolates or baked goods, or if they drink alcohol, a bottle of wine could be a nice choice.

(2) How to give: Gifts should be presented in wrapping paper or a gift bag and given when you arrive, or there may be a designated table where you can drop off your gift. It's common for Americans to open gifts right away.

Don't ask recipients what gift they would like unless it's a close relative or friend. This may make the recipient uncomfortable and feel that they need to give a gift in return. Instead, consider their hobbies and interests or ask a friend or family member what they would enjoy. If possible, include a gift receipt. Sometimes it's hard to know what size, color, or style the gift recipient might prefer. This gives the recipient the opportunity to exchange the gift with something that might suit them better. It doesn't mean that your gift isn't appreciated, but it ensures that your gift will be enjoyed.

(3) What to expect: There is evidence that shows "altruistic gift-giving without any hope of reciprocity makes people happy."

If you receive a gift, be sure to thank the gift-giver, and depending on the occasion, you may ask if you should open the present now, or wait until later. If you open the gift in front of the gift-giver, be sure to thank them and give positive comments like, "This is exactly what I need" or "What a lovely color."

If you receive the gift by mail, contact the gift-giver and tell them the gift has arrived. You may feel uncomfortable if you don't have anything to give in return, but you can always send a gift at a later date. What's important is your gratitude as the gesture is meant to show appreciation, and the gift-giver may only be hoping for a simple thank-you in return.

(4) How much to spend: When giving gifts, Americans aim to spend any amount they are most comfortable with, not what they think the other person is spending. Most people receiving gifts are not concerned about the money spent, but rather the effort that was made to give them something to enjoy. Americans often feel uncomfortable when receiving expensive gifts from anyone outside of their immediate family.

单词表

altruistic	*adj.*	利他的；无私的
reciprocity	*n.*	互换；互助

V. Story Links

1. Chinese Dress Code

Business costumes in China are conservative and modest. In a formal setting, the business costumes for men consist of dark colored, traditional suits. Women on the other hand are expected to wear business suits or dresses with a high neckline. For men, business costumes in China consist of shirts or jackets. For more formal situations, men are also expected to wear a tie. Tuxedos are not considered a part of business costumes in China.

Women are expected to dress in conservative business suits or blouses with a high neckline. At times, business costumes in China for women also include long dresses. Flashy and loud colors must be avoided as they are not an acceptable part of business costumes in China. Rather, subdued, neutral colors are more suitable for formal settings. Short sleeve blouses or blouses that reveal too much are not accepted as part of business costumes in China. Similarly, bare backs and low necklines are also frowned upon.

It is important to keep in mind that shorts or jeans are not at all acceptable for business meetings or in formal situations. Clothes that are revealing are considered an offense to Chinese businessmen.

Jewellery forms another important part of business costumes in China. Jewellery should not be something very flashy or gaudy. Simple gold jewellery, with an equally simple watch goes a long way in making a good impression. Women also need to avoid wearing heavy make-up.

Due to the formal culture in China, women are expected to wear either flat shoes or shoes with very low heels. High heels are reserved only for formal evening parties.

2. Western Dress Code

For both men and women, hats corresponding to the various levels of formality exist. As supplements to the standard dress codes, headgear (see biretta, kippah etc.) can be worn. Ceremonial dress, military uniform, religious clothing, academic dress, and folk costume appropriate to the formality level are encouraged.

(1) Formal wear

The dress codes counted as formal wear are the formal dress codes of morning dress for daytime and white tie for evenings. The clothes dictated by these dress codes for women are ball gowns. For many uniforms, the official clothing is unisex. Examples of this are court dress, academic dress, and military full dress uniform.

Typical events: weddings, state dinners and affairs, formal balls, royal events, etc.

(2) Semi-formal wear

Semi-formal wear or half dress is a grouping of dress codes indicating the sort of clothes worn to events with a level of formality between informal wear and formal wear. In the modern era, the typical interpretation for men is black tie for evening wear and black lounge suit for day wear, corresponded by either a pant suit or an evening gown for women.

Typical events: theatre opening nights, charity balls, etc. There is some variation in style depending on whether it is summer or winter. See black tie and stroller for more details.

(3) Informal wear

Informal wear or undress, also called business wear, corporate/office wear, tenue de ville or dress clothes, is a Western dress code for clothing defined by a business suit for men, and cocktail dress or pant suit for women. On the scale of formality, it is considered less formal than semi-formal wear but more formal than casual wear. Informal or undress should not be confused with casual wear such as business casual or smart casual; most situations calling for "informal wear" will usually tolerate casual dress to varying extents.

Typical events: diplomatic and business meetings, many social occasions, everyday wear

(4) Casual wear

Casual wear (or casual attire or clothing) is a Western dress code that is relaxed, occasional, spontaneous and suited for everyday use. Casual wear became popular in the Western world following the counterculture of the 1960s. When emphasizing casual wear's comfort, it may be referred to as leisurewear or loungewear. Casual wear encompasses business casual, smart casual, etc.

VI. Did You Know?

1. Cultural Background of Gift Giving in China

Thanks to its long history of being a predominantly Confucian society, gift giving is a big part of Chinese culture.

The principles of Confucianism are largely about keeping the peace and harmony not only in a family, but in society at large. This means showing respect and developing relationships with people throughout your life. As such, it should come as no surprise that gift giving is important. Gifts are given to family members, friends, colleagues, teachers—you name it. Gifts are commonly given on holidays (especially for Spring Festival) and birthdays. They're also given for first-time or important meetings, at weddings, and at other special events. When invited into someone's home, it's also common to bring along a gift.

"Courtesy demands reciprocity"（礼尚往来）is a famous Chinese saying that tells a lot about the gift giving culture of China. Whereas gift giving in the West is often simply for fun (think secret Santa or bachelor parties and the gifts one might bring to those), it's critical that one keep a tally of gifts both given and received in China. If a friend treats you to a nice meal, it's important that you remember that and return the favor sometime in the future. Similarly, if you give someone a gift, you can expect to receive one from them somewhere down the road. You can't give something that is much cheaper or much more expensive than the gift they gave you, either—try to keep it at about the same level.

2. The Origins and History of Gift Giving in the West

The giving of gifts may be one of the oldest of human activities that pre-dates civilization and may go back to the origin of our species.

Even in primitive cavemen culture, the giving of gifts was fairly common as it was used to show love and affection towards one another. The bestowing of gifts was also inferred as a status symbol when leaders of tribes or clans would show their appreciation for the contributions of those who were part of an important achievement. Whether it was an unusually shaped rock, a tooth from an animal, the bark from a tree or some other item that was natural in origin, the giving of gifts was certainly common behavior long before we became an advanced civilization. As tools were developed, the gifts started to become more elaborate, for example, holes were drilled into animal teeth and stones so they could be displayed on necklaces and many other objects were fashioned as well.

Later during the Egyptian era, gifts were most notably given to their pharaohs who built massive pyramids to store their wealth for afterlife and produced idols to support their beliefs of idol worship.

In Roman times people would present each other with good luck tokens, which lasted for centuries and later influenced all of Western civilization onwards. Such tokens of good luck were used as presents to carry favors and show allegiance, which is still the case today.

By the Medieval age, gifts were used to secure the personal favor of the king or show allegiance in times of war. Also, personal gifts of betrothals were given as dowries which ranged from coins to precious metals to a herd of cattle, goats or sheep. In many cultures, dowries and other similar expressions still exist today.

Today gift giving is still part of our everyday culture and defines who we are and the message we want to send with our gift. Gifts are given for all occasions and celebrations and are a means of us communicating with each other and expressing ourselves.

VII. Cultural Reflection

通过对中西社会交往进行多重层面的对比，帮助学生深入了解中西方文化差异对社交互动的影响，培养跨文化沟通和交往的能力。

首先，学生将意识到不同文化背景下的社交行为规范和价值观的差异。这有助于他们培养跨文化意识，理解并尊重不同文化的差异，避免文化冲突和误解。其次，学习中西社会交往对比可以帮助学生了解在不同文化环境中如何适应和调整自己的行为方式。他们将学会根据文化背景和场合的要求，运用适当的礼仪和行为准则，提升他们在跨文化交往中的表现和信任度。

再次，对比中西方商务交往的差异，有助于学生了解在国际商务场合中的行为准则和商务礼仪。这对于有意进入跨国公司工作、开展国际贸易或拓展国际市场的学生尤为重要，能够增强他们在跨文化商务环境中的竞争力。最后，通过对比中西社会交往，可培养学生对细微文化差异的敏感性。他们将学会观察、理解并尊重他人的文化表达方式，从而避免冒犯他人或造成误解。这对于建立良好的人际关系、促进跨文化合作和跨国交流至关重要。通过学习中西社会交往的对比，学生将增强他们的文化自信心和自我认同，他们将意识到自己所处文化的独特性，并能够以开放和包容的心态面对其他文化的差异，这有助于个人的成长和自信心的培养。

除此之外，通过中西社会交往对比的研讨与学习，可以更加深入和生动地了解中西文化的差异，以及这些差异所隐含的价值内涵。

通过对比中西社会交往，我们可以反思不同文化中的价值观差异对社交互动的影响。例如，在中西方文化中，对个人权利、集体利益、面子观念、礼貌与直率等价值的不同看法，会导致在社交场合中的不同表达方式和行为规范。这样的反思有助于我们理解并尊重其他文化的差异。

中西社会交往的对比还能使我们深入思考文化因素对社交行为的塑造。例如，中国文化中强调的尊重长辈和权威、社会地位的重要性，与西方文化中强调平等、自由表达和个人主义的特点形成对比。通过这种反思，我们可以思考不同文化中社交行为的根源，并了解这些行为背后的文化意义。

中西社会交往对比还可以引发学生对文化传统与变革的思考。文化是动态的，随着社会的变化和发展，社交行为也会发生变化。通过比较中西社会交往，我们可以反思自己的文化传统在现代社会中的变革，以及与其他文化交流中的文化借鉴和变化。这有助于培养学生开放的思维和包容的态度。

中西社会交往对比让我们意识到跨文化交际所面临的挑战和机遇。了解和尊重不同文化的社交行为规范是有效跨文化交流的基础。通过反思中西社会交往的对比，我们可以认识到自身文化与其他文化之间的差异，并积极寻求跨文化交际的机遇，提高我们的跨文化沟通能力。

这些文化交往的细节对比，不仅有助于我们超越简单的对比和判断，更深入地理解中西社会交往的文化差异,并在跨文化交流中更加灵活地应对。而且对比学习能够促进我们的文化反思，提升个人的文化敏感性和跨文化交际能力，促进文化的相互理解与和谐发展。另外，还需要指出的是，在现实中，文化是多元而复杂的，每个人和每种文化都可能有其独特的价值观。理解中西社会交往的文化价值观需要更深入的研究和对具体文化背景的理解。

VIII. Homework

1. 学生选择一个特定的社交行为或社交场合（例如家庭聚会、商务会议等），并比较中西方在这方面的交往方式和行为规范。要求学生研究相关的文化背景、价值观和社交准则，并撰写一篇论文，分析两种文化之间的差异和相似之处。

2. 视频演示：学生分成小组，每个小组选择一个特定的社交场景，例如餐桌礼仪、商务交流等。要求每组制作一段视频，展示中西方在该场景下的交往方式的对比。学生可以扮演角色，展示不同文化下的行为规范和交往方式。

参考资料

一、书籍

Langford, Beverly. The etiquette edge: Modern manners for business success [M]. New York: Amacom, 2016.

De Mente, Boye Lafayette. The Chinese mind: Understanding traditional Chinese beliefs and their influence on contemporary culture [M]. North Clarendon, Vt.: Tuttle Publishing, 2009.

Morrison, Terri, & Conaway, Wayne A. Kiss, bow, or shake hands: The bestselling guide to doing business in more than 60 countries [M]. Avon, Massachusetts: Adams Media, 2006.

LeBaron, Michelle. Cultural conflicts: A new approach for a changing world [M]. San Francisco: Jossey-Bass, 2009.

列维 - 斯特劳斯，克洛德 . 神话学：餐桌礼仪的起源 [M]. 周昌忠译 . 北京：中国人民大学出版社，2007.

克尼格 . 世界上最伟大的礼仪书 [M]. 童伟芳、陈明慧译 . 西安：陕西人民出版社，2010.

纪亚飞 . 优雅得体中西餐礼仪 [M]. 北京：中国纺织出版社，2014.

张国刚 . 从中西初识到礼仪之争：明清传教士与中西文化交流 [M]. 北京：人民出版社，2003.

二、网站

1. Culture Crossing (https://www.culturecrossing.net)：提供全球不同国家和地区的文化礼仪指南和交流策略

2. Executive Planet (https://www.executiveplanet.com)：提供商务文化和礼仪指南，涵盖多个国家和地区

3. COMMISCEO Global (https://www.commisceo-global.com/resources/country-guides)：提供各个国家的商务礼仪指南和国际沟通习俗

4. Kwintessential (https://www.kwintessential.co.uk)：提供全球商务礼仪指南以及不同文化之间的比较和对比

三、影视资源

1. 纪录片《食尚中国》

2. Ted-Ed: “Cross-Cultural Communication”

3. 电影：《迷失东京》(*Lost in Translation*)、《窈窕淑女》(*My Fair Lady*)、《末代皇帝》(*The Last Emperor*)

图书在版编目（CIP）数据

中西文化对比教程：英文 / 刘春芳主编 . -- 2 版 . 北京：中国人民大学出版社，2025. 1. --（新视界商务英语系列教材）. -- ISBN 978-7-300-33316-8

Ⅰ. H319.39

中国国家版本馆 CIP 数据核字第 20245HG136 号

新视界商务英语系列教材
中西文化对比教程（第二版）
主　编　刘春芳
副主编　马　骞　张　洁　马海歆　张　续
Zhong-xi Wenhua Duibi Jiaocheng (Di-er Ban)

出版发行	中国人民大学出版社		
社　址	北京中关村大街 31 号	邮政编码	100080
电　话	010-62511242（总编室）		010-62511770（质管部）
	010-82501766（邮购部）		010-62514148（门市部）
	010-62515195（发行公司）		010-62515275（盗版举报）
网　址	http://www.crup.com.cn		
经　销	新华书店		
印　刷	北京七色印务有限公司	版　次	2017 年 6 月第 1 版
开　本	889 mm × 1194 mm　1/16		2025 年 1 月第 2 版
印　张	17.5	印　次	2025 年 1 月第 1 次印刷
字　数	347 000	定　价	52.00 元

中国人民大学出版社读者信息反馈表

尊敬的读者：

感谢您购买和使用中国人民大学出版社的 ____________________________ 一书，我们希望通过这张小小的反馈表来获得您更多的建议和意见，以改进我们的工作，加强我们双方的沟通和联系。我们期待着能为更多的读者提供更多的好书。

请您填妥下表后，寄回或传真回复我们，对您的支持我们不胜感激！

1. 您是从何种途径得知本书的：

□书店　□网上　□报纸杂志　□朋友推荐

2. 您为什么决定购买本书：

□工作需要　□学习参考　□对本书主题感兴趣　□随便翻翻

3. 您对本书内容的评价是：

□很好　□好　□一般　□差　□很差

4. 您在阅读本书的过程中有没有发现明显的专业及编校错误，如果有，它们是：

____

____

____

5. 您对哪些专业的图书信息比较感兴趣：

____

____

____

6. 如果方便，请提供您的个人信息，以便于我们和您联系（您的个人资料我们将严格保密）：

您供职的单位：________________________________

您教授的课程（教师填写）：____________________

您的通信地址：________________________________

您的电子邮箱：________________________________

请联系我们：黄婷　程子殊　王新文　王琼　鞠方安

电话：010-62512737，62513265，62515580，62515573，62515576

传真：010-62514961

E-mail：huangt@crup.com.cn　chengzsh@crup.com.cn　wangxw@crup.com.cn　crup_wy@163.com　jufa@crup.com.cn

通信地址：北京市海淀区中关村大街甲59号文化大厦15层　邮编：100872

中国人民大学出版社